Women Deacons
400 Years of B

MW00849729

Women Deacons and Deaconesses
400 Years of Baptist Service

Charles W. Deweese

Baptist History and Heritage Society
Brentwood, Tennessee

Mercer University Press
Macon, Georgia

June 2005

ISBN 0-86554-438-7   MUP/P321

The paper used in this publication meets the minimum requirements
of American National Standard for Information Sciences—
Permanence of Paper for Printed Library Materials, ANSI Z39.48-1984.

Library of Congress Cataloging-in-Publication Data

Deweese, Charles W.
    Women deacons and deaconesses : 400 years of Baptist service /
    Charles W. Deweese. — 1st ed
        p. cm.
    Includes bibliographical references and indexes.
    ISBN 0-86554-438-7 (pbk. : alk. paper)
        1. Deaconesses—Baptists. 2. Baptists—History.
    3. Women in church work. I. Title.
    BX6346.D49 2005
    262'.1461'082—dc22

2005008881

Contents

Dedication

To
Mary Jane
Who has wonderfully exhibited
the New Testament spirit of diakonia *(service)*
As my wife for almost thirty-eight years,
Daughter of Murray and Mary Eisenhauer
Mother to Dana and Julie,
Mother-in-law to Alan and Kristopher,
Grandmother to Hannah and Chase,
Teacher to thousands of public-school children,
Faithful member of a Baptist church

Preface

Complexity, conflict, and resilient defense of the right to exist characterize the history of Baptist women deacons and deaconesses. Unlimited sources relate to them, including the records of thousands of churches and information on tens of thousands of internet websites. Views of whether they have a biblical base and should be ordained vary dramatically. Concepts of how they should be structured in local churches go many directions. Strong advocacy and intense opposition dominate discussions about them. Factors affecting interpretations of their viability, qualifications, and duties run the gamut of biblical, historical, theological, practical, and cultural possibilities. Their history is multifaceted and international. Through it all, women deacons and deaconesses have secured permanent places for themselves in the Baptist story.

In this book I do not attempt to provide a definitive treatment. However, this does represent a serious effort to capture the large trends that have permeated four centuries of development. Illustrative material from a wide array of source materials reveals the essence of most major patterns. Baptists in the United States receive primary attention; Baptists in England serious attention; and Baptists in selected other countries minor attention.

"Baptists" emerged into world history in circa 1609. Immediately, they began to make deacons (male and female) an official part of their congregational life and documents. The determination to maintain a healthy deaconship, then, has characterized most Baptists on a global scale for almost 400 years. Many factors have encouraged that emphasis: the permeating value of the servant motif in the life and teachings of Christ and in New Testament theology and practice, the presence of deacons and deaconesses in the New Testament and in subsequent Christian traditions, and every church's need for voluntary ministry and exemplary leadership.

Across these four centuries, Baptist churches have approached deacons (male and female) in different ways. Some have included women; most have not. Some have selected deacons through nominating committees; others have chosen them via popular vote. Some have ordained deacons; others have not. Some have placed them in office for life; others have used rotation policies. Some have primarily assigned them church business functions; others have mainly placed them in ministry roles. Most churches have retained deacons; some have abolished deacons in favor of "elders." Some have placed all deacons on a par with all church members in the common priesthood of all believers; others have placed them (and all other church members) in a submissive role under pastoral authority or elder rule. Some have made deaconesses submissive to male deacons; others have assigned to deaconesses and women deacons a status equal to that of male deacons. Such diversity is inevitable, given the democratic nature of Baptist polity, especially the autonomy of local churches.

In this study, I pinpoint positive and negative developments relating to women deacons and deaconesses. Models of deacon leadership and service will be put forward to illustrate that Baptist history can teach modern deacons some valuable lessons. Perhaps the chief point of this book is to connect history with possibilities. Looking for, finding, and sharing these links fueled the preparation of this manuscript.

This writing will lay out big points of tension Baptists have faced in deciding whether even to have women deacons and deaconesses, in taking the steps to add women to their deacon bodies, and in deciding whether to ordain them. At times, this study will also question attitudes toward women deacons and deaconesses that seem to counter New Testament intentions, teachings, and practices, and that seem to depart from the best ideals of Baptist heritage.

This book focuses first and foremost on the history of Baptist women in the diaconate. Women deacons, whether ordained or not, have existed, for the most part, in two periods of Baptist life: 1609–1612 according to some writings in Amsterdam by John Smyth and Thomas Helwys, the first two Baptist pastors, and since about 1950 in the United States and certain other parts of the world. A few churches had women deacons prior to 1950. Alongside male deacons, these women have typically received equal treatment in nomination, election, ordination (or nonordination), and duties. Some churches with women deacons have elected them as deacon chairs; some have not. Today, gender-free language characterizes the deacon policies of many churches.

In most cases where women deacons have not been ordained, neither have male deacons, as is the prevalent approach in churches related to the American Baptist Churches, USA. Women deacons typically do not operate in organizations separate from those of men. Instead, male and female deacons serve together in the same deacon body.

Baptist literature apparently said little about women in the diaconate in the period from 1613 until after 1650. In England, widows (possibly functioning as deaconesses) existed in the 1650s, and the first recorded deaconess showed up in 1662. Deaconesses predominated in Baptist life in the period from the early 1660s through the 1940s, the bulk of Baptist history. Even today, thousands of churches continue to use deaconesses, especially in black Baptist traditions in the United States and in various Baptist traditions in other countries. Deaconesses have tended to be subordinate to male deacons; typically, they have not engaged in matters of church business or in the distribution of the Lord's Supper. Deaconesses have normally met in separate organizations and have often been viewed as assistants to deacons, sometimes described as inferior to deacons. Generally, deaconesses have not received ordination, but some have. Some churches have treated deaconesses as equals to deacons.

Though usually referring to women in local-church ministries, "deaconess" at times designated women who served voluntarily in institutional sisterhoods: they lived in special homes or "motherhouses" in large urban areas and provided spiritual and social ministries outside of local churches. Such sisterhoods existed between 1890 and the second half of the 1900s.

This book attempts the following goals: to identify the issues at stake; to assess background influences on the rise of women deacons/deaconesses in Baptist life, including both the Bible and patterns in general church history prior to the rise of Baptists in the early 1600s; to describe and evaluate key features and patterns of the history of Baptist women deacons/deaconesses in the 1600s–2000s; to present personal stories of women deacons today, along with affirmations of their ministries; and to offer some lessons from history for the future of women deacons.

Five motivations have guided the research, writing, and publication of this book. These motivations have biblical, historical, theological, practical, and personal aspects.

First, the creation of woman in God's own image, the emancipation thrusts in the life and teachings of Jesus, the freedom themes that run throughout the New Testament, the significance of women behind key advancements in church history, and the presence and achievements of Baptist women in the diaconate since 1609 provide powerful foundations for diaconal roles for women today. These foundations support the urgent need for Baptist churches worldwide to place women in diaconal roles fully equal to the roles of male deacons. Sexual discrimination against women in the diaconate misreads Jesus, the New Testament, and the historic principles of Baptists; further, it is as wrong as racial prejudice. Church ministry and service are at stake; women are fully capable of handling diaconal opportunities.

All Baptists possess the right to reach their own conclusions about women deacons. However, if Baptist churches reluctant to create policies favoring women deacons will move past the diverse translations of and opinions surrounding Romans 16:1 and 1 Timothy 3:11, as well as misunderstandings and misapplications of the apostle Paul's comments about women's submission and keeping quiet in church, and will engage in an honest, soul-searching study of the freedom-based intentions of Jesus for women, many of those churches will take immediate action to effect positive change in behalf of women qualified to serve as deacons.

Second, the implications of Baptist origins for Baptists today influenced the preparation of this work. The writings of Smyth and Helwys, for example, plainly called for deacons, male and female. That call reflected an advanced stage of Protestant development and should penetrate the conscience of all Baptists today who prepare to celebrate Baptists' four-hundredth birthday in 2009. An excellent way to honor the founding fathers of English Baptists (and of all Baptists) would be to implement their intentions for women in the diaconate.

Third, this book is intended to counter the mindset of recent fundamentalist Baptist leaders and pastors who, especially since the 1970s, have registered intense opposition to the ordination of women. New attitudes favoring women's rights inside and outside the church in the 1960s and 1970s undoubtedly helped precipitate the harsh reaction against women deacons and ministers. That reaction is unjustified. The life and teachings of Christ move in a different direction—a direction that properly places women in all kinds of diaconal and ministry roles.

Fourth, my interest in the topic has taken previously published forms. In 1977, I prepared the article, "Deaconesses in Baptist History: A Preliminary Study," for the journal *Baptist History and Heritage*. Then, in 1979, Broadman Press published my book, *The Emerging Role of Deacons*, which included limited historical information on Baptist women in the diaconate. I collected materials on the topic, particularly through research in three libraries: the American Baptist Historical Collection in Rochester, New York, the Library of Congress in Washington, and the Southern Baptist Historical Library and Archives in Nashville. In addition, I secured information through study of multiple sources, examination of many websites, and extensive postal and e-mail correspondence with numerous individuals, churches, associations, Southern Baptist state conventions, American Baptist regions, and Baptist historians in other countries.

Fifth, personal reasons also come into play. Evelyn Underwood, one of my history professors at Mars Hill College in 1963–1967, was named deacon chair at the Mars Hill Baptist Church in 1976, one of the earliest women in Baptist life in the South to occupy that role. In 1982, the First

Baptist Church in Asheville, North Carolina, ordained my mother-in-law, Mary Eisenhauer, as one of the church's first three women deacons. In 1993–1997, Anita Rolf, deacon at First Baptist Church in Waco, Texas, served as a mother away from home for our daughter, Dana, while Dana attended Baylor University. In 2000, I served alongside several women deacons in my role as deacon chair at First Baptist Church, Nashville, Tennessee. Across the years, my wife, Mary Jane, and I have been members of six Baptist churches in North Carolina, Kentucky, and Tennessee that either had women deacons when we were members or later adopted them. Throughout my career, and especially during the preparation of this manuscript, I have communicated with dozens of women deacons and learned about their joys and achievements, challenges and pressures.

Thousands of Baptist churches in the United States incorporate women deacons or deaconesses into vital roles of service and leadership, and thousands more do the same in other countries. The number of churches with women deacons is growing, and the number of deacon bodies with women chairs is also increasing. Simultaneous with these forward trends, some Baptist organizations, especially the Southern Baptist Convention, have strongly objected to women's ordination through resolutions, agency actions, publications, and other methods.

In this writing, I present in detail key points of opposition and support for women deacons and deaconesses. However, I advocate without apology women's rights to serve as deacons. Biblical evidence, historical precedence, theological common sense, and practical needs demand such advocacy. The life and teachings of Christ confirm that women's equality with men in church leadership and ministry is certain. Past contributions of women in diaconal roles have produced meritorious results. Women's potential as deacons to help shape the future of Baptist church life has no limits.

The presence of women functioning in diaconal roles throughout Baptist history is God's gift for challenging negative church traditions and for elevating women to their rightful place in the forward movement of responsible Baptist faith. Historical fence-sitting is a nonacceptable option when misreadings of scripture, masculine dominance of church life, and a refusal to acknowledge the positive trends of Baptist history characterize the attitudinal landscape that prevents women from serving in diaconal roles that should be rightfully theirs. It is time to undercut discrimination against women in the heart of Baptist life by letting the Bible and history make their case.

My sincere gratitude goes to librarians and archivists who assisted me, to pastors and historians of local churches who provided information, and to women deacons who have graciously shared their stories. Bill Sumners, director, Taffey Hall, archivist, and Kathy Sylvest, librarian, all of the Southern Baptist Historical Library and Archives, gave special assistance. In addition, Pam Durso, associate director of the Baptist History and Heritage Society (BH&HS), provided excellent suggestions relating to content. Marc Jolley, director of Mercer University Press, helpfully initiated a copublishing arrangement between that press and the BH&HS that made this book possible. Edd Rowell, senior editor of Mercer University Press, significantly improved the layout and readability of the manuscript. I am also grateful to the BH&HS for allowing me to serve as executive director and to use part of my time in preparing this work.

Introduction

The Issues at Stake

Sharply contrasting attitudes toward women deacons and deaconesses characterize Baptist life in the early 2000s. Baptist congregations related to the American Baptist Churches, USA (ABC) and the Cooperative Baptist Fellowship (CBF) routinely incorporate women deacons into their local-church structures and leadership; a large majority of Southern Baptist churches reject them. American Baptists normally do not ordain deacons, male or female; Southern Baptists and CBF Baptists tend to ordain them, including women. Large numbers of black Baptist churches prefer non-ordained deaconesses. Such contrasting attitudes should surprise no one, given the diverse nature of Baptists.

What are the real issues at stake in the history and current status of Baptist women deacons and deaconesses? At least nine major issues (or sets of issues) seem pertinent to a responsible discussion of this topic: the gift or curse of women deacons, controversy and crisis, authority issues, women's equality or subordination, diverse attitudes about ordination, the credibility and integrity of the Southern Baptist Convention (SBC), counterattacks against assaults on women deacons and pastors, what women think, and divergent views of scripture and theology.

Women Deacons: Gift or Curse?

Baptists, past and present, differ intensely about the pros and cons of women deacons—even about whether the topic is important enough to merit attention in print. In fact, few topics evoke stronger reactions, positive and negative. In 2000, Mike Clingenpeel, editor of Virginia Baptists' *Religious Herald*, wrote: "Excluding women as deacons seems a terrible squandering of human giftedness."[1] In sharp contrast, the editor of the *Baptist Messenger*, newspaper for the Baptist General Convention of Oklahoma, recently described the issue of women deacons as a "can of worms."[2] Upon learning of my involvement in writing this book, the editor

---

[1]Mike Clingenpeel, "The changing face of leadership" *Religious Herald* (23 March 2000): 8.

[2]John Yeats, e-mail to author, 10 August 2004.

of the *Christian Index*, newspaper for the Georgia Baptist Convention, questioned the study by stating that "surely there is some more compelling work in which to invest your research and writing skills."[3]

Thousands of Baptist churches in the United States provide wonderful outlets for women by electing and, in some cases, ordaining them as deacons. A Maryland pastor wrote in 1989 that women had served on his church's deacon body for twelve years. "Not only has our experience been a positive one, it is hard to imagine life in our church—and in our Ministry of Caring—without the leadership of our women. My counsel to a church dealing with this issue would be: Try it, you'll like it."[4]

Some Baptist leaders wish more churches had women deacons. The editor of the *Montana Baptist* wrote in 2004 that "as far as I know, in our short fifty-one-year history, we have never had any women deacons in Montana—and the work is the poorer for it. I strongly believe women deacons are scriptural and our Baptist work in the state would be better off to have them."[5]

Controversy and Crisis

Ernest A. Payne, general secretary of the Baptist Union of Great Britain and Ireland, wrote in 1954 in his foreword to an important publication on deaconesses in England that "the place of women in the ministry and service of the Church is one of the urgent issues which face Christians in all parts of the world."[6] His point is as valid in the early 2000s as it was in the 1950s. The treatment of women in diaconal positions in Baptist life on a global scale continues to require major discussion. Many key issues remain unsettled.

Controversy and crisis have typically characterized women's issues in the 2,000 years of Christian history. Why else would E. Glenn Hinson, one of the finest church historians in America, write an article titled "The Church: Liberator or Oppressor of Women?" and then observe regarding

---

[3]Gerald Harris, e-mail to author, 10 August 2004.

[4]Stephen C. Hyde, letter to Brian Conner, 19 July 1989; mailed to author by Marion Aldridge.

[5]Jim Edlin, e-mail to author, 28 April 2004.

[6]Ernest A. Payne, foreword to Doris M. Rose, *Baptist Deaconesses* (London: Carey Kingsgate Press, 1954) 3.

women's status in the history of Christian churches that "Christianity in the comprehensive sense has a mixed record on this question?"[7]

Ralph H. Langley, noted Baptist pastor, wrote: "We like to say the New Testament church is 'the light of the world,' but most times it is only the taillight! Equality of the sexes is more evident in other segments of society than inside the church walls. The church has not only been the captive of the culture; it has more often than not resisted change, and nowhere is this resistance more evident than the status of women in the front ranks of church life."[8]

Leon McBeth, distinguished church historian, admonished men for defining women and their roles; interpreting scripture passages about them; passing laws that affected their rights; interpreting their place in history; deciding what they "could do, say, wear, or own"; pronouncing verdicts on whether God could call them and, if so, to what; deciding if they could serve as deacons, teachers, and ministers; and "jello-molding" them to fit the patterns men require. Then McBeth urged women to take up their own cause.[9]

The whole idea of women deacons and deaconesses has generated controversy in Baptist life for generations. Causes of such conflict have included varying interpretations of what the Bible says about women's roles in the church; differences over whether women should even speak, hold leadership positions, or exercise authority in the church; disagreements concerning the ordination of women; concerns about placing women on deacon bodies that have engaged primarily in church business functions; the reality of male-dominating attitudes in church life; and cultural influences.

Such controversy has created major tension in church business meetings as churches have voted to adopt or reject policies providing for women deacons. It has also caused conflict in Baptist associations and state conventions; some associations and conventions have disassociated from churches that have ordained women to the diaconate. Writers with varying viewpoints have expressed themselves in Baptist publications. Fundamen-

---

[7]E. Glenn Hinson, "The Church: Liberator or Oppressor of Women?" *Review and Expositor* 72/1 (Winter 1975): 19.

[8]Ralph H. Langley, "The Role of Women in the Church," *Southwestern Journal of Theology* 19/2 (Spring 1977): 60.

[9]H. Leon McBeth, "Perspectives on Women in Baptist Life," *Baptist History and Heritage* 22/3 (July 1987): 10.

talism, which rose in full force in Southern Baptist life in the late 1970s, was and is dominated by a high degree of antagonism for women's ordination of any kind, as well as for the concept of women serving in church leadership roles over men.

Will Baptists ever resolve issues relating to women, including female deacons? Not likely. However, careful attention to the Bible and historic Baptist ideals can inject meaning into the discussion and can advance women's causes in church life in a healthy fashion.

Authority Issues

Jesus Christ is the supreme model for deacons, male and female. The Bible and Baptist history support that assertion. In fact, all Baptist history, contemporary theology and practices, and future directions must be constantly evaluated according to the example and teachings of Jesus. The following sentences, published in 1869, represent an excellent view of the primary source of authority for deacons' existence and functions: "Christ is the foundation and model of diaconal service. . . . He is the key to the scriptures on this as upon every doctrinal topic. . . . The original charter by which diaconal service is authorized is found in the example of Christ. . . . Jesus Christ became a *diakonos* or servitor [servant] of God. . . . His service was diaconal, and is the model and warrant for employment of diaconal service in the church."[10]

Baptist churches and deacons may find it a healthy exercise to ask and answer several questions relating to authority and to explore the implications of each question for women deacons? Are deacons power brokers of local-church business or servants after the fashion of Jesus himself? How should deacons relate to pastors or elders who assume extraordinary authority in church life? Does ordination convey authority, or does it present opportunity? What actions should a church and deacon body take to guarantee appropriate differentiation between authority and servant-oriented leadership?

Concern about a growing pattern of excessive pastoral authority among Baptists, with special concern for its impact on deacons, male and female, is and has been widespread among Baptists in the United States. LifeWay Christian Resources, SBC published a book on the ministry in 1998 that

---

[10]J. Colver Wightman, "Deacons and the Diaconate," *The Baptist Quarterly* 3 (January 1869): 56.

urged giving extraordinary authority to ministers. It included such statements as the following. "The position of minister is the position of God's authority established in the church. . . . Scripture is clear that God expects both individual and group submission to ministerial authority. . . . Ministers are the rulers of the church."[11] This book was written by Michael D. Miller, director of LifeWay's Church Leadership Division. Paige Patterson, at the time, president of both the Southern Baptist Convention and of Southeastern Baptist Theological Seminary, claimed on the back cover of the book that if "read by every one of our 16 million Southern Baptists," this book "would revolutionize church life among Baptists today."

Miller's book and its endorsement translate into a source of grave concern for Baptists who believe that the concepts of pastoral authority presented in it completely violate historic Baptist emphases on the equality of *all* church members and on the priesthood of *all* believers. Pastors who prefer to rule, rather than to serve, tend to suppress local-church inclinations to elect, ordain, and retain women deacons. Moreover, they do serious damage to women's potential to provide diaconal leadership in Baptist life.

Baptists in other countries face similar authority issues. Three leaders so stated in 1998. Arnoldo Canclini, past president of the national Baptist convention of Argentina, wrote that "Baptist life here is very much disturbed by the so-called 'renewal movement' that gives very little place to Baptist practices and then, believing in a strong pastorate, deacons tend to disappear."[12] Konstanty Wiazowski, honorary president of the Baptist Union of Poland, opined that "The position of deacons is neglected in the churches where pastors are strong personalities."[13] Thorwald Lorenzen, Baptist pastor in Australia and chair of the Human Rights Commission of the Baptist World Alliance (BWA), claimed that "pastoral leadership sometimes is interpreted in an authoritarian hierarchical manner which would both place more emphasis on the pastor as the 'manager' which in turn would of course take away responsibility from the diaconate. I don't think that is a healthy development and I think it is in tension with our Baptist tradition."[14]

---

[11]Michael D. Miller, *Honoring the Ministry: Honoring the Leaders God Gives Your Church* (Nashville: LifeWay Press, 1998) 43, 57.

[12]Arnoldo Canclini, letter to author, 7 April 1998.

[13]Konstanti Wiazowski, letter to author, 8 April 1998.

[14]Thorwald Lorenzen, letter to author, 23 March 1998.

Deacon bodies might also find it useful to consider excessive applications of deacon authority in church life. One reason is that the more
authority churches assign to deacons or that deacons assume on their own,
the less likely those churches will allow for women in the diaconate.
Historically, many Baptists have tended to restrain women from leadership
roles that include authority, especially authority over men.

Two nineteenth-century examples show what can happen. The 1842
circular letter of the Salem (Massachusetts) Baptist Association to its
churches offered a series of reasons why deacons should be "chosen to a
shorter period than life." One reason cited was that "deacons, like other
men, may become ambitious of authority, dictatorial, sour, frigid."[15] Then
the 1850 circular letter of the Woodstock (Vermont) Association stated
unequivocally that deacons "are second in command, in admonition, in
authority, and in the lead of the church only to pastors."[16] Whether in the
1800s or today, those kinds of attitudes have exacted serious damage on the
possibility of women serving in diaconal roles.

Women's Equality or Subordination

Baptists have always struggled with what to do with women in the church,
including, and sometimes especially, women in the diaconate. Should
Baptists treat women as deacons, with all the privileges given to men, or
should they treat them as "deaconesses," with reduced privileges? Or
should they deny to women all possible participation in the diaconate?
These questions have plagued Baptists for centuries, and they show no sign
of abating.

A handwritten, thirty-four-page, unpublished manuscript from 1872
helps to capture some of the basic issues that have preoccupied Baptists
regarding women in the church, including women in the diaconate. Lansing
Burrows, Baptist pastor in Bordentown, New Jersey, presented a lecture to
his church in June of that year titled "Woman's Position in the Church."
This lecture was the first of ten given on ten consecutive Sunday evenings
in a course Burrows titled "Woman's Work in the Church." Burrows would
later distinguish himself as pastor of the First Baptist Churches of Augusta,
Georgia (1883–1899) and Nashville, Tennessee (1899–1909); and in three

---

[15]*Minutes*, Salem Baptist Association (MA), 1842, 14.
[16]*Minutes*, Woodstock Baptist Association (VT), 1850, 11.

SBC roles: recording secretary (1881–1913), statistician (1881–1919), and president (1914–1917).[17]

Burrows's 1872 lecture put forward positions that characterized what he called "The Woman Problem." His positions reflected comparable positions running throughout the Baptist story. Burrows's starting point included women preachers and deaconesses:

> They have ascended the pulpit. . . . The feasibility of ordaining deaconesses—a ministerial, and not simply a temporal office—has not only excited the attention of the magnates of a large body of Christians, but has met with no insignificant support. We cannot close our ears to the loud agitations of the hour. We must see the foam of the disturbed billows. These questions enter into our daily life. They become the themes of conversation. Our journalistic reading presents them continually to our minds. They are not only mere theoretical questions, but they are ever near in practice.[18]

Burrows then discussed women's roles, duties, and rights in the church:

> Woman is in the church . . . because she has a right there, because it is her sphere, her mission, her home. Being there, what are her rights, what are her duties? It is a living question. It is a vital question. It is a question which ought to be discussed—which we cannot afford to ignore.[19]

Burrows then made two contrasting points about woman's position in the church: equality and subordination. First, "In things spiritual, woman's position in the church is one of equality." He asserted New Testament authority for such equality, quoting in full Galatians 3:27-28 (KJV): "For as many of you as have been baptized into Christ have put on Christ. There is neither Jew nor Greek, there is neither bond nor free, there is neither male nor female; for ye are all one in Christ Jesus." Burrows emphasized that women have equal rights in redemption, in the ordinances of the church, and in the benefits of the church. He concluded that

---

[17]Edwin S. Davis, "Burrows, Lansing," *Encyclopedia of Southern Baptists*, vol. 1 (Nashville: Broadman Press, 1958) 211.

[18]Lansing Burrows, "Woman's Position in the Church" (Bordentown NJ: June 1872) 3-4; manuscript located in the Lansing Burrows Papers, AR 25, file folder 55, Southern Baptist Historical Library and Archives, Nashville TN.

[19]Ibid., 4-5.

the distinction of her sex fades away into the fact of a needy hungering soul, fed by Christ, nurtured by Christ, and saved to eternal blessedness by Christ. Palsied be the tongue that would ever deny her this equality, for it would be fearful sin—sin to the death against an immortal soul.[20]

Burrows's second major point would have shocked the first Baptist congregation in 1609 and will shock readers today who favor women deacons, with equal nomination, election, ordination (or nonordination), and duties with male deacons: "In things temporal, woman's position in the church is one of subordination." Burrows quickly acknowledged that "wide difference of opinion" surrounded his claim because "the age has developed a mode of liberal thought which would deny any subordination whatever of woman in the church." Next, he made his ultimate argument: "To honest Christian minds all that is necessary is to appeal to the testimony of the Scriptures."[21]

Burrows hammered home his theme of woman's subordination in the church with specifics: "The position of woman in the church is not one of leadership." The "temporal prosperity of the church" resides "peculiarly [in] the province of pastors and deacons." Biblical evidence is clear: " 'Let the woman learn in silence with all subjection. But I suffer not a woman to teach, nor to usurp authority over the man, but to be in silence' " (1 Tim. 2:11-12). After citing the selection of men only as the apostles, the seven in Acts 6, and other New Testament personalities, Burrows concluded: "Such is the only argument which as men who reverence the Scriptures it is necessary to adduce to prove the subordination of woman in the management of the church." In fact, "the leadership is committed to faithful men."[22]

Burrows pressed his point by excluding women from church leadership: "The leadership . . . of the church is incompatible with the social duties of woman." Besides, "There is much for women to do in the church; concerning that I hope to convince many; but that work effects not the leadership of it."[23]

Finally, Burrows admonished women:

---

[20]Ibid., 13, 14, 16, 17, 19.
[21]Ibid., 20.
[22]Ibid., 21-22, 23-25.
[23]Ibid., 25, 26.

Let no Christian woman chafe beneath this subordination. Let her remember the pit from whence she was digged. Her Saviour has taken her from among the bondslaves of Satan, and placed her in charge of a flowering garden, not amid the dust and blood of the battle.

Further, "Disdain not this humble ministry, my sisters; it is God's plan; it answers your own cravings, it is endorsed by your own tender intuitions."[24]

Burrows's contrasting positions depicted thrusts that existed in Baptist literature long before he made them, and they have continued ever since. Baptists strongly disagree over whether women in church life should be equal to men or in bondage to them.

The following pages of this book will present many more examples of both sides of this issue. Running through it all, however, one may see that the historic, liberty-based values of Baptists offer considerably more support to the equality side of the equation than to the subordinating side.

Diverse Attitudes about Ordination

Throughout Baptist history thorny issues have arisen over the ordination of women as deacons and deaconesses. No concern has caused more interest in women deacons than opposing views of the meaning and implications of ordination in the New Testament and in Baptist history. Baptists, especially SBC Baptists, who claim that ordination conveys authority, tend to oppose women's ordination. Other Baptists, such as CBF Baptists, who assert that ordination symbolizes a door to ministry are more inclined to favor ordination. Still other Baptists, such as American Baptists, approve ministry roles for women deacons but generally disapprove ordination for all deacons, men and women. Black Baptists largely favor deaconesses and oppose ordination. The patterns vary, and exceptions exist to all the preceding trends.

In 2002, Everett C. Goodwin, noted American Baptist pastor, wrote an important book, *Down by the Riverside: A Brief History of Baptist Faith.* In commenting on early Baptist practices of ordination for pastors and deacons, he stated that ordination "was not assumed to endow its recipients with special powers, prestige, or authority, but instead symbolized both the confidence and the expectation of the congregation in fulfilling their

---

[24]Ibid., 28, 32.

respective roles."[25] That is a position that SBC leaders in recent decades have resisted with all their might, to the detriment of women deacons.

Still, some Southern Baptist churches and other kinds of Baptist churches have made serious strides in the past fifty years in electing and ordaining women as deacons. Baptist deacon bodies have made substantial advancements, especially since the 1960s, in choosing women to serve as chairs. (See the appendix for a list of almost 300 selected Baptist churches with women serving as deacon chairs and/or cochairs in the present and/or past.)

General factors contributing to such progress for women deacons and their ordination in some sectors included the Women's Liberation Movement of the 1960s and 1970s prompted by the 1963 publication of Betty Friedan's *The Feminine Mystique*; the adoption of the Civil Rights Act in 1964; the 1971 Supreme Court ruling that treating persons unequally based solely on sex violated the Fourteenth Amendment, which provides equal protection under the law; the 1972 approval of the Equal Rights Amendment by the Senate (the House had approved it in 1971), even though the amendment later failed because not enough states approved it; the American Bicentennial Celebration of 1976, which was saturated with freedom themes; and Baptist President Jimmy Carter's human rights initiatives.

Baptist contributions to more openness for women included the ordination of Addie Davis to the ministry in 1964 by the Watts Street Baptist Church in Durham, North Carolina, as the first Southern Baptist woman so ordained; the adoption of official human rights pronouncements by the BWA in 1970, 1975, and 1980; the adoption of human rights resolutions by the SBC in 1963, 1965, and 1977; SBC adoption of the Declaration of Human Rights in 1978; a Consultation on Women in Church-Related Vocations held in Nashville, Tennessee, in 1978; the holding of the first Conference of American Baptist Women in Ministry in 1974; and the formation of the Women in Ministry SBC organization in 1983 (later Southern Baptist Women in Ministry and still later Baptist Women in Ministry). This latter organization impacted Baptists in many states. For example, in 2001, Virginia Baptist Women in Ministry published in one volume all past issues of their newsletter, *Synergy*, covering the years 1991–2001.

Alongside these developments, ongoing organizations have constantly helped Baptist women, deacons and otherwise, understand their potential,

---

[25]Everett C. Goodwin, *Down by the Riverside: A Brief History of Baptist Faith* (Valley Forge PA: Judson Press, 2002) 90.

whether ordained or not: Woman's Missionary Union, auxiliary to the SBC, which celebrated its one-hundredth birthday in 1988; American Baptist Women's Ministries, which celebrated its fiftieth anniversary in 2001; and the BWA Women's Department, which celebrates its fiftieth anniversary in 2005, although women's participation in BWA Congress meetings dates back to 1905, the year BWA was organized, and although formal women's committee structures date to 1911.

Since the 1960s, Baptists have produced many writings that have both focused on topics relating to women and have influenced the advancement of positive developments for women, including deacons and their ordination. Catherine Allen identified several key issues of Southern Baptist periodicals from the 1970s.[26] Norman Letsinger produced an important dissertation in 1973 on the implication of the women's liberation movement for Southern Baptists.[27] Libby Bellinger described Letsinger's research as "part of the awakening of the consciences of men and women concerning the role of women in the SBC."[28] In 1974, Broadman Press published the book compiled by Harry Hollis titled *Christian Freedom for Women and Other Human Beings.* This volume contained lectures presented at a 1974 seminar on the role of women in the church sponsored by the Southern Baptist Christian Life Commission. More recent writings have also focused on topics relating to Baptist women.[29] In 1978, Westminster Press published an important work by Evelyn and Frank Stagg, *Woman in the World of Jesus.* (Frank Stagg was the longtime, highly esteemed New Testament professor at the Southern Baptist Theological Seminary.) In 1979,

---

[26]Catherine B. Allen, "Women's Movements and Southern Baptists," *Encyclopedia of Southern Baptists*, vol. 4 (Nashville: Broadman Press, 1982) 2561. The issues included *The Baptist Program* (October 1970), *The Quarterly Review* (Spring 1970), *Home Missions* (May 1972), *The Deacon* (April 1973), *The Commission* (November 1974), *Review and Expositor* (Winter 1975), *Baptist History and Heritage* (January 1977), and many Woman's Missionary Union magazines.

[27]Norman Letsinger, "The Women's Liberation Movement: Implications for Southern Baptists" (Th.D. diss., Southern Baptist Theological Seminary, 1973).

[28]Libby Bellinger, "More Hidden than Revealed: The History of Southern Baptist Women in Ministry," *The Struggle for the Soul of the SBC: Moderate Responses to the Fundamentalist Movement*, ed. Walter B. Shurden (Macon GA: Mercer University Press, 1993) 130.

[29]See, e.g., Sheri Adams, *What the Bible Really Says about Women* (Macon GA: Smyth and Helwys, 1994); and Carolyn D. Blevins, *Women's Place in Baptist Life* (Brentwood TN: Baptist History and Heritage Society, 2003).

Broadman Press released Leon McBeth's important work, *Women in Baptist Life*. (McBeth was distinguished professor of Church History at Southwestern Baptist Theological Seminary.)

More specifically, Baptists have released several significant manuscripts and publications that have related to the history and life of women deacons and deaconesses and provided impetus for Baptist churches to consider electing and, in some cases, ordaining women deacons. These have included Donald F. Thomas's manuscript on "The Deacons and the Deaconesses" prepared for the Division of Evangelism of the American Baptist Home Mission Society (September 1960); E. Glenn Hinson's article, "On the Election of Women as Deacons," which appeared in several Baptist state newspapers in 1972 and 1973 and in *The Deacon* (April 1973); Charles Deweese's article, "Deaconesses in Baptist History: A Preliminary Study," in *Baptist History and Heritage* (January 1977); Leon McBeth's chapter on "Women Deacons" in his *Women in Baptist Life* (Broadman Press, 1979); sections throughout Charles Deweese's *The Emerging Role of Deacons* (Broadman Press, 1979); Harold Nichols's *The Work of the Deacon and Deaconess* (Judson Press, 1984); and other writings that will be cited in the following chapters.

In recent years American Baptists and Southern Baptists have taken totally different approaches to women's issues. American Baptists are far more open to women deacons than are Southern Baptists. Fundamentalist influences since 1979 have increasingly led Southern Baptists to oppose the election and ordination of women deacons. This opposition permeates Southern Baptist literature, resolutions, and practices.

The American Baptist Convention and, later, the American Baptist Churches, USA adopted several documents in the 1960s–1980s that provided pivotal support for women. In 1969 the ABC adopted a "Resolution on Increased Opportunities for Women." In 1975, the ABC general board adopted a report by an ABC Task Force on Women. The report included a progressive statement of philosophy regarding the value of women to God and the church and suggested actions that needed to be taken, including a recommended provision for women to serve in key denominational positions and in pastorates. In 1977, the ABC general board adopted a "Resolution on the Empowerment of Women," which called for a reversal in the declining number of positions professionally trained women held in regional, state, city, and national staffs.[30] In 1978, the ABC conducted "A

---

[30]Elizabeth J. Miller, "AB Women's Gains and Losses Three Decades after the

Study of Women in Ministry (S.W.I.M.)." Linda C. Spoolstra, executive minister for the ABC of Massachusetts, claimed that "the S.W.I.M. project was a watershed in the life of the ABC because it resulted in direct action for many people, groups, and institutions who desire the full acceptance of women in pastoral ministry."[31]

In 1985, the ABC general board adopted an "American Baptist Statement on Women and Men as Partners in Church and Society." The document concluded with nine affirmations, the first of which read, "We affirm that the Gospel ministry of Jesus Christ liberates all persons, female and male, to serve in any ministry to which they have been called by God and for which they have God-given talents."[32] Although American Baptists largely prefer not to ordain any deacons, actions such as these have facilitated the fact that a high percentage of American Baptist churches do have women deacons.

SBC Credibility and Integrity

Leon McBeth, noted Baptist historian, directed an explicit and incisive charge against Southern Baptists, one of the largest Protestant denominations in America:

> Southern Baptists have basically followed their host culture in their teachings and attitudes about women. There is no convincing evidence [McBeth wrote in 1977] that Southern Baptists have ever influenced their culture, or been in advance of the culture, on the question of women's rights. Every significant step in the emerging role of Southern Baptist women was preceded by comparable developments in society.[33]

Integration of the Mission Societies," *American Baptist Quarterly* 20/3 (September 2001): 232-33, 235. See also the "Report of the American Baptist Churches Task Force on Women to the General Board," *American Baptist Quarterly* 20/3 (September 2001): 267-69.

[31]Linda C. Spoolstra, "Project S.W.I.M.: A Study of Women in Ministry," *American Baptist Quarterly* 20/3 (September 2001): 238.

[32]"American Baptist Policy Statement on Women and Men As Partners in Church and Society" (December 1985) <www.abc-usa.org/resources/resol/women. htm>, accessed 8 November 2004.

[33]H. Leon McBeth, "The Role of Women in Southern Baptist History," *Baptist History and Heritage* 12/1 (January 1977): 25.

The SBC adopted a "Resolution on Ordination and the Role of Women in the Ministry" in 1984. This resolution asserted that the Bible makes "man the head of woman," teaches that "women are not in public worship to assume a role of authority over men," and "excludes women from pastoral leadership" in order "to preserve a submission God requires because the man was first in creation and the woman was first in the Edenic fall." The adopted resolution concluded by resolving that "we encourage the service of women in all aspects of church life and work other than pastoral functions and leadership roles entailing ordination."[34] The resolution obviously had negative implications for women deacons. (Chapter 5 will present a full discussion of the 1984 resolution and reactions to it.)

In 1998, the SBC added a new article, "The Family," to the 1963 Baptist Faith and Message (BF&M). This addition stirred up considerable controversy with its claim that "a wife is to submit herself graciously to the servant leadership of her husband."[35] Then the SBC's 2000 adopted revision of the Baptist Faith and Message added a new sentence to the original article on "The Church" as found in the 1963 BF&M: "While both men and women are gifted for service in the church, the office of pastor is limited to men as qualified by Scripture."[36] This continuing Southern Baptist pattern of excluding women from local-church leadership represented a growing separationist mentality toward half the members of Southern Baptist churches.

More recently, on 6 October 2004, the SBC North American Mission Board (NAMB), with the support of seminary leadership, officially positioned itself in opposition to ordained women deacons. NAMB trustees adopted a thirty-four-page position paper on that day that NAMB will use as a guideline to determine what constitutes a "New Testament church." NAMB starts about 1,500 new churches every year. Richard Harris, NAMB's vice president of church planting, said his staff would use the document "to review and guide the agency's church-planting strategies, processes and materials." Titled "Ecclesiological Guidelines to Inform Southern Baptist Church Planters," the position paper was written by Stan Norman, associate professor of theology and director of the Baptist Center

---

[34]*Annual*, Southern Baptist Convention, 1984, 65.

[35]*Annual*, Southern Baptist Convention, 1998, 78.

[36]"Report of the Baptist Faith and Message Study Committee to the Southern Baptist Convention, Adopted June 14th, 2000." <www.sbc.net/2000-bf_m.html>, accessed 2 April 2002.

for Theology and Ministry at New Orleans Baptist Theological Seminary, and was endorsed by the Council of Southern Baptist Seminary Deans and two SBC seminary presidents, Paige Patterson, president of Southwestern Baptist Theological Seminary, and Phil Roberts, president of New Orleans Baptist Theological Seminary.[37]

The adopted document attacked ordained women deacons and, by inference, churches that ordain them:

> The BFM [Baptist Faith and Message] 2000 leaves open the issue of whether or not women can serve as deaconesses in SBC churches. My position is that, if a local church ordains its deacons, then women cannot serve in this capacity. In SBC life, ordination carries with it implications of authority and oversight, and I believe the Bible relegates authority and oversight to men (1 Timothy 2:12-15). If a church, however, does not ordain its deacons, then the authority-oversight prohibitions would not apply. In that case, the generic meaning of the term "deacon" (Greek: *diakonia*) is that of a servant or a table waiter. Thus, any member of the congregation is qualified to serve. Since there is no clear instance recorded in Scripture of the presence of female deacons, I will use masculine language in my references to deacons.[38]

The implications of the NAMB action are serious. Churches with women deacons will likely not be able to start new churches using money from NAMB, and churches started with NAMB money will likely be urged not to elect women deacons. The adopted document is flawed biblically, historically, theologically, and practically. It erroneously claims that "ordination carries with it implications of authority and oversight" and that "the Bible relegates authority and oversight to men." Nothing in the New Testament supports those claims. The writer's assertion that "I will use masculine language in my references to deacons" reflects an antiwoman bias and fails to take into account that thousands of Baptist churches throughout the world, including many in the SBC, have women deacons and deaconesses, ordained and not ordained.

Tony Cartledge, editor of the *Biblical Recorder*, Baptist state newspaper for North Carolina, raised serious questions about the NAMB action.

---

[37]Martin King, "NAMB trustees meet, approve guidelines for church starts." <www.baptistpress.com> (7 October 2004), accessed 20 October 2004.

[38]Stan Norman, "Ecclesiological Guidelines to Inform Southern Baptist Church Planters." <www.namb.net/news/guidelines> (28 September 2004), accessed 20 October 2004.

Claiming that "some NAMB officials and trustees expect the document to have considerable influence," he asserted that because of the NAMB action, "thousands of faithful congregations . . . will find themselves portrayed as something less than true Baptist churches." Cartledge observed that the document delegated authority to pastors and deacons, "who must be men." Therefore, "Say goodbye to the longstanding Baptist belief that the biblical purpose of ordination is to set one apart for special service, as opposed to the Roman Catholic concept of empowering the ordainee with spiritual or supervisory authority." For Cartledge, "the adoption of guidelines that paint an increasingly narrow picture of a 'true' Baptist church is a legitimate cause for concern."[39]

Through amendments to the Baptist Faith and Message, approval of convention resolutions, and actions of its agencies, the SBC has told the world that ordained women deacons are not acceptable in local churches. Some local churches will buy into that concept. Others, using the autonomy of the local church and a more biblical understanding of God's intentions for women, will decide in favor of women deacons. Their number is growing.

Counterattacks against Assaults
on Women Deacons and Pastors

Without question, Baptist developments of the past twenty-five years have incorporated issues relating to women deacons into broader issues relating to women. Two documents printed in *Going for the Jugular: A Documentary History of the SBC Holy War*, published by Mercer University Press in 1996, plainly illustrate this. Speaking to the Southern Baptist Pastors' Conference in 1979, Adrian Rogers described women's liberation as a "unisex movement . . . belched out of hell."[40] The SBC's 1988 Resolution on the Priesthood of the Believer affirmed the authority of the pastor and undercut the priesthood of all other Christians, women deacons included.[41]

Other documents in *Going for the Jugular* reveal counterattacks to what some viewed as a systematic war on women's status in Baptist life. In

---

[39]Tony Cartledge, "Defining a Baptist (?) Church," *Biblical Recorder* (23 October 2004): 2.

[40]Walter B. Shurden and Randy Shepley, comps. and eds., *Going for the Jugular: A Documentary History of the SBC Holy War* (Macon GA: Mercer University Press, 1996) 19.

[41]Ibid., 237.

March 1983, thirty-three women met in Louisville, Kentucky, to take steps to initiate the formation of Women in Ministry, SBC, and that organization was officially launched in June of that year. In 1990, Randall Lolley delivered a sermon to the Forum, a formal national meeting of moderate Baptists, in which he compared *"the dinosaur rhetoric of the past regarding Christian femaleness"* to *"the biblical rhetoric of the future regarding Christian femaleness,"* observing that "the plain and simple fact is that in both the Old Testament and the New Testament women play a surprisingly prominent role in male-dominated religion."[42] Believing that "no issue in the controversy more starkly contrasts the fundamentalist and moderate approach to Scripture than does the role of women in the church,"[43] Walter B. Shurden presented in 1991 an "Address to the Public" on behalf of the CBF Interim Steering Committee in which he described Galatians 3:27-28 "as a clue to the way the Church should be ordered."[44] In concluding *Going for the Jugular*, Shurden claimed that "the SBC has become as chauvinistic in the 1990s as it was racist in the 1890s" and predicted that "just as the SBC apologized for racism in 1995, it will one day apologize for its chauvinism."[45]

A major development took place in the early 1990s with events surrounding the origins of the CBF. In August 1990, the first Consultation of Concerned Baptists met in Atlanta. An Interim Steering Committee convened for the first time in October 1990. Shortly before the second convocation convened in May 1991—at which CBF would be formed—the Interim Steering Committee adopted a document prepared by Cecil E. Sherman and Walter B. Shurden that Shurden presented as an address to the second convocation. The address acknowledged that "Our Understandings Are Different" than those of fundamentalist Southern Baptists on six key issues: Bible, education, mission, pastor, women, and church.[46] The comments about women were critically important since they would generally represent CBF attitudes into the twenty-first century and because

---

[42]Ibid., 255-57.

[43]Ibid., 93.

[44]Ibid., 268.

[45]Ibid., 280.

[46]Daniel Vestal, "The History of the Cooperative Baptist Fellowship," *The Struggle for the Soul of the SBC: Moderate Responses to the Fundamentalist Movement*, ed. Walter B. Shurden (Macon GA: Mercer University Press, 1993) 260-66.

they would help change attitudes toward women deacons as well. They read as follows:

> 5. *Women.* The New Testament gives two signals about the role of women. A literal interpretation of Paul can build a case for making women submissive to men in the Church. But another body of scripture points toward another place for women. In Galatians 3:27-28 Paul wrote, "As many of you as are baptized into Christ have clothed yourselves with Christ. There is no longer Jew or Greek, there no longer slave or free, there is no longer male and female; for all of you are in Christ Jesus" (NRSV).
>
> We take Galatians as a clue to the way the Church should be ordered. We interpret the reference to women the same way we interpret the reference to slaves. If we have submissive roles for women, we must also have a place for slaves in the Church.
>
> In Galatians Paul follows the spirit of Jesus who courageously challenged the conventional wisdom of his day. It was a wisdom with rigid boundaries between men and women in religion and in public life. Jesus deliberately broke those barriers. He called women to follow him; he treated women as equally capable of dealing with sacred issues. Our model for the role of women in matters of faith is the Lord Jesus.[47]

What Women Think

The Baptist version of Christian history has clearly presented special challenges to women. Baptists, especially male Baptists, have questioned whether women should speak and vote in church and conventions, whether they should teach men or exercise authority over men, whether they should be ordained to the diaconate or the pastoral ministry, and whether they should serve as denominational officers and as executives of denominational agencies.

Baptist women have faced discrimination in ministry and deacon functions since the 1600s. Most Baptists have interpreted the Bible to shut women out of many possible avenues of Christian service. This tendency has accelerated in the 2000s, especially in Southern Baptist life, as ultraconservative views against women's ordination to the diaconate and the pastoral ministry have intensified. This book will demonstrate, however, that women deacons and deaconesses have existed and functioned success-

---

[47]Ibid., 265-66.

fully for the past four centuries. Women deacons are alive and well today; their numbers are growing, as are the number of female deacon chairs.

What women think about women's issues is critically important. In 1923, Helen Barrett Montgomery, an ex-president of the Northern Baptist Convention, presented an address titled "The New Opportunity for Baptist Women" during the Third Baptist World Congress meeting in Stockholm, Sweden. In straightforward language, Montgomery declared:

> Jesus Christ is the great Emancipator of women. He alone among the founders of great religions of the world looked upon men and women with level eyes, seeing not their differences, but their oneness, their humanity. He alone put no barriers before women in His religious teaching, but promulgated one law, equally binding upon men and women; opened one gate to which men and women were admitted upon equal terms.
>
> A striking illustration of His casteless, sexless attitude is found in the story of His conversation with the Samaritan woman by Jacob's well. . . . In the mind of the Founder of Christianity there is no area of religious privilege fenced off for the exclusive use of men. In this attitude Jesus stands absolutely alone among religious teachers. . . . God has liberated and equipped them [women] in order that they may offer their whole mind and soul and body in the service of this Saviour in Whom alone rests the hope of the world.[48]

Montgomery admitted that Jesus' teachings created such a dramatic impact on the practices of the rising Christian community that the apostle Paul felt obligated to check the new liberty to protect the church's reputation and the orderly conduct of its life. But the important thing was not Paul's cautions to women but "the presence of a new driving *force* in the rising Christian community, revealed in the activities of the women," such as the seven prophesying daughters of Philip; Priscilla; Phoebe; and "that long list of women who find a place in the closing greetings of Paul's letters." As the churches began to mingle with Greek and Roman civilizations, "much of the beautiful simplicity and freedom of the Way was lost; and women were shut up again in the prison of inhibitions and conventions. But

---

[48]Helen Barrett Montgomery, "The New Opportunity for Baptist Women," *Record of Proceedings. Third Baptist World Congress*, ed. W. T. Whitley (London: Kingsgate Press, 1923) 99, 102. (Montgomery, of Rochester, New York, is perhaps best remembered for her well-known *Centenary Translation of the New Testament*, published in 1924 by the American Baptist Publication Society.)

Christianity never wholly ceased to feel the powerful upthrust of the Master."[49]

Six years later, in 1929, another woman spoke out in a significant setting. Ethlene Cox, president of the national Woman's Missionary Union, addressed the SBC as the first woman ever to do so. Focusing on "The Woman's Part," she made a point to describe Jesus' view of women:

> The attitude of Jesus toward women is meaningful because He revealed the principles and forms of woman's service not only for His day but for every age. He revealed for all time what should be the Christian attitude toward woman as well as woman's responsibility to the world. From the Scriptures we get no intimation that Jesus ever treated woman other than the equal of man. Nor was woman released from any moral or spiritual obligation. Reverently I affirm that only Jesus knew God's perfect plan for woman. . . . Jesus never talked down to woman, rather the reverse; many of His most profound revelations were spoken to her.[50]

Carolyn D. Blevins, associate professor of religion at Carson-Newman College and an astute observer of the role of women in Baptist history, reflected in the year 2000 on Baptists and women's issues in the twentieth century. She concluded that problems affecting Baptist women in the diaconate, the ministry, and other roles were serious at the end of that century:

> One issue dominated women's relationship within Baptists in the twentieth century: who controls the voice of women? When other persons attempted to control that voice, they silenced some women, confused many women, and made ministry difficult for those who refused to be silenced. Baptist women spent the century trying to get a voice in their denominations. By the end of the twentieth century, had woman gained a voice in Baptist life? My conclusion is that she was a strong soloist surrounded by a chorus of opposition.[51]

In 2003, Blevins claimed that one key point overrides all the challenges Baptist women face:

---

[49]Ibid.

[50]*Annual*, Southern Baptist Convention, 1929, 229.

[51]Carolyn D. Blevins, "Reflections: Baptists and Women's Issues in the Twentieth Century," *Baptist History and Heritage* 35/3 (Summer/Fall 2000): 65.

What is women's place in Baptist life? To do whatever God calls them to do. As Lottie Moon said, women are responsible only to God. Baptists take doing God's will and answering God's call very seriously. Women's place in Baptist life first and foremost is to obey God. Others who respect the individual's relationship with God are obligated to honor that call and encourage it. Baptist women have a rich legacy of foremothers who answered the call to serve others as God directed.[52]

That call includes serving as deacons. Blevins herself had served as deacon chair in the First Baptist Church of Jefferson City, Tennessee.

Divergent Views of Scripture and Theology

Baptists worldwide differ in their interpretations of scripture and theology when dealing with the issue of women in the diaconate. Many Baptists, defining their views on the basis of the life and teachings of Christ, ascribe to women full equality in consideration for every position of leadership in the church; for them, women deacons are as biblical as believer's baptism and the Lord's Supper. Many other Baptists, drawing their views from literal readings of restrictions placed on women by the apostle Paul, as well as on traditional patterns of cultural subjugation of women to men, view it as biblical misunderstanding, historical aberration, and theological corruption to adopt ordained women deacons into church life. They will sometimes accept nonordained deaconesses. Exceptions exist to both of these approaches. For example, some churches ordain deaconesses while others do not ordain women deacons.

Theological factors in Baptist history have exerted a powerful influence on the tendencies in Baptist church life both to support and to oppose women deacons. For example, Calvinist theology and church polity, both somewhat negative toward women deacons, especially those who are ordained, have affected every century of Baptist life, sometimes in mild forms, sometimes in strong forms. Among Baptists, past and present, women typically have been excluded from leadership roles, especially those roles viewed as having authority over men. A resurgence of Calvinism in Southern Baptist life in recent years has contributed to a bias against the ordination of women to the diaconate or the ministry. This issue merits careful consideration by scholars studying the relationship of Calvinism and Baptist women and by readers of this book who will discover time and

---

[52]Blevins, *Women's Place in Baptist Life*, 42-43.

again as the chapters unfold that Calvinism has worked hardships on women deacons and deaconesses.

On the other hand, other theological factors have nurtured and encouraged churches to adopt women deacons. Baptists have often appealed to a biblical doctrine of creation featuring equality between men and women, freedom-based concepts of church polity, the priesthood of all believers, the concept of ordination providing opportunity rather than authority, the idea that God does not intend for spiritual leadership and service to be confined to a masculine agenda, and inclusion as opposed to exclusion in church life.

Here are some questions that emerge from historical developments which the reader may want to ponder while exploring the remainder of this book.

- How should Baptists process negative attacks against women in the diaconate that have appeared in every century of Baptist life?
- How do Baptists explain that they read the same Bible and wind up with wildly different perspectives on women deacons, and is that good or bad?
- What importance should Baptists give to the fact that the first two Baptist pastors, John Smyth and Thomas Helwys, both allowed for women deacons with the same ordination and duties as men?
- How should Baptists react to the reality that thousands of Baptist churches today use women deacons or deaconesses?
- In what ways should Baptists today reconcile a growing antagonism toward ordaining women deacons with the fact that more churches are ordaining them in the early 2000s than in any period of the Baptist past?
- What does ordination mean in the Bible?
- What are the implications of Baptist history and theology for whether a church should consider electing and ordaining women deacons?
- How should Baptist women counter the mounting pressures of male leaders of the SBC to suppress all ordained women and to cut off relationships with churches that ordain them?
- In what ways has Baptist theology hurt and helped women deacons?

Chapter 1
Biblical and Historical Backgrounds

One way to enhance an understanding of how and why Baptists chose to incorporate women into the diaconate in the 1600s-2000s is to examine pre-Baptist backgrounds in the larger Christian tradition. Therefore, this chapter will focus on the Bible, especially Baptist views of what it teaches; the Early Church and Middle Ages; and the Protestant Reformation, English Separatism, and Anabaptism. The Bible will receive the most extensive treatment.

The Bible

Two key New Testament verses figure inevitably into discussions of possible biblical evidence for deaconesses or women deacons: Romans 16:1 and 1 Timothy 3:11. The question in Romans 16:1 is how to translate the Greek word *diakonon*, used by the apostle Paul to describe Phoebe. A sampling of sixteen representative translations of the New Testament shows that opinions vary. Of these, five translate *diakonon* as "deaconess," one as "deacon," one as a "woman," six as a "servant," one as a person "who serves," one as a "minister," and one as a "fellow Christian who holds office."[1]

Then in 1 Timothy 3:11, the question centers around the translation of the Greek word *gunaikas*. Again, opinions vary. Of the sixteen translations examined, eight translate *gunaikas* as "women," seven as "wives," and one as "deaconesses."[2]

Baptist scholars have also differed in their views on how to translate the words *diakonon* and *gunaikas* in the two verses in question. A. T. Robertson (1931) believed *deaconesses* were probably the subject of both

---

[1]Translations include "deaconess" (Williams, RSV, Amplified, Phillips, Jerusalem Bible); "deacon" (NRSV); "servant" (KJV, ASV, Weymouth, NASB, NIV, Holman Christian Study Bible); person "who serves" (TEV); "minister" (REB); "woman" (Living Bible); "fellow Christian who holds office" (NEB).

[2]Translations include "women" (ASV, Weymouth, RSV, Amplified, NASB, Jerusalem Bible, NRSV, REB); "wives" (KJV, NEB, Phillips, TEV, Living Bible, NIV, Holman Christian Study Bible); "deaconesses" (Williams).

Romans 16:1 and 1 Timothy 3:11.[3] Frank Stagg (1962) concluded: "Evidence is too scant to determine whether or not the reference in verse 11 [of 1 Timothy 3] is to deaconesses or to the wives of deacons."[4] Robert L. Cate determined that "women deacons developed within the New Testament" and that "the New Testament seems clearly to allow such a practice."[5] Ray Summers believed that Romans 16:1 and 1 Timothy 3:11 provided a "fragile base" for building a case for women deacons," but he concluded: "Service to God is not determined by race, social class, or sex" but by what a "church decides is best in its situation."[6]

A classic illustration of recent Southern Baptist variations is that SBC-sponsored commentaries, from the 1970s and the 1990s, took opposite positions on the key New Testament passages that relate to the women-deacon question. *The Broadman Bible Commentary* concluded that Phoebe was a "deaconess" in Romans 16:1 and that the weight of argument slightly favored translating *gunaikas* in 1 Timothy 3:11 as "deaconesses." In contrast, the New American Commentary volumes viewed Phoebe as a "servant" in Romans 16:1 and the *gunaikas* in 1 Timothy 3:11 as the wives of deacons.[7]

Therefore, one has to move past these verses and examine the larger picture of scripture in order to determine biblical support for and the appropriateness of women in the diaconate. An open-minded reading of scripture relating to God's creation of woman in his own image reveals God's clear intention to provide an equal place for woman in carrying out his purposes.

---

[3]A. T. Robertson, *Word Pictures in the New Testament*, vol. 4 (Nashville: Sunday School Board, Southern Baptist Convention, 1931) 425, 575.

[4]Frank Stagg, *New Testament Theology* (Nashville: Broadman Press, 1962) 264-65.

[5]Robert L. Cate, "Shall We Have Women Deacons?" *Baptist Standard* (17 April 1974): 4.

[6]Ray Summers, "Deacons-Deacon-Deaconess," *Baptist Standard* (3 July 1974): 9.

[7]Dale Moody, "Romans," *The Broadman Bible Commentary*, vol. 10 (Nashville: Broadman Press, 1970) 279; E. Glenn Hinson, "1-2 Timothy and Titus," *The Broadman Bible Commentary*, vol. 11 (Nashville: Broadman Press, 1971) 319. Robert H. Mounce, *Romans*, New American Commentary 27 (Nashville: Broadman and Holman, 1995): 272; Thomas D. Lea and Hayne P. Griffin, Jr., *1, 2 Timothy, Titus*, New American Commentary 34 (Nashville: Broadman and Holman, 1992) 119-20. ("And Holman" signifies the addition of the Holman Bible publishing house to the SBC publishing enterprise.)

The New Testament plainly provides solid foundations for women deacons. These foundations reside in the emancipation-based life and teachings of Jesus Christ and in New Testament perspectives on freedom and on women in general.

D. S. Schaff summarized New Testament origins of deaconesses by stating that

> from the earliest times the need must have been felt for a special class of women who should devote themselves to Christian service at times of baptism, visit the parts of the houses set aside for females, and perform other duties. While Phoebe is the only person in the New Testament distinctly called a deaconess, there are indications, as in the case of Dorcas (Acts ix. 36) and other cases, that woman's service was held in high esteem by the Church and had a distinctive character.[8]

Four Sets of Point-Counterpoint Articles. For centuries Baptists have assessed what the New Testament says (or does not say) about women in the diaconate and their ordination. A frequent approach has been to publish pro and con articles on these topics. By producing detailed arguments, this approach has shown that Baptists have radically disagreed when discussing women in the diaconate.

The 1900s witnessed the printing of many sets of point-counterpoint articles relating to women deacons and deaconesses in the New Testament and to biblical perspectives on women's ordination. Four representative sets of such articles by Baptist professors and pastors appeared in 1929, 1984, 1985, and 1988. A digest of the contents follows. The eight writers lived in North Carolina, Missouri, and Texas; six were men, two were women. Some common denominators ran throughout these writings. Opponents of women deacons and deaconesses and their ordination tended to appeal to selected writings of the apostle Paul, to literalistic views of scripture, and to a pattern of interpretation that forbade anything not specifically taught in the Bible; advocates appealed more generally to the life and teachings of Christ and to broader understandings of Paul's writings, to nonliteralistic views of scripture, and to the larger contexts and meanings of the Bible.

---

[8]D. S. Schaff, "Deaconesses," *The New Schaff-Herzog Encyclopedia of Religious Knowledge*, vol. 3, ed. Samuel Macauley (New York: Funk & Wagnalls, 1909) 374.

First, a classic written debate took place in 1929 in the *Biblical Record-er*, the North Carolina Baptist newspaper, between a leading opponent of the ordination of deaconesses and a leading advocate of such ordination. G. W. Paschal, professor of Greek at Wake Forest College, acknowledged in January 1929 that he had learned of the recent ordination of a deaconess in a Baptist church. He described that development as "a great advance towards modernism, a radical departure from the New Testament, and wholly unauthorized by any American Baptist Confession of Faith." After acknowledging that two verses, Romans 16:1 and 1 Timothy 3:11, were the key verses at stake, Paschal continued, "There is not a word in the New Testament that even hints at the laying on of hands on a woman by way of ordination for any function of the church." He asserted that "there is no proof in the world that Paul meant to say that Phoebe [in Romans 16:1] was a 'deaconess' in the sense of a church officer," and that Paul "had not remotely in his head the idea of deaconess" in the 1 Timothy verse.[9]

After asserting that "on those who are imposing deaconesses on some of our Baptist churches rests the sacred obligation to justify their action," he concluded, "When I see such innovations as this of deaconesses in our Baptist churches I begin to fear for our faith." Paschal revealed his approach to interpreting the New Testament when he claimed that churches that ordain deaconesses "revise the pernicious argument that whatever the Scriptures do not definitely forbid is allowed." Paschal questioned whether churches that departed from scripture "in appointing and ordaining deacon-esses" were even Baptist, calling them "so-called Baptist churches."[10] Livingston Farmer, editor of the *Biblical Recorder*, essentially agreed with Paschal's overall arguments.[11]

A February 1929 issue of the *Biblical Recorder* carried a sharply nega-tive reaction to Paschal's article and views. Written by S. L. Morgan, a noted North Carolina Baptist pastor, this reaction constituted a strong defense of Baptist deaconesses and their ordination. Morgan began by stating that "I had supposed the question of the right of women to be deaconesses had been about as definitely disposed of as the question of woman suffrage. And it has by thousands of Baptist churches." Further, he claimed that Frederick A. Agar, a Northern Baptist leader and writer, had

---

[9]G. W. Paschal, "Deaconesses," *Biblical Recorder* (23 January 1929): 4.
[10]Ibid.
[11]Livingston Johnson, "Doctor Paschal's Article," *Biblical Recorder* (23 January 1929): 6.

recently claimed that there were about three thousand Northern Baptist churches that had deaconesses.[12]

Morgan acknowledged that the verses cited by Paschal "fall somewhat short of making it certain that the women referred to were deaconesses." Still, he admonished Paschal for failing to recognize that "many biblical precepts and customs recognized by law fall short of representing the will of God," claiming that Jesus often "brushed aside a law given by Moses and replaced it with a higher."[13]

Morgan outlined key biblical and theological support for the equality of women both in the diaconate and in other arenas of Baptist life, while decrying the fact that "theologians for 2,000 years have been perpetuating the crime of denying to women equal rights with men in the church." Demonstrably, he asserted that "Jesus never for a moment countenanced the attitude taken by His disciples that a woman was a whit inferior to a man." Claiming that "I know of nothing more regrettable than this persistence of the age-old attempt to hold women to an inferior status in the church, the church founded by Him who so clearly taught that man and woman are essentially equal," Morgan challenged the principle of biblical interpretation that led to such a view:

> The most disastrous blunders in the history of Christianity have been the result of this failure to distinguish between the eternal principles in the Bible and the precepts necessary to meet the ignorance and prejudice in the situation that called forth a Bible passage.[14]

Second, in 1984, *Word and Way*, a Missouri Baptist newspaper, published pro and con articles by two Missouri Baptist pastors relating to biblical perspectives on women's ordination. John H. Hewett, pastor of Kirkwood Baptist Church in St. Louis, presented the pro views. Hewett began by establishing a principle for biblical interpretation which required "approaching each text with two crucial, and sequential, questions: What did this mean in its original context, to its original readers/hearers? and What then does it mean for us today? This 'bifocal' method of biblical interpretation takes the Bible seriously; it does not take it literally." Using that approach, he stated that because of "the hierarchical culture of the

---

[12]S. L. Morgan, "Dr. Paschal and Deaconesses," *Biblical Recorder* (13 February 1929): 4.

[13]Ibid.

[14]Ibid.

day," it is not surprising that women in the New Testament did not serve as bishops, elders, or pastors. However, "Solid evidence does exist to indicate they were accepted as deacons (1 Tim. 3:11, Rom. 16:1)."[15]

Hewett concluded with a question and some answers. Based on New Testament teaching, should the practice of ordination be limited to males only?

> Only if local churches are convinced that God does not endow women with spiritual gifts empowering them to function in enabling and representative ministries. And only if the example of Jesus is to be discounted and the time-bound opinions of Paul elevated to the same level as his timeless proclamations about the equality of men and women "in the Lord." All Christians, male and female, have been commissioned as full-time ministers (servants) of the gospel. As the early Christians frequently affirmed, in baptism we are all "ordained."[16]

Thomas M. McClain, pastor of Glendale Baptist Church in Springfield, then presented the con side of women's ordination. For him the case was simple: "God has not indicated that He wants women ordained as preachers or deacons." In fact, "There are no examples of deacons or preachers who were women on the pages of Holy Writ." Using an outline of scriptural order, offices, and objections, McClain claimed that scripture does not allow women's ordination. According to the scriptural order expressed in Genesis 3:16, 1 Corinthians 11:3, Ephesians 5:22, Titus 3:5, and 1 Peter 3:1, "the woman's role is . . . subordination and submission." According to the scriptural offices, which included apostles, elders, deacons, bishops, pastors, and teachers, "There is no indication that any of them were females. They were all males." According to scriptural objections, a woman must avoid "interrupting a worship service where the Holy Spirit is at work" (1 Cor. 14:34); should "learn Bible doctrine in silence, with earnest concentration and under masculine authority" (1 Tim. 2:8); and "is not permitted to teach Bible doctrine with a dogmatic, authoritative emphasis" (1 Tim. 2:12).[17]

McClain finished by issuing two cautions. First, he warned Baptists that if they "intend to have the New Testament remain their rule of faith

---

[15]John H. Hewett, "Women's Ordination: Biblical Perpectives—Pro," *Word and Way* (17 May 1984): 6.

[16]Ibid., 11.

[17]Thomas M. McClain, "Women's Ordination: Biblical Perspectives—Con," *Word and Way* (17 May 1984): 7.

and practice, they must listen to the scriptural objections to ordaining women as deacons and as preachers." Second, after noting particularly that there were women deacons in First Baptist Church of Oklahoma City, he predicted: "Southern Baptists are headed for grave trouble because of this issue."[18]

A third set of pro and con articles, focusing again on women's ordination, appeared in a 1985 issue of the *Baptist Standard*, a Texas Baptist newspaper. Dan L. Griffin, pastor of Cliff Temple Baptist Church in Dallas, favored women's ordination. Paul W. Powell, pastor of Green Acres Baptist Church in Tyler, opposed it.

Griffin, influenced by Forrest Feezor's presentation on women's ordination at the 1975 meeting of the Baptist Convention of North Carolina in Asheville, and by a sermon titled "The Bible and Women" that he had heard John Claypool deliver in the 1970s at Broadway Baptist Church in Fort Worth, Texas, concluded that "there's not much guidance in scripture regarding ordination" and that "in ordination, a church agrees that a person has the gifts as well as the call to perform the offices of deacon or pastor. There is nothing in the scripture to prevent a woman from being ordained as a deacon or pastor. I believe that ordination is overrated." Griffin continued, "The real question about the ordination of women as deacons revolves around the power structure in the church. . . . To ordain a woman as a deacon means that she is going to share power with the men in the decision-making processes."[19]

Griffin claimed further, "By denying to women a chance to share power and lead, we are denying the church some remarkable gifts given by the Holy Spirit for its own welfare." Then he concluded,

> The church has too often been silent and apathetic regarding liberation movements. Frequently, it's the last organization to grant the freedom or equality won in the secular world. We need to champion the cause of women and open the door to what they can bring to a church sorely in need of committed leadership.[20]

In sharp contrast, Paul Powell expressed strong opposition to the ordination of women as deacons or ministers. "There is no evidence in

---

[18]Ibid., 11.

[19]Dan L. Griffin, "For Women's Ordination," *Baptist Standard* (24 April 1985): 8.

[20]Ibid., 8, 10.

scripture," he wrote, "that women ever served in a governing role as either pastors or deacons as we view the deacon's role in our Baptist churches today. Nor is there any clear evidence in church history of this. Both scripture and tradition agree that the position of overall government in our Christian community should be held by men." For Powell, quite simply, "Men as a group are more suited to a governmental role than are women as a group. . . . It is a matter of temperament." Further, "Women were not put in positions of authority in the church in the New Testament. Nor should they be now. The issue of ordination does not have to do with ministry but with authority." Therefore, "to ordain women is to fail . . . to appreciate how God made us. It is to refuse to accept His order in society."[21]

In July 1988, *Baptist History and Heritage* published still another set of pro and con articles on women's ordination. Of the four sets of such articles described in this chapter, this is the only set written by women. Dorothy Kelly Patterson, a homemaker in Dallas, Texas, and a teacher of seminars in womanhood and family living, opposed women's ordination. She was the wife of Paige Patterson, noted fundamentalist Southern Baptist leader. Jann Aldredge Clanton, member of the Seventh and James Baptist Church in Waco, Texas, favored women's ordination.

Patterson claimed that 1 Timothy 2:8-15 presented a biblical warning regarding women's ordination and that 1 Corinthians 14:33-35 presented a reprimand. Asserting that biblical authority does not exist for ordaining female deacons or pastors, she stated that the only thing that matters is what "God has spoken from eternity in His immutable written Word." And "the Scriptures declare that women are to be submissive because of the order of creation (1 Cor. 11:2-16; 1 Tim. 2:11-13)." Further, "The idea of male headship and female submission is clearly found in the Old and New Testaments as well as in the writings of both Paul and Peter." First Timothy and 1 Corinthians make clear that women "did not teach or exercise authority over men." In conclusion, Patterson insisted that "the Scripture does not support ordination" for women, although it does not "prohibit a woman's serving in the diaconate, if following the New Testament pattern of this office. Subordination in the home, church, school, or marketplace has never abolished equality any more than equality has abolished subordination."[22]

---

[21]Paul W. Powell, "Against Women's Ordination," *Baptist Standard* (24 April 1985): 9-10.

[22]Dorothy Kelley Patterson, "Why I Believe Southern Baptist Churches Should

Jann Clanton strongly favored women's ordination. She launched her article with explicit language:

Southern Baptists cannot overthrow the ordination of women because it is of God. Ordination of women as pastors and deacons stands on solid biblical hermeneutics, an accurate review of Baptist history, and a theology of human beings created in the image of God and redeemed by Christ to be their own priests.

Clanton claimed that "although the Old Testament describes a culture oppressive to women, it shows God working to restore women to full personhood in God's image." Key elements of the New Testament witness include the facts that "Christ leads us to affirm the equality of men and women in every sphere of life, including the ordained ministry" and that a study of Paul's writings reveals that "it is unlikely that Paul gave any blanket prohibitions against women in church leadership." In fact, persons who argue against women's ordination on the basis of Paul's writings "practice selective literalism, violating contextual and historical hermeneutical principles."[23]

After reviewing biblical and Baptist historical accounts relating to women, Clanton concluded that "Baptist history, along with scripture, supports the ordination of women as pastors and deacons" and that "churches which refuse to ordain women as pastors and deacons limit God. Women and men equally reflect the image of God (Gen. 1:27)." Churches opposing women's ordination also "deny the priesthood of women by standing between God and the woman, dictating the form God's call to her must take." Clanton then related women's ordination to the call of God, the gifts of the Spirit, and the life and teachings of Christ: "Exclusion of women from the ordained ministry also places restrictions on the call of God and on the gifts of the Spirit. To deny the gifts of pastor and deacon in women is to deny the actions and teachings of Christ."[24]

The contrasting articles of Patterson and Clanton revealed two illuminating points. First, Patterson's article opposing women's ordination mentioned Jesus only three times; an assessment of Paul's writings dominated her treatment. Clanton's article included numerous paragraphs

---

Not Ordain Women," *Baptist History and Heritage* 23/3 (July 1988): 57-62.

[23]Jann Aldredge Clanton, "Why I Believe Southern Baptist Churches Should Ordain Women," *Baptist History and Heritage* 23/3 (July 1988): 50-53.

[24]Ibid., 53-54.

featuring the life and teachings of Jesus; her treatment of Paul's writings took a more contextual approach. Second, Patterson's sources focused heavily on more conservative publications such as *Christianity Today*, *Journal of the Evangelical Theological Society*, and the *Criswell Theological Review*. Clanton used more progressive Baptist sources, such as the writings of Evelyn and Frank Stagg, William E. Hull, and Leon McBeth.

Contextual Interpretations Emerge. Baptist scholars, male and female, have contributed important writings to this discussion of women's issues, including women deacons, especially since the mid-1970s. The following will feature selected writings of William E. Hull, Peter Rhea Jones, Evelyn and Frank Stagg, T. B. Maston, Sheri Adams, and Molly T. Marshall.

In 1975, William E. Hull, then dean of the School of Theology and professor of New Testament Interpretation at the Southern Baptist Theological Seminary, prepared a penetrating essay titled "Woman in Her Place: Biblical Perspectives."[25] After noting that he had reluctantly agreed to write the article, he cited several reasons why he finally did agree, one of which read: "Among the fifty or so biblical specialists working in our six SBC seminaries, not a single woman is to be found. Nor does one readily think of a woman among twice that number of Southern Baptist colleagues working in scriptural studies at the college level."[26]

Hull reviewed the place of woman in Israel, in Judaism, and in Roman Hellenism. Then he concluded that "on the whole, it is not a pretty picture which our sources paint of the place which woman occupied in the ancient world." However, he asserted that "the issue for us is not how much progress was actually achieved in one corner of the world during the millennium covered by biblical literature but whether God chose that often deplorable situation in which to disclose his ultimate intention for woman."[27]

Hull discussed woman and creation, woman and Christ, and woman and the consummation. Hull labeled Genesis 2:4b-25 as "the oldest and in many ways the most comprehensive biblical witness to the place of woman as defined by creation." Then he claimed that "because this account depicts woman as having been created after man, from man, and for man, some have seen in its concept of complementary companionship a theology of

---

[25]William E. Hull, "Woman in Her Place: Biblical Perspectives," *Review and Expositor* 72/1 (Winter 1975): 5-17.

[26]Ibid., 7.

[27]Ibid., 12.

female subordinationism of which there is no hint in the text." In fact, the creation narrative in Genesis 1:26-31 dispels any doubt about woman's status in creation. God created male and female concurrently in verse 27. "Sexual differentiation was inherent in God's design for mankind from the first; the female was not an accident, an afterthought, or an expedient. Any suggestion of androgyny and the baneful theologies of narcissism on which they are built was explicitly repudiated."[28]

Jesus, Hull affirmed, "was the supreme interpreter of creation theology within the Bible." Paul, unlike Jesus, did occasionally refer "to the subordination of woman rooted in Genesis 3:16 (cf. 1 Cor. 11:3-9, 14-34; Eph. 5:22-24; 1 Tim. 2:11-15)." However, the Pauline perspective on woman in creation cannot be understood apart from his views about woman in Christ in which he carefully maintained "the unity and equality of the sexes in the creative purpose of God (1 Cor. 11:11-12; Eph. 5:28-33; and, by implication, 1 Cor. 6:16)."[29]

In discussing women and Christ, Hull pointed out that the message of Christ "nowhere included references to circumcision, that distinctively male rite of initiation from which Jewish women and female proselytes were excluded." In the place of circumcision, "Jesus focused on faith as the basis on one's standing before God. This immediately put the woman, as well as the foreigner, on equal footing with the Jewish male (e.g., Mk. 5:34; cf. Mt. 8:10)." Even Paul would come to realize that "the ultimate meaning of Christ is that we are saved entirely by grace without regard for race or sex or nation or any other human distinction." That awareness would lead Paul to affirm that "in the clearest expression of his Christocentric faith: 'there is no "male and female"; for you are all one in Christ Jesus' (Gal. 3:28)."[30]

In writing about women and the consummation, Hull noted that both Jesus and Paul set sexuality in the framework of saving history. Both seemed to present three ages or levels in the relationship between man and woman:

(1) The Old Age in which "hardness of heart" led to male dominance, female subjection, unfaithfulness and exploitation; (2) the Messianic Age in which Christ makes possible a realization of the original intention for man and woman in the created order, namely, an equality of reciprocal

---

[28]Ibid., 13.
[29]Ibid., 14-15.
[30]Ibid., 15-16.

loyalty, fidelity, and support; (3) the Age to Come in which even our redeemed sexuality will be abolished and our unity-in-reciprocity will be fulfilled not by oneness with the opposite sex but by a perfect oneness with God-in-Christ.[31]

In 1976, Peter Rhea Jones, also a New Testament professor at the Southern Baptist Theological Seminary, wrote a powerful essay on "The Liberating and Liberated Lord: A Biblical Essay on Freedom."[32] Describing Jesus as "nothing less than a model of freedom," Jones asserted that "Jesus is the most liberated person who ever lived. He is the greatest Liberator the world has ever known."[33]

Jones showed how Jesus was liberated from death, sin, greed and materialism, narrow nationalism, and the traditions of the elders. Further, he was liberated from "the exclusivism of a Judaism that excluded Samaritans" and from a religious austerity (he ate with the nonreligious). He was even liberated on the cross while being persecuted. Jesus liberated children, his disciples, the possessed, the poor, and sought to liberate the rich.

In presenting Jesus as the great liberator, Jones inserted Jesus' attitude and approach towards women:

> Jesus was also liberated from male chauvinism and stereotypical concepts of woman and man. His own sense of maleness was evidently not threatened by gentleness and tenderness. In theological terms he was the incarnation of humanity, not merely maleness, and is a paradigm of freedom for women as well as men.[34]

Further, Jesus "liberated women by raising their self-estimate and sense of value as well as challenging male manipulation."[35] Jones claimed that "the determinative pronouncement stands at Mark 3:35. Jesus rhetorically asked who his brothers and sisters and mother were and answered: 'Whoever may do the will of God, this one is my brother and sister and mother.' The Kingdom means freedom."[36]

---

[31]Ibid., 17.

[32]Peter Rhea Jones, "The Liberating and Liberated Lord: A Biblical Essay on Freedom," *Review and Expositor* 73/3 (Summer 1976): 283-92.

[33]Ibid., 283, 292.

[34]Ibid., 287.

[35]Ibid., 289.

[36]Ibid., 289-90.

In 1978, Westminster Press published the highly important book, *Woman in the World of Jesus*, written by Evelyn and Frank Stagg. Like William E. Hull and Peter Rhea Jones, Frank Stagg was also a New Testament professor at the Southern Baptist Theological Seminary. The Staggs based their book on "the assumption that the New Testament, in particular the tradition centering in Jesus himself, remains for Christians our basic and authoritative witness." Throughout the Gospels, Jesus presented radical correctives to his religious heritage, "and there should be no surprise that this holds true for what he did for woman."[37]

The Staggs reviewed what they called the Domestic Code in Colossians 3:18-4:1, Ephesians 5:22-6:9, 1 Peter 2:13-3:7, Titus 2:1-10, and 1 Timothy 2:1ff., 8ff.; 3:1ff., 8ff.; 5:17ff.; 6:1ff., verses often used to downplay the role of women both in biblical interpretation and throughout church history, including women in diaconal roles. Then the Staggs affirmed that "Paul himself was a great exponent of freedom, and his fight for freedom reached its highest expression known to us in Galatians." In reviewing Paul's non-subordinating vision in Galatians 3:28 (sometimes called Paul's freedom manifesto), in which there is "not any male and female," they asserted that "if this is taken at face value, the whole question is settled as to the dignity, worth, freedom, and responsibility of woman."[38]

The Staggs commented on Romans 16:1 and 1 Timothy 3:11, key verses relating to women in the diaconate, and concluded that ambiguity surrounds both. Phoebe was a deacon, not a deaconess, since the latter term does not appear in the New Testament. Applied to Phoebe, the force of that term is not certain since it can mean servant. However, "possibly she was a 'deacon' in the official sense of that term." Regarding 1 Timothy 3:11, the Greek word here can mean women or wives; the Staggs concluded that "the reference here probably is to wives of 'deacons.' "[39]

After reviewing evidence in the Synoptic Gospels and Acts, the Staggs asserted that in these writings "woman's status . . . is amazingly free. There is no discernible disposition to place limits upon women." Fidelity to Jesus in the Synoptics caused women to occupy a high place of dignity and freedom.[40]

---

[37]Evelyn Stagg and Frank Stagg, *Woman in the World of Jesus* (Philadelphia: Westminster Press, 1978) 9, 10.

[38]Ibid., 163, 187, 204.

[39]Ibid., 180, 202.

[40]Ibid., 232-33.

The Staggs' final assessment of biblical teachings regarding women is critical to a study of women deacons. Not only was the world Jesus entered "prevailingly male-oriented and male-dominated," it is also true that "the church has tended to trust controls more than freedom, and it seems that woman has suffered disproportionately in the result." The Staggs claimed that "it seems to us that a true following of Jesus Christ compels us to recognize the full personhood of woman." In fact, "There are solid biblical bases for a full recognition of the freedom and responsibility of woman in ministry and the freedom of God's Spirit to bestow the gifts for ministry upon men and women alike." For the Staggs, "Jesus was not a woman's liberator. He was a liberator, concerned to set free any person with the courage to receive freedom."[41] One cannot conclude that women have no place in ministry because Jesus chose twelve male disciples. All twelve were also Jews, so does this "exclude all non-Jews from Christian ministry?" The key point is that Jesus "commissioned all his followers to ministry, and he declared ministry to human need to be the basic criterion for the Final Judgment of all (Mt. 25:31-46)."[42]

In February 1985, *The Student* magazine of the SBC Sunday School Board reprinted "The Bible and Women," an article which had originally appeared in the June 1983 issue of *Light*, a publication of the SBC Christian Life Commission. Written by T. B. Maston, retired professor of Christian Ethics at Southwestern Baptist Theological Seminary, this writing connected the biblical and ethical dimensions of issues relating to women. Maston divided his article into four sections featuring the Old Testament and women, Jesus and women, Paul and women, and applications to Baptist life today. Although the article did not focus primarily on women deacons, it provided contextual information and implications for them.

Maston contended that the Old Testament was predominantly a "man's book" and that this was "inevitable since the Old Testament world was largely a man's world." However, parts of the Old Testament show respect and concern for women. The most significant Old Testament passages relating to women are the creation accounts in Genesis 1 and 2. Maston challenged the view of some "who contend that woman is innately inferior and should be subservient to man" and "defend their position on the basis that woman was created or 'built' from the rib or side of Adam." To that, Maston asked if man is inferior to dust since God formed him out of it

---

[41]Ibid., 253, 255-57.
[42]Ibid., 255-56.

(Gen. 2:7), and he also asked whether man is inferior to animals since they were created before him (Gen. 1).[43]

Maston then sketched the attitude of Jesus toward women and his relationship to them. Ironically, Jesus offered "no specific teachings concerning women"; this clearly meant that "he believed that his teachings were equally applicable to men and women." Jesus' attitude toward women and his relation to them "were revolutionary for his day." In fact, he "never permitted any barrier—race, sex, or moral condition—to keep him from reaching out to a person in need." The Gospels record that many women ministered to Jesus, and he accepted their ministry.[44]

In discussing Paul and women, Maston acknowledged the controversy surrounding such Pauline verses as 1 Corinthians 14:34-36 and 1 Timothy 2:11-15 (women should keep silent and be submissive in churches) and 1 Corinthians 11:2-6 (women should dress properly). Maston claimed that "we should not judge Paul's attitude toward women by one or two isolated statements" since they were directed to certain churches with specific needs and are not relevant for every age. Paul's central ideals for women reside in such passages as 1 Corinthians 11:12 (woman was made from man, man was born from woman, but all things come from God), Galatians 3:28 (there is neither male nor female in Christ), and Ephesians 5:21 (husbands and wives should be subject to one another to show reverence for Christ). Paul's ideals in behalf of women were "radical or revolutionary."[45]

Maston's assessment of scripture relating to women led him to apply biblical teachings to Baptist life today. Convinced that "in many, and possibly most, of our churches women are not treated as Jesus would treat them or as our Heavenly Father would have them treated," Maston urged churches and church leaders to rethink church attitudes toward women and the place they should hold in programs and work. He specifically suggested that in our effort to reach answers regarding "the ordination of women as deacons or deaconesses and to the ministry, we need to restudy the whole matter of New Testament ordination." He claimed that Romans 16:1 and 1 Timothy 3:11 may have referred to women deacons. If New Testament ordination was "a simple service of dedication" for persons whom God had set apart for particular work, then a rediscovery of this conception of ordi-

---

[43]T. B. Maston, "The Bible and Women," *The Student* 64/8 (February 1985): 4-5.

[44]Ibid., 5, 6, 47.

[45]Ibid., 47.

nation could lead our churches to "ordain anyone, male or female, who had a special call of God to perform some distinctive ministry for the church." Maston believed that individuals should not seek ordination; rather, the initiative should come only from others.[46]

Sheri Adams, professor in the International Baptist Theological Seminary in Buenos Aires, Argentina, concluded her 1994 book, *What the Bible Really Says about Women,* by claiming that "we have said that the Bible taken as a whole presents us with an ideal: full equality for each and every person born on the face of the earth. We are equals because we are made in the image of God."[47]

Then in 1995, Molly T. Marshall, professor of Theology, Worship, and Spiritual Formation at Central Baptist Theological Seminary, prepared an essay, "Women's Status in Ministry Equals That of Men," in which she observed that opponents of biblical equality for women typically point to such isolated texts as 1 Corinthians 14:34 regarding women keeping silent in church, to 1 Timothy 2:12 relating to whether women should instruct men, and 1 Timothy 3:2 relating to the husband-of-one-wife passage, plus the fact that Jesus chose twelve male disciples.

Then Marshall asserted her view that three aspects of redemption in Christ offer biblical and theological support for the equality of women. First, the risen Lord commissioned women to be the primary proclaimers of the Resurrection. Second, the Spirit of Christ offers gifts for ministry in freedom rather than according to gender or cultural expectation. Third, baptism, not a gender-based circumcision, became the rite of belonging to the new community created by Jesus. She also claimed that interpretations of Genesis that place the blame for the "fall" and "curse" on Eve, thus subordinating her forever to the rule of Adam, deny the "new creation" established by Christ.[48]

Conclusion. The New Testament concept of "service" (*diakonia*) must enter any healthy discussion of New Testament evidence for women deacons. *Diakonia* provides the basis for *diakonos,* "servant" or "deacon,"

---

[46]Ibid., 48.

[47]Sheri Adams, *What the Bible Really Says about Women* (Macon GA: Smyth and Helwys, 1994) 99.

[48]Molly T. Marshall, "Women's Status in Ministry Equals That of Men," *Defining Baptist Convictions: Guidelines for the Twenty-First Century,* ed. Charles W. Deweese (Franklin TN: Providence House Publishers, 1996) 198-200.

which the New Testament applies to Jesus, to men, and to women. Servant-hood is a hallmark trait of true disciples (Mark 9:35; Matt. 20:26, 23:11).

The New Testament "affords unambiguous evidence of the perpetual necessity of *diakonia* as a function of the church on earth."[49] Equally applicable to all Christians, *diakonia* can readily take the shape of general Christian service or of official church officers—male and female. The New Testament makes *diakonia* fully accessible to and the privilege and duty of women in the diaconate.

One final note needs to be made regarding possible New Testament evidence for women deacons. In the Cambridge Bible Commentary on the New English Bible, Anthony Hanson contends that 1 Timothy 5:9-16 "seems to suggest that deaconesses were recruited from the ranks of widows."[50] While this has not been the primary Baptist explanation for the origin of women deacons, some Baptists have clearly related deaconesses to the 1 Timothy passage on widows. E. Glenn Hinson claimed that 1 Timothy 5:10, which focuses on widows in the New Testament church, "may supply a clue to the origin of the office of women deacons." That verse "strongly suggests that widows performed diaconal functions—acts of charity ('good deeds'), hospitality for travelers, care of orphans, nursing of the sick, and the like. But it is not likely that all widows did so." However, "It would appear that women deacons were selected from among widows, whom the churches supported."[51]

The Early Church and Middle Ages

Many variations characterized the approach of Christian churches to deaconesses in the period AD 100–1500. Although this fourteen-century period preceded Baptist origins in the early 1600s, good reasons exist to take a quick look at deaconess patterns in these years. This period shows how Christians in early and later churches interpreted New Testament material relating to women, pinpoints the geographical distribution of

---

[49]C. E. B. Cranfield, "Diakonia in the New Testament," *Service in Christ*, ed. James I. McCord and T. H. L. Parker (Grand Rapids MI: Eerdmans, 1966) 45.

[50]Anthony Tyrell Hanson, *The Pastoral Letters. Commentary on the First and Second Letters to Timothy and the Letter to Titus*, the Cambridge Bible Commentary on the New English Bible (Cambridge UK and New York: Cambridge University Press, 1966) 43.

[51]E. Glenn Hinson, "On the Ordination of Women As Deacons," *Western Recorder* (1 April 1972): 3.

deaconesses in the East and West, describes factors affecting the rise and decline of deaconesses from era to era, offers insights into the roles and functions of deaconesses, and provides a useful contextual awareness of the larger scope of deaconesses in Christian history.

Because of the vast amount of church history covered in this chapter, heavy reliance will be placed on published works that have already carefully investigated and analyzed key documents from the centuries in question. Undoubtedly, the leading, most scholarly book on deaconesses in these centuries is Aimé Georges Martimort's *Deaconesses: A Historical Study* (1986).[52] This work described and, in many cases, quoted major documents dealing with deaconesses through about 1500. Martimort assessed the original texts and provided significant information on the identity and functions of deaconesses treated in the documents.

Two other key book-length sources carefully consulted for this chapter included *The Ministry in Historical Perspectives* (1956), edited by H. Richard Niebuhr and Daniel D. Williams, and Jeannine E. Olson's *One Ministry, Many Roles: Deacons and Deaconesses through the Centuries* (1992). (This latter work contains a twenty-five-page bibliography of sources relating to deaconesses in many Christian traditions worldwide.)[53] Other sources were also consulted.

Martimort introduced his book by claiming that "what is most evident about the history of deaconesses . . . is the complexity of the whole subject."[54] Deaconesses varied in acceptance, meaning, and activity according to era and region. Further, "The Christians of antiquity did not have a single, fixed idea of what deaconesses were supposed to be," and "the institution of deaconesses lasted only as long as adult baptisms were the norm."[55] (Deaconesses often played key roles in the baptisms of adult women.) To the question of whether deaconesses in the pre-Reformation era were viewed as deacons, Martimort concluded that "during all the time

---

[52]Aimé Georges Martimort, *Deaconesses: A Historical Study*, trans. K. D. Whitehead (San Francisco: Ignatius Press, 1986). The original French and Latin edition was *Les Diaconesses: Essai historique*, Bibliotheca "Ephemerides liturgicae" subsidia 24 (Rome: C.L.V.-Edizioni liturgiche, 1982).

[53]H. Richard Niebuhr and Daniel D. Williams, eds., *The Ministry in Historical Perspectives* (New York: Harper and Row, 1956); and Jeannine E. Olson, *One Ministry, Many Roles: Deacons and Deaconesses through the Centuries* (St. Louis: Concordia Publishing House, 1992).

[54]Martimort, *Deaconesses*, 9.

[55]Ibid., 241, 242.

when the institution of deaconesses was a living institution, both the discipline and the liturgy of the churches insisted upon a very clear distinction between deacons and deaconesses."[56]

In the early second century, evidences for deaconesses were virtually nonexistent. Pliny the Younger, governor of Bithinia, sent a letter to Emperor Trajan in which he referred to *ministrae*, who were being persecuted, but "to translate this word simply as 'deaconess' forces the sense of the text unduly."[57] However, many other scholars have disagreed and claimed that *ministrae* clearly designated deaconesses.[58] Writing about the same time, St. Ignatius of Antioch and St. Polycarp made no mention of deaconesses in their writings.[59]

In the early third century in the Latin churches, the theology of Tertullian and St. Hippolytus of Rome excluded any possibility of deaconesses. In fact, there were no deaconesses in the Latin churches in the first five centuries of Christian history. "This may have been the result of the fact that, in Rome as in Alexandria, the *Apostolic Tradition* of St. Hippolytus of Rome remained the ideal for ecclesiastical organization." In fact, "This document envisaged no place for any feminine ministry."[60]

Near the end of the fourth century, another factor contributing to the decline of deaconesses related to a development within the male diaconate, namely, the rise of the view of ministry called *cursus honorum* ("course of honors"), which may have imitated the political *cursus honorum* established among Roman civil servants in the Christianized state set up by Emperor Constantine. This concept involved a hierarchical view of ministry—bishops at the top, then presbyters, then deacons. The diaconate "could no longer be considered a terminal or life ministry. It was merely a rung on a clerical ladder."[61] This bureaucratic development negatively

---

[56]Ibid., 247.

[57]Ibid., 26.

[58]See, e.g., Henry Bettenson, ed., *Documents of the Christian Church*, 2nd ed. (London: Oxford University Press, 1963) 5; Schaff, "Deaconesses," 374; M. H. Shepherd, Jr., "Deaconess; KJV Servant," *The Interpreter's Dictionary of the Bible* (Nashville: Abingdon Press, 1962) 1:786; and E. Glenn Hinson, "The Church: Liberator or Oppressor of Women?" *Review and Expositor* 72/1 (Winter 1975): 21.

[59]Martimort, *Deaconesses*, 26.

[60]Ibid., 187.

[61]George H. Williams, "The Ministry in the Later Patristic Period (314–451)," *The Ministry in Historical Perspectives*, ed. H. Richard Niebuhr and Daniel D. Williams (New York: Harper and Row, 1956) 63.

affected the diaconate for centuries throughout the Middle Ages by making the deacon inferior to the presbyter. Deaconesses obviously suffered even further when the status and function of male deacons began to decline.

Beginning in the sixth century, some deaconesses appeared in Gaul and later in Italy, but by the end of the ninth century, "many members of the Latin Church had fallen into almost complete confusion regarding deaconesses." Deaconesses virtually disappeared in the twelfth and thirteenth centuries.[62]

In the Eastern churches deaconesses first arose along the eastern edge of the Roman Empire. "The first document that specifically mentions deaconesses, one that, in a sense, constitutes their birth certificate as an ecclesial institution, is the document called the *Didascalia of the Apostles*,"[63] written in the first half of the third century. This writing did not mention Phoebe in Romans 16:1 or "the women" in 1 Timothy 3:11. Instead, the author claimed that deaconesses were the women in Matthew 27:55 who "served" (Greek *diakonousai*) Jesus. The document interchangeably used the terms "female deacon," "the women," and "deaconesses."

The *Didascalia* listed duties for deaconesses after asserting that "the ministry of a female deacon is especially required and urgent."[64] They were to visit Christian women who lived in pagan households, especially the sick. Although forbidden to baptize, they assisted in the baptisms of women, since baptism involved complete nudity, by anointing the celebrants. "Deaconesses emerged in the Church in a region of the East where the strict separation of women required a specific ministry to serve other women."[65] Still, deaconesses did not function on the same level as deacons. The *Apostolic Constitutions*, probably written in the last quarter of the fourth century in Antioch or Constantinople, merged the *Didascalia* and other documents, many of which referenced deaconesses.

The Testament of Our Lord Jesus Christ (*Testamentum Domini*), another key document of the Eastern churches, was probably written in Syria in the fifth century. While claiming that the office of widows played a more important role and actually supervised deaconesses, this document added a few pastoral and liturgical functions to the role of deaconesses. Martimort found documents referring to deaconesses in the fifth through

---

[62]Martimort, *Deaconesses*, 208.
[63]Ibid., 35.
[64]Ibid., 38.
[65]Ibid., 43-44.

seventh centuries in Chaldea and Persia, but discovered no references to deaconesses in Egypt or Ethiopia during these early centuries.

Clearly, "from the last quarter of the fourth century on, the presence of deaconesses in the Greek-speaking and eastern regions of the Roman Empire became a notable public fact, well known and attested by church councils, laws enacted by Christian emperors and the works of Christian authors."[66] For example, the Council of Chalcedon of AD 451 acknowledged in canon 15 that deaconesses could be ordained but not until they reached the age of forty and had experienced a rigorous period of probation. An ordained deaconess who married had to be "anathematized" along with the person she married.[67]

Martimort concluded that "by the end of the tenth or eleventh centuries, deaconesses had pretty much disappeared in the East."[68] The baptismal duties of deaconesses ended when adult baptism ended and infant baptism became the norm. Then deaconesses often became associated with abbesses or convents. But even these deaconesses disappeared.

Jeannine Olson summarized deacon and deaconess developments between the time of Constantine and Luther. By the third century, deacons, deaconesses, and widows had functions relating to baptism, and deacons and deaconesses had teaching duties. In the fourth and fifth centuries, church polity changes began to subordinate deacons to presbyters, deaconesses to deacons, and widows to deaconesses. The monastic movement eventually absorbed deaconesses and widows.[69]

The Protestant Reformation,
English Separatism, and Anabaptism

One would perhaps conjecture that the Protestant Reformation opened new doors for women in Christian life. However, in a bold and sweeping assessment, Molly Marshall claimed that "the Protestant Reformation effectively curtailed religious vocations for women among the Lutheran, Reformed, and Anglican churches (the magisterial reformers), at least in the early centuries of their influence." Even "Luther's emphasis on the 'priesthood of

---

[66]Ibid., 101.
[67]Ibid., 108.
[68]Ibid., 183.
[69]Olson, *One Ministry, Many Roles*, 82.

all believers,' with its radically egalitarian impulse, did not substantively change the status of women."[70]

In 1542, John Calvin recommended four church officers in a key document that he presented to the government of Geneva: "There are four orders of office instituted by our Lord for the government of his Church. First, pastors; then; doctors [teachers]; next elders; and fourth deacons."[71] In assessing the ministry during the Reformation, William Pauck concluded that Calvin's Genevan church order "became the most influential of all that were produced by the Reformation."[72] Transplanted to many other countries, this church order provided a pattern for "the English Puritans and their descendents, particularly among those denominations which later shaped American Protestantism."[73] Noticeably, this order did not include women. In a commentary on 1 Timothy, Calvin plainly asserted that 1 Timothy 3:11 did not refer to women in the diaconate. In fact, Calvin wrote, "He [the writer of 1 Timothy] means the wives both of deacons and bishops, for they must be aids to their husbands in their office."[74]

Derived from English Puritanism, English Separatism generally adopted Calvin's fourfold list of church officers, but tended to add a fifth, variously named widows, relievers, helpers, deaconesses, and women deacons. (Later, some early English Baptists would retain John Calvin's fourfold list of church officers, as reflected in Baptists' 1644 London Confession).[75] In 1591, English Separatist leader Henry Barrow claimed that "Christ being ascended gave unto his church apostels, prophets, evangelists, pastors, teachers, elders, deacons, widdowes."[76] Although for Barrow the

---

[70]Marshall, "Women's Status," 201.

[71]John Calvin, "Draft Ecclesiastical Ordinances," in *Calvin: Theological Treatises*, trans. J. K. S. Reid, Library of Christian Classics 22 (Philadelphia: Westminster Press, 1954) 58.

[72]William Pauck, "The Ministry in the Time of the Continental Reformation," *The Ministry in Historical Perspectives*, ed. H. Richard Niebuhr and Daniel D. Williams (New York: Harper and Row, 1956) 130.

[73]Ibid., 131.

[74]John Calvin, *Commentaries on the Epistles to Timothy, Titus, and Philemon*, trans. William Pringle (Edinburgh: Calvin Translation Society, 1856) 87.

[75]See William L. Lumpkin, *Baptist Confessions of Faith*, rev. ed. (Valley Forge PA: Judson Press, 1969) 166.

[76]Henry Barrow, "A Plain Refutation of M. G. Giffardes Reprochful Book, Intituled a Short Treatise against the Donatists of England," in *The Writings of Henry Barrow, 1590–1591*, ed. Leland H. Carlson, Elizabethan Nonconformist

first three offices had ceased, the last five were fully effective. He observed that "there remain by a perpetual decree these offices to the ministrie, government, and service of the church: pastors, teachers, elders, deacons, relievers."[77] Barrow described the duties of deacons and relievers as follows: "The deacon to collect and distribute the benevolence and contribution of the sainctes. The relievers to attend to the sicke, impotent, etc."[78]

In 1596, the English Separatist confession, "A True Confession," included these four officers. However, it also added a fifth: "Helpers," likely a reference to widows or deaconesses.[79] Perhaps of some consequence is the fact that this confession was written primarily by a group of English Separatists residing in Amsterdam, a center for Mennonite Anabaptism which had a history of openness towards women in the diaconate.[80]

The writings of English Separatist John Smyth, pastor in Gainsborough, England, are critical to this discussion since he would become the first pastor of the first Baptist congregation in human history in Amsterdam in 1609. In 1605, in a writing titled "A Patterne of True Prayer," Smyth provided a list of church offices and officers:

> The first office is teaching, and that officer is called a Doctor. The second is exhorting, and that officer is called a Pastor. The third office is ruling, and that officer is called an Elder. . . . The fourth office is distributing, and that officer is called a Deacon. The fifth office is shewing mercie, which officer is called a widow. These are all set downe. Rom. 12, 7. 8.[81]

Then in 1607, Smyth wrote his "Principles and Inferences Concerning the Visible Church," in which he reduced his list of church officers from five to two: bishops and deacons. Bishops, also called elders or presbyters, included pastors, teachers, and governors. Deacons included men and women, whom he called women deacons and widows. Smyth stated explicitly that "The Deacons ar 1. men 2. or woemen deacons or widowes. Act. 6, 2. Rom. 16, 1." Differentiating the duties of male and female deacons, he wrote that "Men Deacons collect and distribute with simplicity the

---

Texts 5 (London: George Allen and Unwin, 1966) 188.

[77]Ibid., 189.

[78]Ibid., 190-91.

[79]See Lumpkin, *Baptist Confessions of Faith*, 88.

[80]Ibid., 81.

[81]John Smyth, "A Patterne of True Prayer," in *The Works of John Smyth*, 2 vols., ed. W. T. Whitley (Cambridge UK: Cambridge University Press, 1915) 1:158.

churches treasury according to the necessities, and the Saincts occasions," and that "Woemen deacons or widowes are of 60 yeers of age, qualified according to the Apostles rule. 1 Tim. 5, 9. releeving the bodily infirmities of the Saincts with cheerfulnes. Rom. 12, 8. and 16, 1." Further, "The widowes cheef office is to visite and relieve the widow, fatherless, sick, lame, blind, impotent, woemen with child, and diseased members of the church. 1 Tim. 5, 9. Rom. 12, 8. Mat 25, 35-40."[82]

Smyth recommended ordination, including fasting and prayer, for all church officers, so this applied equally to women deacons. While this represented a significant advancement for women, Smyth opposed women preachers: "Weomen are not permitted to speak in the church in tyme of prophecy."[83]

Because of the close relationships the English Separatists and earliest Baptists had with the Mennonites in Amsterdam in the early 1600s and because of the possible influence Mennonites may have had on some of these groups, it is important to note that deaconesses did exist among some of the early Mennonites in Holland. In 1575, Thomas Cartwright and Walter Travers spoke of "deacons of both sorts, namely, men and women."[84] *The Mennonite Encyclopedia* claimed that "among the Anabaptists the deaconess office was always based on the apostolic pattern" and that "in several Dutch Mennonite congregations the office of deaconess has been preserved from the beginning."[85]

In 1632, Mennonites of the Netherlands and Germany adopted the Dortrecht Confession, perhaps the most influential of all Mennonite confessions. This statement noted that

> honorable old widows should be chosen as deaconesses, who, besides the deacons are to visit, comfort, and take care of the poor, the weak, afflicted, and the needy, as also to visit, comfort, and take care of the widows and

---

[82]John Smyth, "Principles and Inferences Concerning the Visible Church," in *The Works of John Smyth*, 2 vols., ed. W. T. Whitley (Cambridge: University Press, 1915) 1:258-61.

[83]Ibid., 256.

[84]Thomas Cartwright and Walter Travers, "A Full and Plain Declaration of Ecclesiastical Discipline out of the Word of God and of the Declining of the Church of England from the Same," cited by D. S. Schaff, "Deaconesses," 375-76.

[85]L. M. S., "Deaconess," *The Mennonite Encyclopedia* (Scottdale PA: Mennonite Publishing House, 1956) 2:22.

orphans; and further to assist in taking care of any matters in the church that properly come within their sphere, according to their ability.[86]

Conclusion

Deaconesses made their initial breakthroughs in the New Testament and in the early centuries of Christianity. Although they had little success in Western churches, they did have some success in Eastern churches. However, they essentially disappeared from the known world in the twelfth and thirteenth centuries. They made their next appearance among some English Separatists and Anabaptists in the 1500s and 1600s. English Separatist John Smyth even began to write about women deacons. He set the stage for the rise of Baptists in 1609, whose writings would immediately begin to recommend ordained women deacons.

---

[86]Lumpkin, *Baptist Confessions of Faith*, 73.

Chapter 2

Patterns in Early Baptist Development, 1600s–1700s

"Baptists" emerged in human history in 1609 in Amsterdam. In 1609–1612, they prepared statements of faith favoring women deacons, with full equality in nomination, election, ordination, and duties. There are, however, gaps of information about women in the diaconate in English Baptist life after 1612 into the early 1650s.[1] In 1654, the South Wales Baptist Association presented duties for widows, described as assistants to deacons. By "widows," the association possibly meant deaconesses since the functions matched those of early Baptist deaconesses. The Broadmead Baptist Church in Bristol chose its first "deaconess" in 1662. Deaconesses did not have equality with male deacons—lacking, for example, ordination. An increased number of deaconesses existed in England in the late 1600s. Neither women deacons nor deaconesses are mentioned in the extant literature of Baptists in America in the 1600s. In the 1700s, deaconesses declined in English Baptist life, but they experienced growth among Baptists in America, especially among the Separate Baptists.

Women Deacons in Baptist Origins

Early Baptist documents, especially confessions of faith, prepared by John Smyth, pastor of the first Baptist congregation in Amsterdam, and by Thomas Helwys, who would become the first Baptist pastor in England, explicitly emphasized women deacons (sometimes listed as "widows"). In fact, women deacons occupied a central place in the initial ideals of Baptist church life. These writings showed possible English Separatist and/or Anabaptist influence regarding women deacons. Four of the earliest Baptist

---

[1]To illustrate, in pivotal writings and research, two key English historians and a researcher made no reference to women in the diaconate during these years: B. R. White, *The English Baptists of the Seventeenth Century*, vol. 1 of A History of the English Baptists, ed. B. R. White (London: Baptist Historical Society, 1983; rev. and exp. ed., 1996); John Briggs, "She-Preachers, Widows, and Other Women: The Feminine Dimension in Baptist Life Since 1600," *The Baptist Quarterly* 31/7 (July 1986): 337-52; and Steve Wright, e-mail to author, 21 September 2004.

documents referred to women "deacons," not to "deaconesses"; and all four were created in Amsterdam, where Smyth had led his English Separatist congregation in 1608–1609, soon to create the first "Baptist" church in human history.

First, in what possibly constituted the first reference to women deacons in Baptist literature, John Smyth claimed in a 1609 writing that "the church hath power to Elect, approve & ordeyne her owne Elders, also: to elect, approve, & ordeine her owne Deacons both men & woemen."[2]

Second, Smyth soon concluded that his baptism and that of a few others whom he had baptized was invalid. Therefore, he wrote a twenty-article confession of faith on behalf of his small party and submitted it along with an application to join the Mennonite community in Amsterdam. Dated 1609, this confession claimed that "the ministers of the church are, not only bishops ('Episcopos'), to whom the power is given of dispensing both the word and the sacraments, but also deacons, men and widows, who attend to the affairs of the poor and sick brethren."[3]

Third, after Smyth's death in 1612, his followers, still waiting for admission into the Mennonite community of Amsterdam, wrote a follow-up confession in 1612–1614. This statement of faith claimed that the church has "two sorts of ministers: viz., some who are called pastors, teachers or elders, who administer in the word and sacraments, and others who are called Deacons, men and women: whose ministry is, to serve tables and wash the saints' feet (Acts vi. 2-4; Phil. i. 1; 1 Tim. iii. 2, 3, 8, 11, and chap. v.)."[4] 1 Timothy 5 describes widows, whom these Baptists apparently viewed as women deacons.

Fourth, in 1611, Thomas Helwys, who succeeded Smyth as leader of the original Baptist congregation in Amsterdam, wrote the first English Baptist confession just prior to this congregation's return to England. Helwys's confession described church officers as

> either Elders, who by their office do especially feed the flock concerning their soules, Act. 20.28, Pet. 5.2, 3. or Deacons Men, and Women who by their office releave the necessities off the poore and impotent brethren

---

[2]John Smyth, "Paralleles, Censures, Observations," *The Works of John Smyth*, 2 vols., ed. W. T. Whitley (Cambridge UK: Cambridge University Press, 1915) 2:509.

[3]William L. Lumpkin, *Baptist Confessions of Faith*, rev. ed. (Valley Forge PA: Judson Press, 1969) 101.

[4]Ibid., 138.

concerning their bodies, Acts. 6.1-4. . . . [Further, all] these Officers are to bee chosen when there are persons qualified according to the rules in Christs Testament, I. Tim. 3.2-7. Tit. I. 6-9. Act. 6.3. 4. By Election and approbacion off that Church or congregation whereoff they are members, Act. 6.3. 4 and 14.23, with Fasting, Prayer, and Laying on off hands, Act. 13.3 and 14.23.[5]

Admittedly, Smyth's and Helwys's writings may or may not have described the actual existence of early Baptist women deacons at the time the confessions were written. They did, however, certainly approve the concept and appropriateness of women deacons.

Deaconesses in England

Helwys's 1611 confession was the only major confession of faith among seventeenth-century English Baptists to mention women deacons or deaconesses. Particular (Calvinist) Baptist confessions—such as the London Confession of 1644, the Somerset Confession of 1656, and the Second London Confession of 1677—did not mention them. Neither did General (Arminian) Baptist confessions—such as the Faith and Practice of Thirty Congregations in 1651, the Standard Confession of 1660, and the Orthodox Creed of 1679—mention them. As John Briggs, English Baptist historian, put it, following the references to women deacons in the 1611 confession, "There the matter ends as far as confessions are concerned: women are not specifically identified in any of the later confessions of faith of either General or Particular Baptists in the seventeenth century."[6] Some confessions, such as the Standard Confession and the Second London Confession, made it clear that deacons were *men.*[7] The Somerset Confession stated unequivocally that "THE women in the church [are] to learn in silence, and in all subjection (I Tim. 2:11; I Cor. 14:37."[8]

Leon McBeth, after carefully studying primary sources of Baptists in the 1600s, reached two conclusions. First, he claimed that evidence made it clear

that the earliest Baptists accepted women deacons. Apparently these women deacons were on an equality with men deacons, with the same

---

[5]Ibid., 121-22.
[6]Briggs, "She-Preachers, Widows, and Other Women," 337.
[7]Lumpkin, *Baptist Confessions of Faith*, 231, 287.
[8]Ibid., 210.

election, ordination, and duties. . . . [Second,] local church records in England amply demonstrate that the woman deacon, or deaconess, was a fixture, especially in churches of the General Baptist persuasion. The more Calvinistic group, called Particular Baptists, allowed less active roles for women, in both England and America.[9]

After reviewing English Baptist life in the 1600s, William Brackney concluded that

the role of women in the early Baptist churches tended to be passive and submissive to male leadership. The membership roles reveal large numbers of women in the early congregations (sometimes over 50 percent), and some churches elected female deacons.[10]

At times, British Baptist records of the 1600s referred to widows as assistants to deacons. In 1654, the South Wales Baptist Association printed a lengthy list of duties for church officers. One item stated that "for the assistance of deacons there are widows, of whom, see 1. Tim. 5.16, who are likewise to serve the church, Ro. 16.1 most probably in looking to the poor and sick."[11] Although not designated as "deaconesses," three things suggest these widows likely functioned as deaconesses. First, the association appealed to Phoebe in Romans 16:1, whom many early Baptists viewed to be an example of a New Testament deaconess. Second, the duties assigned matched duties assigned to early deaconesses. Third, early Baptists sometimes used the terms deaconesses and widows interchangeably. (The Broadmead Church in Bristol, described in the next few paragraphs, will illustrate this.)

Precise evidence shows irrefutably that deaconesses did exist and function in English Baptist life during the 1600s, though probably in only a small number of churches. Records of the Broadmead Baptist Church in Bristol provide detailed information on the qualifications, selection, setting apart, and duties of deaconesses. The following reveals the details, including the close relationship between widows and deaconesses.

---

[9]Leon McBeth, *Women in Baptist Life* (Nashville: Broadman Press, 1979) 30, 140.

[10]William H. Brackney, ed., *Baptist Life and Thought: 1600–1980: A Sourcebook* (Valley Forge PA: Judson Press, 1983) 64.

[11]H. Leon McBeth, *A Sourcebook for Baptist Heritage* (Nashville: Broadman Press, 1990) 62.

In June 1662, the Broadmead Church, having already elected several officers, convened for "fasting and prayer." A "Sister West, a widow woman, was set apart to the office of a widow or deaconess in the church."[12] A May 1671 letter of the church invited Thomas Hardcastle to become the church's pastor. Signed by ninety-eight church members, the list of signees included "Mary West, the deaconess."[13] Then in July 1673, "by reason of the decease of Sister West, the widow or deaconess of the church . . . it being a day of prayer, the congregation chose . . . Sister Murray to be a widow or deaconess to the church." Being "set apart," Murray was "recommended to the work upon trial," as was a deacon who was set apart the same day.[14]

Key developments took place in early March 1679. The church chose four female members, Sister Smith, Sister Spurgeon, Sister Webb, and Sister Walton, who were "widows, each of above sixty years of age, to be deaconesses for the congregation, to look after the sick sisters." Later that month, on a day of prayer, the church's elders sent two sisters to visit each of the four candidates to make certain they would be willing to serve. Only sister Spurgeon was unwilling to serve. Then by fasting and prayer, the church commended Smith, Webb, and Walton "to the work and office of widows, or deaconesses," and "they were set apart to that work of looking after the sick members of the congregation."[15]

The Broadmead records provide detailed information on an important requirement for these deaconesses and on five specific duties. Using 1 Timothy 5:11, a verse relating to "widows," as a base, the three women had to agree not to marry. Duties assigned to them included the following (this list is perhaps the earliest detailed list of deaconess duties in Baptist literature).

1. To visit the sick, to have their eye and ear open to hearken and inquire who is sick, and to visit the sick sisters; in an especial manner to see what they need, because it may not be so proper for men in several cases.
2. To visit not only sick sisters, but sick brethren also; and therefore some conceive [this] may be the reason why they must be sixty years

---

[12]Edward Bean Underhill, ed., *The Records of a Church of Christ, Meeting in Broadmead, Bristol, 1640–1687* (London: Hanserd Knollys Society, 1847) 72.

[13]Ibid., 136.

[14]Ibid., 195.

[15]Ibid., 396-97.

    of age, that none occasion [of offence] may be given; and as 1 Tim.
    v. 14.

3.   Not only to take care of their sick bodies, of the brethren and sisters,
      but that their wants may be supplied; and therefore to make reports
      back of their condition, to the elders and deacons of the congregation.

4.   It is their duty also to speak a word to their souls, as occasion
      requires, for support or consolation, to build them up in a spiritual
      lively faith in Jesus Christ. For as some observe, there is not an office
      of Christ in his church, but it is dipped in the blood of our Lord Jesus.

5.   Some think it is their duty to attend the sick; and if so, then they are
      to be maintained by the church.[16]

In 1685, the church admonished one of these three deaconesses when
it agreed to send two members to her to "stir [her] up to her work, in
visiting, &c., as a deaconess."[17]

English Baptist historian John Briggs carefully studied primary sources
relating to the feminine dimension in English Baptist life, many of which
undoubtedly affected deaconess developments. He discovered evidence in
the 1600s that women exercised informal leadership gifts in churches,
actually became preachers, played key roles in the developing life of
churches, suffered persecution because of their dissent, and "constantly encountered the problem of the Pauline prohibition—but against this were
cited 'legitimising' scriptures such as Joel 2.28-9, John 8.36, and Galatians
3.28, a textual battle that still rumbles on [in 1986]."[18]

Briggs claimed that "opportunities for women to participate in church
life seem to have shrunk by the early eighteenth century, with some chapels
even seating men and women separately," and women's right to vote in
church life "was not general practice." Still, Baptist women in the 1700s
produced important writings, and participated in educational, business, and
charitable enterprises.[19]

The English General Baptists, who favored a general atonement, had
favored deaconesses far more than the Particular Baptists, who preferred
atonement for the elect. One major reason deaconesses declined in the
1700s in England is that General Baptists declined. Reasons for decline in
the 1689–1730 period included theological controversies over the person

---

[16]Ibid., 397-98.
[17]Ibid., 493-94.
[18]Briggs, "She-Preachers, Widows, and Other Women," 338-41.
[19]Ibid., 342.

of Christ, fragmented denominational organization, lack of strong leadership, denominational isolation, and exclusion from the Particular Baptist Fund, which provided money for a theological education for prospective ministers.[20] Causes for decline in the 1730–1770 period included Christological and Trinitarian controversy, with more and more ministers questioning the Trinity and deity of Christ; disagreements about hymn singing in churches; inadequate ministerial leadership; low standards of morality for some ministers; and transferring church membership to Methodist churches.[21]

John Gill, eminent Baptist pastor and theologian who was noted for his strong emphasis on extreme Calvinism, published his systematic theology, *A Complete Body of Doctrinal and Practical Divinity*, in 1769. In discussing the office of deacons, Gill admitted the possibility that "there were women-deacons, or *deaconesses*" in scripture. After briefly surveying possible biblical and historical evidence for deaconesses, Gill concluded that "indeed, something of this kind seems not at all unnecessary, but of service and usefulness; as to attend at the baptism of women, and to visit the sisters of the church, when sick, and to assist them."[22] However, Gill did not directly advocate that churches elect deaconesses, and he likely would have opposed their ordination.

In 1786, Dan Taylor, a leader of the English General Baptists, published *A Dissertation on Singing in the Worship of God*. Taylor presented a high view of woman and her potential: "Women as well as men have rational capacities; they, as well as men, have immortal souls; they, as well as men, are made for eternal duration; they, as well as men, are the creatures of God."[23] He defended the abilities and rights of women to sing. And he affirmed the right of women to speak in church. In fact, he asserted that "This may be applied particularly to the admission of new members, and the choice of officers, pastors, or deacons in the church."[24] Taylor's attitude toward women certainly provided support for the cause of deaconesses.

---

[20]Raymond Brown, *The English Baptists of the Eighteenth Century*, vol. 2 of A History of the English Baptists, ed. B. R. White (London: Baptist Historical Society, 1986) 21, 24, 25, 27.

[21]Ibid., 57, 58, 63, 64, 67.

[22]John Gill, *A Body of Divinity* (Grand Rapids MI: Sovereign Grace Publishers, 1971) 885. This is a reprint of the original 1769 edition.

[23]McBeth, *A Sourcebook*, 109.

[24]Ibid., 110.

Deaconesses in America

Selected church records and other sources related to Baptist life in America in the 1600s and early 1700s show no evidence of deaconesses. Deaconesses did not appear, for example, in the records of such noted churches as First Baptist Church, Providence, Rhode Island, formed in the late 1630s; First Baptist Church, Newport, Rhode Island, formed in the 1640s; First Baptist Church, Boston, formed in 1665; Kittery Baptist Church, Kittery, Maine, formed in 1682; Pennepack Baptist Church, Pennepack, Pennsylvania, formed in 1688; and First Baptist Church, Philadelphia, formed in 1698. Before 1700, members of the Kittery Church would found the First Baptist Church, Charleston, South Carolina, as the first Baptist church in the South. There is no mention of deaconesses in the latter's early records.

In 1697, in London, Elias Keach published his *The Glory and Ornament of a True Gospel-Constituted Church*. In the early 1700s, this writing "was brought into unexpected prominence in America, where, in the late 1600s, Elias had worked"[25] as a pastor in the Middle Colonies. In fact, he had served as pastor of the first Baptist church in the Middle Colonies, at Pennepack, Pennsylvania, from 1688 to 1692, the year he returned to England. During his stay in America, he helped found three other churches in New Jersey.

Keach's publication preceded the rise of the Philadelphia Baptist Association in 1707—the oldest continuing Baptist association in America—and may have influenced some of its thought and practices. The writing described the role of church officers and included special material on deacons. Excluding women from the diaconate, it claimed that "a church thus constituted ought forthwith to choose them a Pastor, Elder or Elders, and Deacons, (the *Church* reading of no other Officers, or Offices abiding in the Church) and what kind of Men they ought to be, and how qualified, is laid down by Paul to Timothy, and to Titus."[26]

In the 1700s, the Philadelphia Association became a highly influential association throughout the country. This association appointed the writing of, and approved, two Baptist treatises (or church manuals) on church discipline, one in 1743, the other in 1798. Each included a section on deacons.

---

[25]Edward C. Starr, ed., *A Baptist Bibliography*, vol. 13 (Rochester NY: American Baptist Historical Society, 1968) 29.

[26]Elias Keach, *The Glory and Ornament of a True Gospel-Constituted Church* (London: n.p., 1697) 7-8, 10-11.

Neither included women in the diaconate. In fact, the 1743 manual made perfectly clear in the opening sentence that "Deacons are Men called forth by the Church."[27] In addition, an important statement of church discipline adopted in 1773 by the Charleston Baptist Association, formed in 1751 as the first association in the South, did not include women in the diaconate.[28] All these documents had a strong Calvinist base.

Various other writings of the late 1700s also excluded women from diaconal roles. David Thomas, a Regular (Calvinist) Baptist pastor in Virginia, published his *The Virginian Baptist* in 1774. This work provided for three kinds of church officers—ministers, elders, and deacons. All were to be male.[29] Then in 1796, the Warwick Baptist Association in New York adopted its annual circular letter to its churches; the topic was "The Character and Office of a Deacon." This letter declared that 1 Timothy 3:11 refers to deacons' wives, not to women deacons.[30]

In the 1700s, deaconesses in America were confined largely, though not exclusively, to the Separate Baptists in the South. Separate Baptist churches in New England apparently were not as open to deaconesses. For example, the Backus Memorial Baptist Church in North Middleboro, Massachusetts, formed in 1756 as a Separate Baptist congregation with the noted Isaac Backus as pastor, did not include women in its diaconate either in its first minutes or in the ordination of the church's first deacon later in 1756.[31]

Morgan Edwards served as pastor of the First Baptist Church of Philadelphia in 1761–1771 and later as an evangelist for the Philadelphia Baptist Association. As the first historian of Baptists in America, his writings of the early 1770s contained the most detailed descriptions of Baptist deaconesses in America. As he traveled throughout the eastern states, he discovered deaconesses in three Separate Baptist churches in North Carolina, nine in Virginia, and one in South Carolina. He also found them in a few Particular (Calvinist) Baptist churches in South Carolina, although he gave no

---

[27]Benjamin Griffin, *A Short Treatise of Church-Discipline* (Philadelphia: printed by B. Franklin, 1743) 17-18; Samuel Jones, *A Treatise of Church Discipline and a Directory* (Lexington KY: T. Anderson, 1805; originally published in Philadelphia by S. C. Ustick, 1798) 13-14.

[28]James Leo Garrett, Jr., *Baptist Church Discipline*, Broadman Historical Monograph (Nashville: Broadman Press, 1962) 34.

[29]David Thomas, *The Virginian Baptist* (Baltimore: Enoch Story, 1774) 27-28.

[30]*Minutes*, Warwick Baptist Association (NY), 1796, 7-8.

[31]*Minutes*, Backus Memorial Baptist Church, 16 January 1756; 14 August 1756.

examples, and in a few Tunker (German) Baptist churches in Pennsylvania.[32]

The three North Carolina churches included those at Sandy Creek, Shallow Fords, and Haw River. Writing in 1772, Edwards described the Sandy Creek Church, formed in 1755 as the mother church of Separate Baptists in the South:

> So called from a little creek near to which the meeting house stands, in the forks of Capefear-river . . . in the county of Guilford, 250 miles NW from Newburn, and about 560 SSW from Philadelphia. The place of worship is 30 feet by 26, built in 1762, on land given by Seamore York. No estate. No salary, except presents, to the amount of about 20 [pounds]. Here ruling elders, eldresses, and deaconesses are allowed; also the 9 christian rites: *baptism*; *Lords-supper, love-feast; laying-on-of-hands; washing feet; anointing-the-sick; right-hand of fellowship; kiss of charity; devoting children.*[33]

Shallow Fords had ruling elders and deaconesses and practiced six of the nine rites, and Haw River had ruling elders, eldresses, and deaconesses and practiced all nine rites.[34]

The nine Separate Baptist churches in Virginia with deaconesses in 1772 included those at Fall-Creek, which admitted "Evangelists, Ruling elders, deaconesses, laying on of hands, feasts of charity, anointing the sick, kiss of charity, washing feet, right hand of fellowship, and devoting children"; Blackwater, with "Ruling elders, laying on of hands, deaconesses, devoting children, washing feet, and other ancient rites"; Bedford, with "Ruling elders, laying on of hands, deaconesses, and all the christian rites"; Amherst, Lower-Spotsylvania, Upper-Spotsylvania, Rapid-Ann, and Buckingham, all admitting ruling elders, deaconesses, and the nine Chris-

---

[32]G. W. Paschal, "Morgan Edwards' Materials towards History of the Baptists in the Province of North Carolina [1772]," *The North Carolina Historical Review* 7 (July 1930): 384-89; Morgan Edwards, "Materials towards a History of the Baptists in the Provinces of Maryland, Virginia, North Carolina, South Carolina, Georgia" (1772; microfilm copy of the original handwritten manuscript, located in the Southern Baptist Historical Library and Archives, Nashville) 5, 48, 56-84; Morgan Edwards, *Materials towards a History of the American Baptists*, vol. 1 (Philadelphia: Joseph Crukshank and Isaac Collins, 1770) 67.

[33]Paschal, "Morgan Edwards' Materials . . . North Carolina," 384.

[34]Ibid., 388, 389.

tian rites; and Goochland, with "Ruling elders, deaconesses admitted, but divided about some of the 9 rites."[35]

Two factors helped account for the rise and expansion of deaconesses, especially among the Separate Baptists, by the early 1770s. First, the Great Awakening, coupled with a mounting emphasis on liberty as the American Revolution approached, may have contributed to a new respect for the roles of women in the church. Baptist historian Leon McBeth claimed that the Separate Baptists "expected their women to take considerable leadership in the church, including serving as deaconesses, praying and exhorting in public, and sometimes preaching."[36] (Another surge of emphasis on women in the diaconate would take place two centuries later during the freedom focus of the American Bicentennial.)

Second, the presence of deaconesses in the Sandy Creek Baptist Church in North Carolina was significant because that church, through the leadership of its pastor, Shubal Stearns, led in forming many other churches in several states. According to Edwards, by 1772, the Sandy Creek Church had become the mother, grandmother, and great-grandmother of forty-two churches out of which had come 125 ministers; and the church had spread its branches west to the Mississippi River, south to Georgia, east to the Atlantic and Chesapeake Bay, and north to the Potomac River.[37] (This influence may be one reason Baptist churches in the early 2000s in North Carolina and Virginia, two states where Separate Baptists made a big impact, have more women deacons and women deacon chairs than any other states in the South.)

Edwards also provided an account of the German Tunkers, who had come to Pennsylvania in 1719 from Schwartzenau, Germany. These Baptists practiced foot washing, the kiss of peace, the love feast, anointing the sick with oil, and trine immersion in which the administrator baptized the candidate head forward three times in the name of the Father, Son, and Holy Ghost. According to Edwards in 1770, the Tunkers "had not published any system or creed"; held to general redemption; used "great plainness of language and dress, like the Quakers; and like them will neither swear nor fight"; would not "go to law" or "take interest for money they

---

[35]Edwards, "Materials towards a History . . . Virginia," 56, 63, 64, 66, 71, 77, 81, 83, 84.

[36]McBeth, *A Sourcebook*, 165.

[37]Paschal, "Morgan Edwards' Materials . . . North Carolina," 385.

lend"; and "commonly wear their beards." In addition to ministers, "They also have deacons; and ancient widows for deaconesses."[38]

In 1768, Edwards released a few copies of his new book, *The Customs of Primitive Churches*, that he intended to serve as a manual on the polity and practices of churches in the Philadelphia Baptist Association. However, the association had not commissioned the manual, and it refused to give its approval to the writing.[39] Edwards's inclusion of material on and support for deaconesses may have been one of the reasons the association refused to endorse his manual. That association held highly restrictive views toward women in the church. For example, in 1746, it replied to a query about whether women should have the right to vote in church. The association replied in no uncertain terms that "the silence, with subjection, enjoined on all women in the church of God, is such a silence as excludes all women whomsoever from all degrees of teaching, ruling, governing, dictating, and leading in the church of God."[40]

Because Edwards was a major player in Baptist life in America in the late 1700s, his comments about deaconesses are instructive for understanding his personal views. He favored deaconesses and identified Romans 16:1 and 1 Timothy 3:11 as biblical bases for them.

> The office of *deaconesses* is of divine original and perpetual continuance in the church. It is the same in general with the office of deacons, only it is chiefly limited to the care of the sick, miserable, and distressed poor. The scripture marks of their office are, *showing mercy, succouring, &c.* The way they are put in the office is by choice of the people, ordination, and other forms as in case of deacons. Their qualifications are laid down negatively and positively by the apostle Paul. Their reward is *honour,* and *maintenance.* Their number should be proportionable to the need of the church. Their manner of performing the office is, with *chearfulness.* Rom. xii. 8.[41]

Edwards questioned why anyone would claim that 1 Timothy 3:11 refers to deacons' wives since 1 Timothy 3 says nothing about the wives of bishops. He observed that ancient church history frequently mentioned

---

[38]Edwards, *Materials towards a History of the American Baptists* 1:66-67.

[39]A. D. Gillette, ed., *Minutes of the Philadelphia Baptist Association from A.D. 1701 to A.D. 1807* (Philadelphia: American Baptist Publication Society, 1851) 141.

[40]Ibid., 53.

[41]Morgan Edwards, *The Customs of Primitive Churches* (Philadelphia: printed by Andrew Steuart, 1768; repr. 1774) 42-43.

deaconesses. He claimed in more detail that the office of deaconesses related especially to meeting the needs of the poor and sick and was "chiefly confined to those things wherefor men are less fit. The helpless poor must be kept clean, and fed. The sick must be nursed, and tended, etc., for which women are the most proper." Finally, he noted that "We cannot give any historical narrative of the ordination of deaconesses, as no such transaction hath fallen under our notice. But think the history of the ordination of deacons may serve for a pattern, only varying some words."[42] Edwards's advocacy of women's ordination may have stimulated additional negative reaction to his writing and to women's ordination, as evidenced by the fact that key documents of the Philadelphia Association would continue to oppose such ordination.

Four key points emerge from Edwards's writings on deaconesses. First, in his travels he discovered deaconesses in fifteen or more Baptist churches, mostly Separate Baptist congregations, in at least four states. Second, he provided no details regarding the actual role and functions of such deaconesses in the specific churches where they served. Third, while he favored the ordination of deaconesses, he admitted that he had never witnessed or heard of a deaconess ordination. Fourth, although he personally believed that 1 Timothy 3:11 referred to deaconesses and even used his 1768 writing, *The Customs of Primitive Churches*, to urge churches to adopt deaconesses and to consider using them, he encountered stiff resistance.

William L. Lumpkin, distinguished Virginia Baptist pastor and historian, wrote a valuable article titled "The Role of Women in 18th-Century Virginia Baptist Life." He claimed that with the coming of the American Revolution "there was much talk of freedom and rights. This must have encouraged many women to reflect on the rights of their own sex" during an era when men dominated church and civil affairs.[43]

But Lumpkin's most significant comments related to his assessment of the influence of early Virginia Baptists on Baptists throughout colonial America: "Baptist churches of colonial Virginia contributed largely to the eighteenth-century revival of the Protestant passion for individual responsibility. They offered to women the appeal of primitive Christianity to enter the faith on the same basis as men, and they argued that women are

---

[42]Ibid., 43.

[43]William L. Lumpkin, "The Role of Women in 18th-Century Virginia Baptist Life," *Baptist History and Heritage* 8/3 (July 1973): 160.

accepted equally with men as children of God. The call to voluntary decision appealed strongly to women, with the result that in most Virginia Baptist churches, women came to outnumber men before 1800." Then to illustrate his point, Lumpkin pointed out that the Bedford Church, the oldest in the Strawberry Association, had deaconesses by the early 1770s.[44]

Baptist deaconesses in America in the 1700s had little hope of making much progress. Many key documents that shaped large portions and wide geographies of Baptist life simply did not mention or support deaconesses; at times, they deliberately opposed them. Men ran most churches and associations. Most major Baptist documents opposing deaconesses had a Calvinist foundation and thrust. In the late 1700s, deaconesses began to decline as Separate Baptists began to merge with Regular (Calvinist) Baptists to form United Baptists.

Two points merit acknowledgment. First, church life in the 1700s did not have elaborate committee structures like today, and many churches tended to have half-time or quarter-time pastors. Therefore, who would take care of church affairs if the deacons did not handle them? Some churches had ruling elders to manage such affairs, but most did not. Second, in a 1795 letter to the Warren Baptist Association in New England, Isaac Backus noted that in Massachusetts, "a law of this State, made in 1756, empowers the deacons of every church to receive and hold estates or donations which were given for religious purposes, and to manage the same at the direction and for the good of the church."[45] This law, and perhaps others like it, may have led deacon bodies in some churches to begin to give increased focus to the business side of deacon duties. All these factors worked against the possibility of women being allowed into the diaconate. Women and business did not go together in Baptist life in the eighteenth century.

Conclusion

Baptists emerged in human history in 1609 in Amsterdam. Immediately, 1609–1612 writings of their first two pastors, John Smyth and Thomas Helwys, who prepared confessions of faith in behalf of their congregations, included a focus on "women deacons," as did a confession prepared by

---

[44]Ibid., 160-61.

[45]Isaac Backus, "Letter to the Warren Association," 1795, in T. B. Maston, *Isaac Backus: Pioneer of Religious Liberty* (Rochester NY: American Baptist Historical Society, 1962) 86.

Smyth's congregation after he died. These deacons enjoyed equality with male deacons—in election, ordination, and function. Whether these writings reflected ideals or reality for women deacons is impossible to determine due to the lack of actual church records from those years. Still, the writings clearly reflected openness to women deacons. For several decades after 1612, extant Baptist literature seldom, if ever, discussed women in the diaconate. Then, in the 1650s and 1660s, new deaconess developments began to emerge. Occasional references did appear to widows (sometimes used interchangeably with deaconesses) in broader British Baptist materials. Deaconesses declined in England in the 1700s.

Extant Baptist literature offers no evidence that deaconesses existed in Baptist life in America in the 1600s, and they existed in only a small percentage of Baptist churches in America in the 1700s. Most Baptist writings of the eighteenth century did not include deaconesses in discussions of church officers. Deaconesses achieved their most significant development in the 1700s among the Separate Baptists in the South.

The shift from women deacons to deaconesses involved a subtle change in the installation procedures. In 1609–1612, women deacons were "ordained," complete with fasting, prayer, and the laying on of hands. In the 1660s and 1670s, the first Baptist deaconesses in the Broadmead Church in Bristol, England, were all "set apart," including fasting and prayer, but church records did not mention laying on of hands. The removal of full ordination, a sticking point for including Baptist women in the diaconate, would have two important implications for the future: deaconesses would lose their equality with male deacons for the next three centuries, and more churches would consider using them because of their subordinated, nonordained status.

The shift from women deacons to deaconesses in the 1600s likely related to the surging impact of Particular Baptists, with their Calvinist orientation, and their increasing dominance over the General Baptists, who tended to be somewhat open to women in church leadership. The distinctively Calvinist 1644 London Confession, of which Lumpkin claimed that "perhaps no Confession of Faith has had so formative an influence on Baptist life as this one,"[46] followed John Calvin's recommendation that church officers consist of pastors, teachers, elders, and deacons—none of which were to include women.[47] Neither would the Calvinist-based Second

---

[46]Lumpkin, *Baptist Confessions of Faith*, 152.
[47]Ibid., 166.

London Confession of 1677 or the Philadelphia Confession of 1742 make a place for women among church officers. The merging of Separate and Regular Baptists in the late 1700s introduced an increasing element of Calvinism into Baptist life, and deaconesses entered a period of decline.

Chapter 3

Deaconess Decline, Affirmation, and Renewal, 1800s–1950s

Baptist deaconesses in local churches experienced continuing decline in England and in the United States throughout the 1800s. Many factors, biblical, historical, theological, and cultural, accounted for those developments. Although women's leadership in diaconal roles plunged to low levels, some writers kept the dream alive and some churches incorporated deaconesses into their life for the first time. Moving into the twentieth century, the number of churches and writers willing to defend the deaconess cause began to grow, although disagreement continued. By the 1950s, an increasing number of ordained women deacons began to emerge, especially in the United States.

Toward the end of the 1800s, professional deaconesses emerged, first in the larger Protestant community and then among Baptists. These deaconesses lived as sisterhoods in motherhouses, wearing distinctive dress, and committed initially to meeting critical social needs of humanity and later, primarily in England, to serving in pastoral functions. Although they died out in the 1900s, these deaconess organizations prompted new consideration of deaconesses in local churches.

Deaconess Decline in Local Churches

The decline of deaconesses in local churches in England and in the United States accompanied rigid views that women generally should keep silent and submissive in church. Literal interpretations of selected statements from the writings of the apostle Paul dominated Baptists' approach to the treatment of women in church life. When some Baptists in the twentieth century initiated renewed emphasis on the freedom-based teachings of Christ and of the apostle Paul, substantial changes begin to take place in women's roles in church life.

Decline among English Baptists. Melissa A. Ziegler, an Oxford Scholar from Carson-Newman College who studied in England in 2003, provided important insights into the role of deaconesses in England in the 1800s in her paper, "Women in British Baptist Life." After examining a large array of sources relating to English Baptists in the nineteenth century, Ziegler concluded that among the majority of Baptists during the first half of that century, "the prevalent belief, founded on 1 Corinthians 14:34, was that women were not to speak in any way, shape, or form while in church"; consequently, "women played a very minimal role in Baptist congregations during the first half of the nineteenth century."[1] Ziegler even cited an Oxford University dissertation on women in British nonconformity which claimed that "among Baptists, the numbers of women deacons plummeted in the early nineteenth century."[2]

However, many Baptist publications in the 1800s, while acknowledging the decline of deaconesses, advocated that churches consider using them. In 1814, *The Baptist Magazine* of London published an anonymous article titled "Deaconesses." The writer reviewed comments by many former writers on the topic and acknowledged that "this matter has, in a considerable degree, been neglected in many of our churches." Then he stated:

> Females whose qualifications are suited to such services (and many such there are in our churches) might, I think, be usefully employed in Christian societies; not only to assist females in baptism, and visit the sick of their own sex, but might also be deputed by the church to give admonition, to obtain information, to administer temporal relief and spiritual comfort to the poor and distressed sisters in their respective connexions; and in many other services for which they are not deficient either in piety or prudence.

The writer concluded with a question: "Would it not be consistent with the order of the primitive churches, to have one or more (as circumstances may render necessary) of the sisters in our respective connexions especially appointed to act, on all proper occasions, as a deaconess or deaconesses?"[3]

In 1841, *The Baptist Magazine* published another anonymous article titled "Deaconesses." This article reprinted information from the records of the Broadmead Baptist Church in Bristol that had deaconesses in the 1600s. The writer claimed that this information "has evident reference to the directions given to Timothy by Paul in the fifth chapter of his first epistle," thus implying that the writer equated deaconesses with the "widows" described in 1 Timothy 5. The writer concluded by stating that

---

[1] Melissa A. Ziegler, "Women in British Baptist Life," 23 June 2003, 14, 21.

[2] Ibid., 13, citing L. E. Lauer, "Women in British Nonconformity, circa 1880–1920, with Special Reference to the Society of Friends, Baptist Union, and Salvation Army" (Ph.D. diss., University of Oxford, 1979) 79.

[3] "Deaconesses," *The Baptist Magazine* 6 (1814): 402-403.

"We have never yet learned the reasons why the practice [of deaconesses] to which it [the Broadmead Church] relates should have fallen into general disuse."[4]

In 1842, *The Baptist Magazine* reprinted an excerpt from the October 1841 circular letter of the Norfolk and Norwich Association of Baptist Churches. Because this letter represented the thought of an entire association, and because it built a case for deaconesses on the bases of biblical teaching and practical need, the entire text follows.

> We ought not, we think, on this occasion, to leave unnoticed an early practice of the Christian church, which has been neglected generally, though not universally, but which with great advantage might be restored. We refer to the practice of choosing deaconesses from the female members of the church.
>
> Of the existence of this class of officers in the apostle's time there can be little doubt. We believe that Phoebe was a deaconess, and Euodia and Syntyche, with some others; and there is reason to suppose that to such ones the apostle referred, when, in 1 Timothy iii.11, he spake of women who were to "be grave, not slanderers, sober, and faithful in all things." That he is not there speaking of the wives of deacons, is maintained by very competent authorities, with whom we are inclined to agree.
>
> At all events "it amounts to a query," says one of our best practical divines, "worthy of very serious consideration, whether we are perfectly justified in laying aside an office which certainly appears to have once existed in the church, and which, amidst all its varying circumstances, might be rendered eminently useful. How many cases are continually occurring, in which the official ministrations of a female would at once be more effectual and more discreet than those of the opposite sex? How many scenes of half penitent profligacy are there, into which it would be hazardous to a *man's* character to venture? How many cases of sickness amongst the female members, which none can so effectually relieve as one of their own sex?"
>
> Now, when we think of the expediency and obvious fitness of such an officer as thus suggested, and remember that there is very strong, if not certain, proof that such a class of officers as deaconesses existed in the apostolic times, we seriously commend to the associated churches the immediate consideration of the question, whether they will not appoint deaconesses themselves, who shall be solemnly set apart to their appointed duties by the word of God and prayer. We believe we should thereby

---

[4]"Deaconesses," *The Baptist Magazine* 33 (1841): 113.

approximate more nearly to New Testament order, and promote very considerably the welfare of the church.[5]

In 1863, Charles James Middleditch published *The Office of Deacon*, a forty-eight-page tract that he had originally prepared, to a great extent, several years earlier as a circular letter on "The Deacon's Office," and the Bristol Association of Baptist Churches had unanimously adopted.[6] Middleditch included only one paragraph on deaconesses, but he viewed them as having an explicit presence in the New Testament. He believed deaconesses "were plainly recognized in apostolic times as specially engaged in the service of the Church," including Phoebe in Romans 16:1, Euodia and Syntyche in Philippians 4:2, and "several others whose names are mentioned in the New Testament," such as the aged women in Titus 2:3 and the widows in 1 Timothy 5. Further, "it is also of Deaconesses, and not of the wives of Deacons," that he speaks of in 1 Timothy 3:11.[7]

In 1881, John W. Ashworth delivered an address on deacons and deaconesses to the Debon Association of Baptist Churches in England in which he claimed that "the Church has lost much by not using its holy women more." Then he appealed, "If ever Deaconesses were required, they are required now," and he gave three reasons why. First, "our male officials are so absorbed in business and in professional duties that, in too many instances, their discharge of duty is confined to the Lord's-day." Second, "there are Female Prayer-Meetings which such sisters might conduct, and Classes for our younger members for Bible study, and suggestions respecting countless things on which none but women are capable of giving advice and guidance." Third, "our Deacons would be largely relieved from obligation as to details of work which now press upon many by far too heavily, and would set free their energies to assist the pastor in more direct missionary enterprise, in extending the knowledge of Christ throughout their neighborhood."[8]

---

[5] "On Deaconesses," *The Baptist Magazine* 34 (1842): 68; additional paragraph breaks added to aid readability.

[6] Charles James Middleditch, *The Office of Deacon* (London: J. Heaton and Son, 1863) v.

[7] Ibid., 13-14.

[8] John W. Ashworth, *Deacons and Deaconesses, Address Delivered at Totnes, June 14th, 1881, before the Debon Association of Baptist Churches* (London: Yates and Alexander, 1881) 16-17.

Decline among Baptists in the United States. In 1813, Baptist historian David Benedict acknowledged that the Separate Baptist churches of the late 1700s had tended to have deaconesses and eldresses. However, he claimed that by the early 1800s "the offices of eldresses and deaconesses have fallen into disuse"[9] in churches in the Sandy Creek Association, formed in 1756 as the first and most influential Separate Baptist association in the South. One likely cause of this decline was that while "many of its [the association's] members were formerly thought to lean considerably towards the Arminian system; but they have now become generally, and some of them strenuously Calvinistick."[10] In their church manuals, J. L. Reynolds asserted in 1849 that deaconesses have "fallen into desuetude,"[11] and Edward T. Hiscox wrote in 1894 that "a few churches retain the practice."[12]

Various kinds of evidence illustrate the continuing decline of deaconesses among Baptists in the United States. For example, many publications published biographies and obituaries, in the form of full-length articles, on deacons;[13] deaconesses, however, did not tend to receive such coverage.

Many Baptist associations published and distributed to their churches circular letters that focused on deacons—their necessity, qualifications, ordination, duties, and terms of service. Fifteen such letters published between 1804 and 1895 by fourteen associations in eight states (Connecticut, Georgia, Indiana, Massachusetts, New York, Pennsylvania, Rhode Island, and Vermont) plus a New Jersey association's statement on church discipline, with a section on deacons, all discussed male deacons only; none

---

[9]David Benedict, *A General History of the Baptist Denomination in America, and Other Parts of the World*, vol. 2 (Boston: Manning and Loring, 1813) 107-108.

[10]Ibid., 107.

[11]J. L. Reynolds, *Church Polity* (Richmond: Harrold and Murray, 1849) 138.

[12]Edward T. Hiscox, *The New Directory for Baptist Churches* (Philadelphia: American Baptist Publication Society, 1894) 116.

[13]See, e.g., "Character and Last Days of Deacon Jonathan Merriam," *The American Baptist Magazine* (January 1829): 3-15; three 1842 articles in *The Baptist Memorial and Monthly Chronicle* (April, 110; July, 215; October, 299-303); and Lynn C. Dickerson II, "Joel B. Lemon, 1828–1910: Portrait of a Nineteenth-Century Baptist Deacon," *The Virginia Baptist Register* 25 (1986): 1275-85.

mentioned deaconesses.[14] Closed attitudes toward deaconesses dominated most associational life in the North and South.

Following a pattern initiated in the 1700s, Baptist churches and associations in the 1800s increasingly described diaconal functions in administrative, business, and management categories, with an emphasis on deacons as managers, trustees, and board members, and as treasurers, assessors, collectors, and disbursers of church funds, often to the neglect of the more caring and supportive ministries. To illustrate, one church described deacons as "the chief managers in the church" as early as 1773.[15] Three associations in three states viewed deacons as "trustees" of the church in 1804, 1809, and 1824.[16]

Variously, associations assigned the following functions to deacons: "to superintend the secular concerns of the Church" and to serve as "the official agent of the Church";[17] to serve as "the assessors, collectors and disbursers of the churches' funds";[18] and to lead in "managing the secular

---

[14]In chronological order, the circular letters are located in the following sources: Shaftsbury Association (VT), 1804, printed in Stephen Wright, comp., *History of the Shaftsbury Baptist Association* (Troy NY: A. G. Johnson, 1853) 95-99; *Minutes*, Georgia Association (GA), 1808, 7-12; *Minutes*, Warren Association (RI), 1809, 9-13; *Minutes*, Hartford Association (CT), 1824, 10-13; Georgia Association (GA), 1825, printed in Jesse Mercer, *A History of the Georgia Baptist Association* (Washington GA: n.p., 1838) 283-88; *Minutes*, Bradford Association (PA), 1839, 12-19; *Minutes*, Stephentown Association (NY), 1840, 2-19; *Minutes*, Salem Association (MA), 1842, 10-14; *Minutes*, Fairfield Association (VT), 1846, 7-10; *Minutes*, Woodstock Association (VT), 1850, 10-13; *Minutes*, Buffalo Association (NY), 1850, 11-15; *Minutes*, Madison Association (NY), 1855, 12-16; *Minutes*, New York Association (NY), 1861, 20-23; *Minutes*, Curry's Prairie Association (IN), 1862, 5-8; and *Minutes*, Euharlee Primitive Association (GA), 1895, 7. Also see "An Outline of Church Discipline" in *Minutes*, New Jersey Association (NJ), Jersey), 1846, 19.

[15]*Records of the Welsh Tract Baptist Meeting*, vol. 2 (Wilmington DE: Historical Society of Delaware, 1904) 8.

[16]Wright, *History of the Shaftsbury Association from 1781 to 1853*, 98; *Minutes*, Warren Association (RI), 1809, 10; *Minutes*, Hartford Association (CT), 1824, 12.

[17]*Minutes*, Stephentown Association (NY), 1840, 11-12.

[18]*Minutes*, Fairfield Association (VT), 1846, 10.

affairs of the churches."[19] In contrast, one association opposed using deacons as church treasurers.[20]

Baptists questioned the biblical basis for deaconesses, their necessity, and their ordination. For example, in response to an 1842 query from a church, "Would it not be well for the churches to have Deaconesses now as well as in the days of the Apostles?" the Big Hatchie Association in Tennessee studied the matter for a year and then refused to act on it in 1843.[21] Near mid-century, two books on Baptist church polity considered deaconesses "unnecessary."[22]

Few writers contributed as significantly to the concept of deacons as church managers as did R. B. C. Howell, pastor of First Baptist Church, Nashville, and editor of *The Baptist*, an influential Tennessee Baptist newspaper. In 1846, Howell published his book, *The Deaconship: Its Nature, Qualifications, Relations, and Duties*. This work may have been the most influential writing on deacons and deaconesses published in the United States in the 1800s (Judson Press published the eleventh edition in 1977). Howell's influence would increase through his service in 1851–1858 as the second president of the Southern Baptist Convention.

Although Howell favored deaconesses, his writing guaranteed that many churches using his book would keep deaconesses subordinate to deacons. Deacons were men; deaconesses were women. Male deacons were full-fledged deacons; deaconesses were "female assistants to deacons." Deacons were to be ordained; deaconesses were not to be ordained. Howell made a distinct mark on the Baptist trend in the 1800s to assign administrative, business, and financial matters to male deacon bodies, thereby excluding women who typically were not allowed to participate in those kinds of leadership roles in church. He claimed that deacons "of right have the full control" over the church's temporalities. They must exercise "management" over the church's "property and funds," although he did make clear that such management "is not absolute, but limited to such uses as the church may order." Deacons were both "the financial officers of the church" and "a BOARD OF OFFICERS, or the *executive board* of the church, for her temporal department." (This designation of a deacon body

---

[19]*Minutes*, New Jersey Association (NJ), 1846, 19.

[20]*Minutes*, New York Association (NY), 1861, 21.

[21]*Minutes*, Big Hatchie Association (TN), 1842, 6; 1843, 5.

[22]Reynolds, *Church Polity*, 138; William Williams, *Apostolical Church Polity* (Philadelphia: Bible and Publication Society, 1859?) 29-30.

as a "board (of managers)" continues to have implications for many Baptist churches in the early 2000s.)[23]

In 1867, J. M. Pendleton published his *Church Manual*, which was still in print more than one hundred years later. Pendleton, a leader of the Landmark Movement that made a strong impact on Southern Baptist development, urged deacons to be the trustees and treasurers of churches. He gave substantial thrust to the idea of relating deacons heavily to the business side of church life.[24] That made it difficult for women to be elected deaconesses, and it virtually prohibited women's ordination.

Because churches minimized women's participation in administrative roles, following the lead of American culture, the growing tendency of churches and writers to assign business functions to deacons undoubtedly contributed to the decline of deaconesses in the 1800s. So did the expanding influence of Calvinism in Baptist life, with its theology of male leadership.

Continued Affirmation of and Disagreement about Deaconesses

In spite of the decline of deaconesses, Baptists published several major affirmations of deaconesses, almost all of which opposed their ordination. Three appeared in 1846. First, William Bullein Johnson (1782–1862), first president of the Southern Baptist Convention, claimed that deaconesses could be "particularly useful" and "exceedingly valuable" in certain duties, namely, "in visiting the female poor, and in attending to the interior of the meeting house."[25]

Second, a Kentucky Baptist newspaper presented the history of deaconesses and determined that their existence and ministry in the primitive churches were clear. While deaconesses are "to visit the sick, the miserable, and the helpless of their own sex" and to assist women being baptized, the

---

[23]R. B. C. Howell, *The Deaconship: Its Nature, Qualifications, Relations, and Duties* (Philadelphia: American Baptist Publication Society, 1846) 8, 18, 60, 95, 97, 107-108.

[24]J. M. Pendleton, *Church Manual* (Philadelphia: American Baptist Publication Society, 1867) 30-31, 35, 39-40.

[25]William Bullein Johnson, *The Gospel Developed through the Government and Order of the Churches of Jesus Christ* (Richmond: H. K. Ellyson, 1846) 97.

publication concluded that "Deaconesses were not, as Deacons are, formally ordained."[26]

Third, R. B. C. Howell included in *The Deaconship* an entire chapter on deaconesses in which he reviewed biblical evidence and concluded that "the word of God authorizes, and in some sense, certainly by implication, enjoins the appointment of deaconesses in the churches of Christ." For Howell, Romans 16:1, regarding Phoebe, "must be regarded as conclusive evidence of the Scripture warrant for deaconesses," and 1 Timothy 3:11 referred to women in the diaconate. He viewed deaconesses to be as necessary as they were in the times of the apostles.[27]

Howell also suggested qualifications and duties for deaconesses. For one thing, "they should be women whose reputation for piety, and whose kind, intelligent, and courteous deportment, will give force to their ministrations." They were "to visit the sick, the miserable, and the helpless, and ought to feel for them an abiding sympathy, and be ready and able, at all times, to hold forth to them the consolations of the gospel of Christ. They are . . . to attend their neophyte sister at baptism." Howell concluded by claiming that "all that seems to be wanting among us, is the selection and approval by the churches, of the persons to be employed; and, generally, more regular and systematic attention to this department, so as to secure the performance of its duties well, promptly, and faithfully."[28] However, Howell opposed the ordination of deaconesses and their equality with male deacons, following the tenor of his times.

In 1879, J. R. Graves, the noted Landmark Baptist leader, claimed that "There is no good reason why saintly women should not fill the office of deaconess to-day in most churches. In fact, they often perform the duties of the office without the name."[29] He opposed their ordination, however. In the 1890s, a Baptist church manual and a book on Baptist ecclesiology approved deaconesses.[30]

Although deaconesses experienced a general state of decline, and perhaps because of published affirmations of their possible usefulness,

---

[26]"Deaconesses," *The Western Baptist Review* (February 1846): 235-36.

[27]Howell, *The Deaconship*, 100-101, 104

[28]Ibid., 105, 106, 108.

[29]J. R. Graves, "Woman's Work in the Church," *The Baptist* (22 February 1879): 4.

[30]Hiscox, *The New Directory*, 116; Edwin C. Dargan, *Ecclesiology: A Study of the Churches* (Louisville: Charles T. Dearing, 1897) 121.

deaconesses did exist in some churches in the 1800s. After reviewing the sources, Baptist historian Leon McBeth concluded:

> The evidence suggests that in the nineteenth century many Southern Baptists approved deaconesses and regarded the office as biblical. Moreover, at least some churches acted upon these views and regularly set aside deaconesses as well as deacons. Probably Southern Baptists have never been without deaconesses.[31]

Churches in three states illustrate the presence of deaconesses in the late 1800s. The minutes of the Rock Creek Baptist Church in Morgan County, Alabama, for September 1867 indicated that the church was organized that month by several persons including nine "decons" (deacons). Three of the nine were women: Martha J. Holmes, Sarah A. Denson, and Lioceretia Smith.[32] The First Baptist Church of Raleigh, North Carolina, elected four deaconesses in 1874: Sallie Towler, Mrs. A. M. Lewis, V. B. Swepson, and Anna Justice.[33] The First Baptist Church of Waco, Texas, chose six deaconesses in 1877 when B. H. Carroll was pastor; however, Carroll did not favor the ordination of deaconesses and refused to allow them to share in church leadership.[34]

In 1884, an early agenda item at the Baptist General Convention of Texas raised a question, "Do the Scriptures Authorize the Appointment of Women as Deacons?"[35] Though unanswered in the minutes, the question at least showed an interest in the topic.

In 1897, Edwin C. Dargan, professor of homiletics at the Southern Baptist Theological Seminary, published a book on the church. He claimed that Romans 16:1 and 1 Timothy 3:11 did not make deaconesses obligatory, but because of this trace of biblical authority "there should be no objection to establishing it [the deaconess] office should it be found expedient and clearly promotive of good so to do."[36]

---

[31]Leon McBeth, *Women in Baptist Life* (Nashville: Broadman Press, 1979) 143.

[32]*Minutes*, Rock Creek Baptist Church, Morgan County AL, included in an e-mail from Ted Holmes, 26 April 2004.

[33]Caralie Brown and Jane Purser, "Deaconesses: A Long History of Service" (Raleigh NC, n.d.) 2-3; manuscript located in the Baptist History File Folder "Deacons," Southern Baptist Historical Library and Archives, Nashville TN.

[34]Alan J. Lefever, *Fighting the Good Fight: The Life and Work of Benajah Harvey Carroll* (Austin TX: Eakin Press, 1994) 28-29.

[35]*Minutes*, Baptist State Convention of Texas (4-6 October 1884): 53.

[36]Edwin C. Dargan, *Ecclesiology: A Study of the Churches* (Louisville: Charles

Deaconesses sometimes made extraordinary contributions to Baptist life. Violet A. Johnson was an African-American deaconess. In 1897, she helped create a new Baptist mission in Summit, New Jersey. She shared in furnishing the mission's first meeting room, and she personally paid the first month's rent. In 1898, that mission became the Fountain Baptist Church, the first African-American Baptist church in Summit.[37] Johnson, born in 1870 in Wilmington, North Carolina, had moved at an early age to Brooklyn, New York, as a "domestic servant," and then, at age 27, to Summit, New Jersey. There, in addition to helping to found the Fountain Baptist Church, she served as president of the church's board of deaconesses. Eventually, she also provided leadership for the New England Missionary Baptist Convention Women's Missionary Society and as a trustee of the Nannie Burroughs Training School for Girls in Washington, D.C.[38]

The 1800s ended and the 1900s began with Baptist writers disagreeing about the validity of deaconesses and, eventually, women deacons. Wayne Flynt, distinguished professor of Southern History at Auburn University, provided valuable insights into attitudes toward deaconesses and women in general in Alabama in the late 1800s and early 1900s. A thorough examination of primary sources led Flynt to discover that most Alabama Baptist leaders opposed deaconesses, especially their ordination, and even appealed for women's subordination and silence in church. However, some Baptists favored deaconesses. E. B. Teague, an influential denominational leader in the nineteenth century, contributed an article to the Alabama Baptist newspaper in 1870 in which he advocated the election of deaconesses. Willie Kelly, Alabama's most influential missionary between 1893 and 1943, made herself a deaconess in her Shanghai church and opened the office of deaconess to Chinese women as well.[39]

The 1910 edition of *Women in the Churches: Their Rights and Restrictions*, prepared by J. B. Moody, who had served as editor of the Tennessee Baptist state newspaper in 1886–1889, claimed, after reviewing biblical evidence for female deacons, that "If the Bible provides for female dea-

T. Dearing, 1897) 121.

[37]"Fountain Baptist Church, Historic Profile." <www.fountainbaptist.org/history/history.html>, accessed 11 November 2004.

[38]"Fountain Baptist Church, Violet Johnson (1870–1939)." <www.fountainbaptist.org/violet.html>, accessed 11 November 2004.

[39]Wayne Flynt, *Alabama Baptists: Southern Baptists in the Heart of Dixie* (Tuscaloosa: University of Alabama Press, 1998) 154, 178, 240.

cons, then they are needed, and the cause will suffer without them, yea, it is suffering now." Moody commented that "All over the land women are doing the deacon's work." However, "For one to say that he does not believe in female deacons and at the same time is using and encouraging women in the work of deacons is a shameful inconsistency." Moody concluded: "An honest examination of all scriptures on any subject is a cure-all for all heresy. I recommend this course to all my readers. *Why not be right, especially on Woman's Rights?*"[40]

Opponents of deaconesses and their ordination were always close by. P. E. Burroughs, head of the Church Administration Department of the SBC Sunday School Board, claimed in his *Honoring the Deaconship*, a popular study-course book published in 1929, that

> we must enter protest [against any who would suggest that] *deaconesses* should be ordained as officers of the church and should constitute a part of the diaconate or official body of the church. Such procedure would seem to contradict both the precedents and the teachings of the New Testament.

Reluctantly, Burroughs did defer to the local church the options of setting apart some women as deaconesses or deciding whether to regard all women in the church "as unofficial servants or deaconesses."[41]

Burroughs's book set in motion the publication throughout the twentieth century of millions of copies of books and other resources on deacons by the SBC Sunday School Board (later LifeWay Christian Resources) that opposed or, at least, refused to advocate the ordination of deaconesses and women deacons in Southern Baptist churches.

In 1955, Broadman Press published *The Baptist Deacon* by Robert E. Naylor, president of Southwestern Baptist Theological Seminary. Hundreds of thousands of copies would be distributed in the next fifty years; the book is even listed in the 2005 catalog of the R. H. Boyd Publishing Corporation of National (African-American) Baptists. Naylor's book assumed throughout that all deacons are (and should be) men. In commenting on 1 Timothy 3:11, Naylor wrote:

---

[40]J. B. Moody, *Women in the Churches: Their Rights and Restrictions: or, Paul Harmonized with the Law and the Gospel*, 2nd ed, rev. and enl. (Martin TN: Hall-Moody Institute, 1910) 105-107.

[41]P. E. Burroughs, *Honoring the Deaconship* (Nashville: Sunday School Board, SBC, 1929) 43-44.

There are those who want to translate the word "wives" as "women," but the context suggests the first. It is certainly consonant with this book that a wife should enter into the responsibilities and sweet promises of this office without being publicly set apart by the church in an ordination service.[42]

The Renewal of Deaconesses and the Rise of Women Deacons

Prior to 1960, deaconesses reemerged and some churches began to adopt women deacons in several states. North Carolina was a classic example. Illustrations from that state of churches with women deacons and the years they first elected them are First Baptist Church, Ahoskie (1920); Louisburg Baptist Church, Louisburg (1921); Pullen Memorial Baptist Church, Raleigh (1927); Goshen Baptist Church, Leland (1928); Knightdale Baptist Church, Knightdale (1931); Zebulon Baptist Church, Zebulon (1939); Weldon Baptist Church, Weldon (early 1940s); and Warrenton Baptist Church, Warrenton (1955). In addition, First Baptist Church, Shelby, elected *deaconesses* in 1921.

In 1921, the Forks of Elkhorn Baptist Church in Kentucky, whose pastor was J. R. Sampey, professor at the Southern Baptist Theological Seminary, elected several deaconesses and junior deaconesses. They received an "earnest charge" rather than laying on of hands in ordination. Sampey divided his congregation into groups; deacons and deaconesses ministered to the groups.[43] A Baptist church manual largely representing practices among Northern Baptists reported in 1935 that "an increasing number of churches parallel the board of deacons with a board of deaconesses."[44]

Churches in other states also had deaconesses. For example, by 1950, the Third Baptist Church of St. Louis, Missouri, had sixty deaconesses and had had a board of deaconesses for many years.[45] In 1944, this church published an annual report that included separate reports by the chairmen of the

---

[42]Robert E. Naylor, *The Baptist Deacon* (Nashville: Broadman Press, 1955) 121.

[43]Ermina Jett Darnell, *Forks of Elkhorn Church* (Louisville: Standard Printing Co., 1946) 52-53.

[44]William Roy McNutt, *Polity and Practice in Baptist Churches* (Philadelphia: Judson Press, 1935) 94.

[45]McBeth, *Women in Baptist Life*, 143.

board of deacons and the board of deaconesses. Deaconess chair Mrs. Harry W. Barber reported significant achievements in the previous year by the board of deaconesses, which had fifty-five members. Deaconesses had "assisted 394 women and girls who offered themselves for membership in our church." Further, "During the year, 4,665 calls were made, 1,906 of which were made upon the sick, 318 evangelistic and 2,441 other calls. A total of 2,130 telephone calls were also made and 2,382 items of correspondence were mailed to members of our church." In sharp contrast, deacon chair L. R. Main reported, disappointedly, that "Some calls have been made by the deacons but we have not measured up to our full capabilities through this avenue of service."[46]

On 5 January 1954, C. Oscar Johnson, pastor of Third Baptist Church in St. Louis, responded to a request for information on deacons in Baptist churches from Porter Routh, executive secretary of the SBC Executive Committee. Johnson sent Routh a copy of the church's 1944 book of reports and told Routh in his letter that "You might write something about Deaconesses, too, while you're at it because I believe you'll find the Greek work for Deacon is also feminine. That would give us a pretty good scriptural background for having Deaconesses which we've had for many years."[47]

Virginia Baptists also experienced deaconess growth in the early 1900s. In 1934, the Baptist state newspaper of Virginia reported: "Some of our churches have not only deacons but deaconesses. They have scriptural authority for using this office."[48] Peakland Baptist Church in Lynchburg, Virginia, was founded in 1955 with both a board of deacons and a board of deaconesses. Each board had both a chairperson and an equal number of members.[49]

In the early 1900s, several approaches characterized deaconess/women deacon developments in the South. Some churches had separate boards of deacons and deaconesses. Most churches ordained deacons but not deaconesses. A few churches did ordain deaconesses. A few other churches began

---

[46]"Third Baptist Church, St. Louis, Missouri, Constitution and By-Laws Annual Report for 1944" in Executive Committee, Southern Baptist Convention Papers, AR Folder 46-3, Southern Baptist Historical Library and Archives, Nashville.

[47]C. O. Johnson, letter to Porter Routh (5 January 1954) in Executive Committee, Southern Baptist Convention Papers, AR Folder 46-3, Southern Baptist Historical Library and Archives, Nashville.

[48]"Still on the Trail of Deacons," *Religious Herald* (27 September 1934): 10.

[49]Steve McNeely, e-mail to author, 22 October 2004.

to delete the "deaconess" terminology and to start using the term "women deacons." Most churches with female and male deacons merged them into one deacon body with full and equal opportunities for leadership. Most churches with women deacons tended to ordain them.

To illustrate selected patterns relating to ordination, three examples will be cited. First, the 22 April 1928 minutes of the Goshen Baptist Church in Leland, North Carolina, indicated that the church elected "Sister Margaret Biggs" as a deacon and set her ordination for "the 4th Lord's Day in May."[50] The First Baptist Church of Raleigh, North Carolina, which had had deaconesses since 1874, first ordained its deaconesses on 2 February 1941.[51] The Second Baptist Church of Petersburg, Virginia, first ordained deaconesses in 1950.[52]

Ironically, one factor which may have contributed to a renewed emphasis on deaconesses and women deacons in the early part of the twentieth century was a counterreaction to widespread and harsh criticism directed towards male deacons by Baptist papers, especially in the North, between 1915 and 1934. Because deacons came under harsh review in denominational publications, many Baptists may have given thought to whether women could do better.

Article titles reveal a pattern of publishing hard-hitting articles and editorials about deacons. *The Baptist Commonwealth*, newspaper of the Pennsylvania Baptist General Convention, published "The Deacon Who Failed." *The Baptist World* of Louisville, Kentucky, published "The Revenge of the Deacons." *The Standard* of Chicago, Illinois, released an editorial on "Dehorning or Encysting Deacons." *The Baptist*, newspaper of the Northern Baptist Convention, printed an editorial on "Muley Deacons." *The Christian Index* of Philadelphia, Pennsylvania, editorialized on "Rum Selling Deacons." *The Baptist World* of Mansfield, Massachusetts, editorialized on "The Decline of the Diaconate," expressing concern that churches were too careless in their elections and expectations of deacons.[53]

---

[50]*Minutes*, Goshen Baptist Church, Leland NC, 22 April 1928.

[51]Brown and Purser, "Deaconesses: A Long History of Service," 7.

[52]Joe Lewis, e-mail to author, 27 October 2004.

[53]T. P. H. Holloway, "The Deacon Who Failed," *The Baptist Commonwealth* (9 September 1915): 3; William Thomas Tardy, "The Revenge of the Deacons," *The Baptist World* (21 October 1915): 8-9 and (28 October 1915): 11; "Dehorning or Encysting Deacons," *The Standard* (23 September 1916): 75-76; "Muley Deacons," *The Baptist* (30 October 1920): 1351-52; "Rum Selling Deacons," *The Christian Index* (20 August 1831): 117; Richard K. Morton, "The Decline of the

Some articles seriously belittled deacons. "The Bucking Deacons," another article in *The Standard*, claimed that "a church with a bucking deacon is an utter impossibility." This paper described a bucking deacon as "an animal of a different color. He is sort of a religious zebra, with black and white stripes, a hybrid, a compound of good and bad, with the bad predominating in the bucking."[54] *The Watchman-Examiner* of New York ridiculed deacons:

> While a deacon should be grave, he should not be a graveyard. We have seen deacons whose lips seem set for biting a ten-penny nail in two. Their countenance suggested that their regular diet was cayenne pepper and sauerkraut, while their whole appearance suggested an animated vinegar cruet. A long face does not signify that its wearer is long on religion; but short on faith and grey matter.[55]

The Watchman-Examiner published an editorial that cited negative comments about deacons made by a denominational leader in an address to a state convention:

> "The most serious thing faced by the churches today is furnished by the deacons, many of whom are nothing more than moral thermos bottles and fireless cookers. . . . A great number of deacons are moral parasites who throttle the work of the minister."[56]

Northern Baptists tended to be far more receptive to deaconesses and women deacons than did Southern Baptists. Consider the following examples from the 1920s–1930s, most published by Judson Press.

Frederick A. Agar, well-known Stewardship and Church Efficiency Secretary of the Northern Baptist Convention, published two key books. His writings influenced progressive developments in Northern, later American, Baptist life regarding deaconesses and women deacons.

First, Agar's 1923 deacon manual, *The Deacon at Work*, received widespread usage. Agar strongly advocated deaconesses. In discussing the

---

Diaconate," *The Baptist World* (1 October 1933): 224-25.

[54]William Thompson Dorward, "The Bucking Deacon," *The Standard* (15 September 1917): 8.

[55]J. W. Porter, "Duties of Deacons," *The Watchman-Examiner* (16 August 1934): 901.

[56]"Fair Play for the Deacons," *The Watchman-Examiner* (24 February 1921): 229.

organization of the New Testament church, he acknowledged Christ as the head of the universal and local church and claimed that "under his leadership in the person of the Holy Spirit, an under-shepherd was to be sustained by the local body as a visible leader. He was to be assisted by deacons and deaconesses."[57] Agar viewed Phoebe in Romans 16:1 as a deaconess and interpreted the "women" in 1 Timothy 3:11 to be "deacons-deaconesses."[58]

Agar opined that "for many years the local church has suffered seriously from an unchristian prejudice against women and has made sex distinctions that are unwise and harmful. The Scriptures make plain the fact that there should be no sex discrimination regarding spiritual functions, for the promises and powers of God are to every one alike, as Paul makes plain in Galatians 3:28."[59]

Although Agar recommended the use of deaconesses, he followed the typical pattern of the time: he did not treat deacons and deaconesses on an equal basis. Deacons and deaconesses should have separate boards with separate monthly meetings; still, the two boards should also meet together at least once a month. Some of the work of deaconesses should be restricted to "the care of the female members."[60] In the absence of a minister, deacons (but not deaconesses) could perform baptisms; even with the minister present, only deacons could distribute the elements of the Lord's Supper.[61] Church members subjected to corrective church discipline would appear before the board of deacons only.[62]

Agar gave much attention to the duties of deacons and deaconesses to promote stewardship, greet strangers, prepare for baptismal services, attend worship services and prayer meetings, urge every-member participation in church ministries, facilitate church Bible study, support strong family life among church members, provide for the pastor's spiritual and financial needs, share in evangelism, lead training classes for converts and other members, follow up with absentees from worship, and engage in preventive church discipline.[63] Agar urged a "unit system" approach to caring for church members in which "a deacon and a deaconess are paired, and to

---

[57]Frederick A. Agar, *The Deacon at Work* (Philadelphia: Judson Press, 1923) 5.

[58]Ibid., 8.

[59]Ibid., 16-17.

[60]Ibid., 17, 54.

[61]Ibid., 44-45.

[62]Ibid., 81.

[63]Ibid., 41-44, 46, 51-52, 58-59, 62, 69, 71, 74, 83.

them are given about thirty-five of the members for special oversight and ministry."[64]

American Baptists today tend not to ordain deacons, male or female. Agar's manual contributed to that development, claiming that "the so-called ordination of deacons is a dangerous practice because it leads many people to wrong conclusions concerning the import of a setting-apart service."[65] He noted that a careful reading of Acts 6:1-8, which is usually the passage pointed to as the basis for ordaining deacons, makes plain that the seven chosen were not deacons. Further, "The laying on of the hands of a minister or other deacon does not confer special powers upon an officer, and therefore such a procedure is not essential to the formal setting apart of a deacon."[66] He did not mention deaconesses in his discussion of ordination, possibly because most Baptist churches in the United States with deaconesses did not ordain them anyway.

Then in 1937, Agar released another important book, *Church Women at Work*. Claiming that "the office of deaconess is plainly Scriptural," he asserted in the opening paragraph of his first chapter that

> There are no vital sex distinctions in the New Testament. Men and women are dealt with on exactly the same plane in connection with spiritual processes and responsibility for Christian service and developments. . . . [Further,] Contrary to the general tenor of New Testament teaching, men have always assumed to control and lead the churches, with the result that some very important phases of work have not had a proper setting and opportunity in the life and activity of the average church membership.[67]

Agar noted that the church "has continued to minimize the place of women in the leadership of the church" for several reasons. It has misunderstood the social position of women in Bible times. It has mishandled the teachings of Christ in which as he "laid out his plans for the future a large place was made for womenfolk." It has misapprehended the thrusts of the apostle Paul by using his writings "as authority for the preeminence of men in the leadership and work of the church." It has subscribed to translations of the Bible prepared by "men afflicted with the then prevailing idea

---

[64]Ibid., 52.

[65]Ibid., 13.

[66]Ibid., 33.

[67]Frederick A. Agar, *Church Women at Work* (Philadelphia: Judson Press, 1937) 1, 36-37.

and practice of male superiority." And it has failed to observe that "women constitute two-thirds of the average church membership, men only one-third." Agar cautioned, however, that he did not want to be viewed as trying "to feminize the churches" since that would be "as great a drawback as to continue its masculine dominance."[68]

In 1935, a new Northern Baptist church manual reported that "an increasing number of churches parallel the board of deacons with a board of deaconesses." The manual writer, William Roy McNutt, expressed confidence that the practice of deaconesses "will justify itself and grow ultimately into a feature so stable as to be an accepted part of Baptist polity." He further supported deaconesses by identifying a principle of New Testament polity, namely, "its fluidity or adaptability to meet new needs. Churches, therefore, that see a need which they think can be best met by deaconesses are entirely scriptural in appointing them."[69]

Professional Deaconess Movement

Baptist deaconess sisterhoods, organizations of professional deaconesses affiliated with deaconess homes, arose in the late 1800s outside traditional deaconess bodies in local churches. The background of this development lay within an international Protestant model that originated in German Lutheranism. In 1836, Theodor Fliedner, a Lutheran pastor, established the first Protestant order of deaconesses by creating a deaconess motherhouse in Kaiserswerth, Germany. The purpose was to train women to provide Christian service in hospitals and in social work. This movement spread rapidly throughout the Protestant world. Fliedner's approach to deaconesses served as a model for the rise of other deaconess motherhouses in such countries as Germany, Switzerland, Sweden, England, and the United States.

In 1871, more than three hundred deaconesses were connected to the deaconess house at Kaiserwerth. They took no vows, agreed to serve at least five years, and wore a uniform. The home's ministries were diverse. It functioned as a hospital, training school for teachers, a female "lunatic asylum," a refuge for prostitutes and for discharged female convicts, an orphanage, a school for infants, and a home for the "infirm."[70] Based on the Kaiserswerth model, there existed in several countries in 1891 "sixty-three

---

[68]Ibid., 1-4.
[69]McNutt, *Polity and Practice in Baptist Churches*, 94.
[70]Lottie Moon, "Ministering Women," *Religious Herald* (23 March 1871): 1.

mother houses, which had . . . 8,478 sisters" working in hospitals, institutions for invalids and the poor, orphanages, schools, kindergartens, reformatories, homes for young women, mental institutions, industrial settings, insane asylums, schools for the blind, prisons, hospices and lodging houses, and as parish visitors among the sick and poor.[71] The German pattern spread to England and the United States in the late 1800s, fed heavily by moral and social conditions in both countries that created conscience problems for Christians.

The Mennonite Encyclopedia countered a claim found in some Mennonite circles that Fliedner based his institutional concept of deaconesses on a Dutch Mennonite model. Deaconesses among the Dutch Mennonites in the 1800s served in the context of local churches. Fliedner's approach was different: "Not the single congregation, but in a sense all Protestantism became the bearer of the work of charity." After discussing the rapid expansion of deaconess motherhouses based on Fliedner's model, the encyclopedia claimed that "in 1921 there were over 100 such homes, with about 20,000 deaconesses. These deaconess houses bear a denominational stamp."[72]

Developments in England. John Briggs, noted English Baptist historian, established the context within which professional deaconesses arose in England in the late 1800s: "The obligation of Christian conscience to aid the destitute and disadvantaged of every age weighed heavily on the consciousness of nineteenth-century Baptists, leading them to become active both locally and nationally in the causes of amelioration and redress."[73]

Two important writings have focused at length on the institutional approach to deaconesses among English Baptists. In 1954, Carey Kingsgate Press in London published a thirty-six-page booklet by Doris M. Rose titled *Baptist Deaconesses*. This pivotal work treated the deaconess sisterhood movement in England from 1890 through 1954. Although undocumented and without a bibliography, this writing quoted many primary sources and provided valuable information. The second work, *Sisters of the People: The*

---

[71]Charles R. Henderson, "The Work of Deaconesses," *The Standard* (11 April 1896): 5.

[72]L. M. S., "Deaconess," *The Mennonite Encyclopedia* (Scottdale PA: Mennonite Publishing House, 1956) 2:23.

[73]J. H. Y. Briggs, *The English Baptists of the Nineteenth Century*, vol. 3 of A History of the English Baptists, ed. Roger Hayden (Didcot, England: Baptist Historical Society, 1994) 320.

Order of Baptist Deaconesses, 1890–1975, by Nicola Morris, represents work that Morris undertook toward an M.A. at the University of Bristol in Bristol, England. Published in 2002 by the Centre for Comparative Studies in Religion and Gender of the University of Bristol, this fifty-eight-page book is a more academic, comprehensive, and interpretive study than the work by Rose. Thoroughly documented, relying routinely on such sources as the earliest annual reports of the Baptist Deaconess Home and Mission, Morris's work also includes an eight-page bibliography on Baptist deaconesses in England.[74]

English Baptist deaconess work began in 1890 under the leadership of F. B. Meyer, minister of Regent's Park Chapel and honorary superintendent of the London Baptist Association Forward Movement. The Baptist Deaconess Home and Mission was dedicated in London on 6 June 1890. By 1891, the home had trained several deaconesses "in the work of visiting and nursing the sick poor."[75] Meyer was "the genius behind the birth of the Baptist deaconess order, which equipped and trained women to give leadership to the churches to engage with the social problems, particularly the absence of medical care, in the inner city."[76]

Beginning in the early 1890s, deaconesses were appointed to such ministries as counseling and visitation, often including medical training. They took the churches' ministries of compassion into the communities. The shortage of men in the workplace during World War I contributed to expanded roles for deaconesses. In 1919, the Baptist Union of Great Britain and Ireland assumed responsibility for the work formerly done by the Baptist Deaconess Home and Mission and eventually expanded its scope. Thereafter, the formal office of deaconess continued to exist but began to decline. During World War II, deaconesses began to enter pastoral ministry when so many male ministers were called into military service. After the war, they continued to engage in pastoral tasks, but at a smaller remuneration. Eventually, as the state engaged increasingly in social work, deacon-

---

[74]Doris M. Rose, *Baptist Deaconesses* (London: Carey Kingsgate Press, 1954); Nicola Morris, *Sisters of the People: The Order of Baptist Deaconesses 1890–1975*, CCRG research paper 2 (Bristol UK: University of Bristol, Faculty of Arts, Centre for Comparative Studies in Religion and Gender, 2002).

[75]Rose, *Baptist Deaconesses*, 5-8.

[76]Briggs, *The English Baptists of the Nineteenth Century*, 324.

esses focused more and more on pastoral work.[77] Deaconesses tended to
receive small stipends for their service.

A document published by the Baptist Union of Great Britain and Ireland described the role of English Baptist deaconesses near the mid-1900s:

> In 1919 the Baptist Union assumed responsibility for the work which
> had been carried on by the Baptist Deaconess Home and Mission, and
> decided to enlarge its scope. It was agreed to found a college in London,
> and "to call out and train Baptist women who were qualified and ready to
> devote themselves to some specialized form of ministry in the Church, and
> more particularly to the work of deaconesses among the poor, to mission-
> ary work, and in positions of leadership in the Church, Institute, Sunday
> School, and Christian social work."
>
> A Special Committee was set up by the Baptist Union Council to
> survey the organization and the function of the Order and the College, and
> its findings were presented to the Council in March, 1941. Attention was
> drawn to the variety of work the deaconess was called upon to do. "We do
> not aim at training Women Ministers, but some deaconesses have been
> virtually put in the position of Ministers and given the responsibility of
> organizing and maintaining churches. Others act as assistants to ministers,
> with special responsibility for the conduct of Women's Meetings, for
> Sunday school work and the care of young women and children.
>
> By-laws were drawn up and approved by the Baptist Union Council
> in 1948, setting forth rules governing the relationship of deaconesses to
> the Baptist Union on the one hand and to the churches on the other, and
> dealing with recognition, settlement and sustenance.
>
> At the settlement of a deaconess in a church a Service of Induction
> and Recognition is usually held.
>
> The fact that deaconesses are increasingly doing the work normally
> undertaken by a minister raises questions about their status and the training
> necessary for them, and we would call the attention of the Denomination
> to these matters.[78]

Although English Baptist sisterhood deaconesses originally focused
heavily on rendering services to the poor and sick, their ministries had
become much more extensive by the 1950s. Rose claimed that their work
typically found expression in one of seven areas: colleague to a minister in

---

[77]John Briggs, letter to author, 25 March 1998.

[78]"The Doctrine of the Ministry" (London: Baptist Union of Great Britain and
Ireland, 1961) appendix 4, quoted in H. Leon McBeth, *A Sourcebook for Baptist
Heritage* (Nashville: Broadman Press, 1990) 382.

general church work; minister's assistant responsible for a church mission or some special church work; deaconess in charge of a church, churches, or a mission; pioneer in new districts, especially in laying foundations for a new church; reviver of causes whose vitality and interest have declined; specialist in women's work, youth leadership, Sunday School work, or moral and social concerns; and a participant in general church visitation.[79]

Deaconesses wore distinctive uniforms. Rose described the development of the deaconess dress codes:

> From the beginning, the Sisters wore a distinctive form of dress which at first served not merely as a mark of office but also as a protection in days when it was unwise for a woman to be about the streets of London alone once darkness had fallen. When the Baptist Union assumed responsibility for the work, an official uniform was approved which comprised a tailored navy-blue coat, or coat and skirt, worn with a close fitting navy-blue bonnet from which hung a grey veil. A navy-blue hat with a distinctive badge was adopted as an alternative to the veil twelve years ago [about 1942], and since 1949 the hat has become the regulation head-dress for new members.[80]

Gwenyth Hubble, who had been ordained a Baptist Union minister twenty-one years earlier, wrote honestly in 1961 that

> the existence of an order of deaconesses has been, for us as a denomination, an escape route by which we have avoided facing the real issues of women in pastoral ministry, and we have been content, because of the shortage of male ministers, to let women do the work of the pastoral ministry and call them by another name.[81]

To prove her point, she noted that in 1959, fifty-two deaconesses were working under the Baptist Union. Forty-one had full pastoral charge of churches; the other eleven worked as colleagues to male ministers. Hubble's explanation for the Baptist Union's using deaconesses to do the work of ministers was direct: "It is obvious that a church will be prepared to have a deaconess when it cannot afford a minister because she is cheaper."[82]

---

[79]Rose, *Baptist Deaconesses*, 34.

[80]Ibid., 30-31.

[81]Gwenyth Hubble, "Women in the Ministry," *Fraternal* no. 119 (January 1961): 14.

[82]Ibid.

In 1967, forty deaconesses in the Baptist Union were engaged in active service; thirty were involved in pastoral work. "There was a double injustice in paying these women on a lower salary scale [than men in pastoral work] and in denying them full ministerial title, when their work was often indistinguishable from that of ordained ministers."[83] The Order of Baptist Deaconesses was dissolved in 1975 when all serving deaconesses were transferred to the official, accredited list of ministers serving in the Baptist Union of Great Britain.

Nicola Morris summarized well general thrusts relating to the English Baptist deaconess movement. Beginning as a medical mission to the poor of London with only a few sisters participating, it "evolved into a national association of women church leaders whose very presence caused the Baptist Union of Great Britain to reconsider attitudes towards female modes of ministry." Factors fueling changes in deaconesses' roles included two world wars, increased government involvement in health and social care, and twentieth-century contributions to the emancipation of women. Therefore, "When the Baptist Union decided to transfer *en bloc* all serving deaconesses to the list of accredited ordained ministers, they were in fact merely ratifying what in practice was already taking place."[84]

Morris concluded that while "this integration of women ministers into the structures of the Union has indeed given women greater opportunities," one has to admit that "the nature of the deaconesses' original work has been all but lost." In fact, "The price of integration has been the loss of a distinctively female form of ministry." Still, "The Order of Baptist Deaconesses represents the Baptist Union's most distinctive form of female ministry in the twentieth century and as such contributes to the ongoing debate about how gender-inclusive models of ministry can develop."[85]

Developments in the United States. In the United States, by the end of the 1800s, Congregational, Episcopal, German Reformed, Lutheran, Methodist, and Presbyterian churches had developed deaconess organizations. Methodists had as many deaconesses as all the other denominations combined. One report indicated that "a hundred and fifty well-equipped deaconess institutions arose between 1885 and 1900. Under the circum-

---

[83]John Briggs, "She-Preachers, Widows, and Other Women: The Feminine Dimension in Baptist Life Since 1600," *The Baptist Quarterly* 31/7 (July 1986): 346.

[84]Morris, *Sisters of the People*, 1.

[85]Ibid., 44.

stances, this was amazing progress, reflecting as nothing else did the impact of the social crisis upon conventional modes of religious behavior."[86] In the early 1900s, the numbers of deaconesses would begin to decline: "Perhaps their quaint hats and distinctive dress militated against any continuing popularity."[87]

How did Baptists fit into this picture? Lottie Moon, who would serve as the consummate Southern Baptist missionary to China for thirty-nine years, 1873–1912, was working in 1871 in Danville, Kentucky, where she taught at Danville Female Academy. That year, the *Religious Herald*, Baptist state paper of Virginia, published a two-part article by Moon titled "Ministering Women."[88] Part one presented the history of the Lutheran deaconess institutions formed in Kaiserswerth and Strasburg, Germany, respectively, in 1836 and 1842. Part two began by detailing the story of a deaconess organization in the Protestant Episcopal Church and noted similar developments among Presbyterians.

Moon then zeroed in on Baptists in part two: "There is a latent power in our churches which, following the wise example of other denominations, we should seek at once to develop," she urged. Although she claimed that "we do not advocate expensive machinery, such as the purchase of a home or the establishment of a hospital," she did believe that

> each church, especially in our large cities, could set apart and sustain, say, two deaconesses. These could make it their business to minister to the poor and suffering, establish Sunday schools, sewing schools, night schools and mothers' meetings. In a large city, such an instrumentality would be invaluable in reaching the poor, the degraded and the ignorant.[89]

Moon concluded with a rhetorical question and some assertive statements:

> Does anyone object that women cannot be found to devote themselves to this work? All history refutes this imputation on woman's readiness for self-consecration. The last at the cross, the first at the sepulcher, she is still ready for every good work. . . . [Further,] All such women would ask,

---

[86]Aaron Ignatius Abell, *The Urban Impact on American Protestantism, 1865-1900* (Cambridge UK: Cambridge University Press, 1943) 194.

[87]Winthrop S. Hudson, *Religion in America* (New York: Charles Scribner's Sons, 1965) 297.

[88]Moon, "Ministering Women," *Religious Herald* (23 March 1871): 1; (13 April 1871): 1.

[89]Moon, "Ministering Women" *Religious Herald* (13 April 1871): 1.

would be the assurance of a moderate maintenance. Let the churches but guarantee this, and we doubt not that a new impulse would be given to the efficiency of the female element in our churches.[90]

Walter Rauschenbusch, pastor of the Second German Baptist Church in New York City in the 1890s, and leader of the Social Gospel Movement, wrote an article, later published as a sixteen-page leaflet, titled "To the Deacons of Our Churches." He admonished deacons:

My fear, my brethren, is that you have been faithful to the letter of your office, but not to its spirit. . . . In some cases you have even lost sight of the essence of your office altogether, thinking more of serving at the Lord's Supper and in the worship of the church, and of making your influence felt in the management of the church than of the lowly work of service which might be so dear to your Master.

He suggested that deacons, in contrast,

ought no longer to confine your work to the poor of your own church. . . . The deacons of today ought to grapple with the problems of poverty in the world . . . [and] ought not to be content with healing physical misery after it has come, but ought to prevent it before it comes.[91]

One way Rauschenbusch responded to this concern was to play a strong role in helping to create a deaconess sisterhood in New York City to help meet social and spiritual needs created by industrialization, urbanization, and immigration.

A key development took place in 1894. Two Baptist pastors in New York City, Leighton Williams, pastor of the Amity Baptist Church, and Rauschenbusch, jointly led their churches to establish the Baptist Deaconess Home at 312 West 54th Street. An 1895 article in *The World* described this development, noted that it was based on an English Baptist model, indicated that two women were already in training, and provided the following details:

They [deaconesses] will be taught how to take care of the sick, to prepare food and to do everything that may be needed in the places they are called to minister in. The candidates, after a course of training, are ordained, but

---

[90]Ibid.

[91]Walter Rauschenbusch, "To the Deacons of Our Churches" (New York: Samuel Batten, n.d.) 11, 14.

take no vows and may marry if they choose, or retire from the work at any time. They will receive no salary, but will have a home, and all their expenses will be paid. In old age they will be cared for. . . . Some will be nurses, others teachers, and others will go from house to house, talking to mothers and aiding when necessary in the household cares. The garb adopted will be very like that of the Methodist deaconesses, a brown or black dress, simply made, for winter wear and a gray for summer.[92]

By 1907, the garb was "dark blue, altogether unobtrusive, and yet sufficiently distinctive to be a recognition and a safeguard of her sacred trust."[93]

The first officers of the home included Mrs. William R. Williams as president and Mrs. Walter (Pauline) Rauschenbusch as vice president. Leighton Williams, Samuel Batten, and Walter Rauschenbusch served on the advisory committee.

A leaflet on the Baptist deaconess home (portions adapted from Frederick Meyer's *Handbook*) included among the conditions of admission that candidates had to be between twenty-one and thirty-five years old, that an application had to include reference letters and a medical certificate from a physician, that a candidate accepted had to undergo a two-year probationary period, that probationers would receive four dollars a month the first year and six dollars the second, and that ordained sisters would receive eight dollars. The leaflet cautioned that "all outer clothing be as plain as possible" and that candidates were to bring the following articles of clothing: "Six sets of plain underwear. Two plain wash dresses. Two dark underskirts. Six gingham aprons. Six single sheets. Six pair pillow slips. Six towels. Two pairs of shoes. One pair of rubbers. A rain coat, umbrella, and three pairs of dark gloves."[94]

The leaflet listed nine qualifications each candidate had to possess.

1. Sound health, strength enough for the labor and strain of the calling, and sufficient endurance and elasticity not to grow weary and succumb prematurely.

---

[92]"Baptists Fall in Line: Amity and Second German Churches Organize an Order of Deaconesses," *The World* (13 April 1895) n.p.; located in the *Scrapbook* of Amity Baptist Church, New York NY, housed in the archives of the American Baptist Historical Society in Rochester NY.

[93]May Field McKean, "The Baptist Deaconess Home," *The Standard* (31 August 1907): 11.

[94]"Baptist Deaconess Home," undated leaflet, 1-2, 4; located in the archives of the American Baptist Historical Society in Rochester NY.

2. A consistent Christian character and reputation attested by reliable testimony.
3. A mind teachable and capable of development.
4. Adaptability to the associated life, in which self-surrender, modesty, forbearance, sincerity, unselfishness, and freedom from jealousy and over-sensitiveness are very important.
5. A joyous spirit and cheerful heart free from predisposition to gloominess or melancholy are needed for successful service.
6. Habits of order and neatness in dress and appearance.
7. Willing and loving helpfulness toward all and readiness to obey, for the Lord's sake, those in authority and ability to subordinate personal will and desires to those of others.
8. A spirit of loyalty to the work and management of the Home, and a disposition to do all that is possible for its establishment and prosperity.
9. But above all there should be the deep sense of an earnest desire to serve our Lord and Master in the person of His poor and the candidate should be distinctly conscious of a divine call to this service.[95]

In 1896, Charles R. Henderson prepared an article titled "The Work of Deaconesses" for *The Standard* (published in Chicago). He noted the earlier establishment of the Baptist deaconess home in New York in 1894 and called for the formation of a similar organization in Chicago.[96]

By 1901, two other churches had joined in sponsoring the Baptist deaconess home founded in New York in 1894, and still other churches were considering becoming sponsors. A 1901 report indicated that "there are now in the home three deaconesses who, having finished the course of two years' training, have been ordained to the work, five probationers, now in course of training, and one associate deaconess worker." The report concluded that "we believe God means to accomplish great things through the instrumentality of these consecrated, recognized, voluntary workers."[97]

In 1903, the Baptist Deaconess Society of New York City ordained as deaconesses in the Amity Street Baptist Church two women who had been in training for two years at the deaconess home there. Elizabeth Dorsett, of Asbury Park, New Jersey, had chosen the ministry of visiting deaconess, and Lorina Coppoe, of Chambus, Nebraska, had chosen to be a nurse

---

[95]Ibid., 2-3.

[96]Henderson, "The Work of Deaconesses," 5.

[97]May Field McKean, "Deaconesses, Ancient and Modern," *The Standard* (20 April 1901): 7.

deaconess. During the ordination, Frank Kaiser, pastor of the Second German Baptist Church, presented an address on Christian service. Then Leighton Williams, pastor of the Amity Church, offered "the prayer of ordination during which the pastors and deacons present laid hands upon the bowed heads of the candidates."[98] With these ordinations, the deaconess society had advanced to the point that it had ordained seven sisters.

A 1906 article in the *New York Herald* titled "Workingmen Now Building a Church" revealed the support of working classes for deaconesses. The Amity Baptist Church was in the process of raising $100,000 to build "new edifices for the church work, including an auditorium and a deaconesses' home and hospital." Noting that the primary persons contributing money for the project were the "labor classes," the article showed how this particular effort to aid the Baptist deaconess movement related to Christian socialism:

> Christian socialism is realizing one of its ideals in the raising of $100,000 for the building of the new Amity Baptist Church and connected structures in West Fifty-fourth street by small subscriptions. Owing to the radical views of the Rev. Dr. Leighton Williams, who is a socialist of the Fabian persuasion and a member of the Intercollegiate Socialistic Society, the church is to a large degree cut off from the receipt of funds which might come from the wealthy classes.[99]

In 1916, Elizabeth Dorsett, who had been ordained in 1903 by the Baptist Deaconess Society of New York, published an article in *The Baptist Commonwealth*, newspaper of the Pennsylvania Baptist Convention. She described the various ministries of deaconesses by identifying hypothetical activities in one day's work of a visiting deaconess and one day's work of a nurse deaconess. She claimed that "a true deaconess is literally one who serves Christ by serving his people."[100]

---

[98]May Field McKean, "The Baptist Deaconess Society of New York City" (10 December 1903) no publication information or page number; located in the *Scrapbook* of Amity Baptist Church, New York NY, housed in the archives of the American Baptist Historical Society in Rochester NY.

[99]"Workingmen Now Building a Church," *New York Herald* (9 December 1906) n.p.; in the *Scrapbook* of Amity Baptist Church, New York City, housed in the archives of the American Baptist Historical Society in Rochester NY.

[100]Elizabeth Dorsett, "The Baptist Deaconess Society of New York City, the Deaconess on Her Field," *The Baptist Commonwealth* (12 October 1916): 19-20.

On 11 May 1923, Johanna Langhorst died; her life was significant because it had included involvements in Baptist deaconess homes in three cities. Born in Germany fifty years earlier, she had moved to the United States in the early 1890s. She was "regenerated" in early 1896 under the preaching of Walter Rauschenbusch at the Second German Baptist Church of New York; she joined that church the same year. Under the influence of the deaconess home in New York, she decided to become a deaconess. In late 1896, she entered the Deaconess Hospital in Dayton, Ohio, and graduated in 1899. She was ordained to deaconess work in November of that year back in the Second German Baptist Church in New York.

Following years of deaconess service in New York, Langhorst moved to Chicago in early 1914 and took charge of the German Baptist Deaconess Home as superintendent. She was serving in that position when she died in 1923. At her funeral on May 14, five deaconesses and one female missionary served as pallbearers.[101]

The strongest developments regarding deaconess sisterhoods among Baptists in America occurred among the German Baptists. Although professional and volunteer deaconess organizations arose in New York, Chicago, Philadelphia, and Dayton in the late nineteenth century, in the United States the movement did not gain the level of acceptance that it achieved in Europe. As the twentieth century progressed, the movement gradually died out.

Conclusion

Baptist deaconesses in England and the United States experienced decline in the 1800s. Between 1800 and 1960, Baptist churches that included women in the diaconate typically preferred deaconesses, not women deacons. A renewal of deaconesses took place in the early 1900s, and women deacons began to emerge as the 1900s progressed. Most deaconesses were not ordained, but some were, especially in the 1900s. Women deacons tended to be ordained, but some were not, especially in Northern Baptist churches. The late 1800s and early 1900s witnessed the rise of professional deaconess organizations in England and the United States.

This period set the foundation for growing opposition to and support for Baptist women deacons in the United States. Southern Baptists would

---

[101]C. A. Daniel, "A Beautiful Life," no publication publication information or page number; located in the *Scrapbook* of Amity Baptist Church, New York NY, housed in the archives of the American Baptist Historical Society in Rochester NY.

increasingly oppose the act of ordaining women deacons. American Baptists would begin to shift from deaconesses to women deacons, although they would generally oppose ordaining all deacons, men and women. Black Baptists would largely retain the practice of using deaconesses without ordination. Cooperative Baptist Fellowship Baptists in the 1990s and early 2000s would eventually cultivate a strong preference for ordained women deacons. Exceptions would exist among most groups of Baptists. Only a minority of Baptist churches in the United States would include women in the diaconate in any form.

Chapter 4

Women Deacon Resurgence and Opposition, 1960s-1970s

The 1960s–1970s witnessed several new trends relating to women deacons and deaconesses. Southern Baptist churches began to elect and ordain more women deacons, and the pattern of electing women to serve as deacon chairs gained momentum. Cautiously, the Southern Baptist Sunday School Board produced more materials on deaconesses and women deacons in the 1970s than it ever had. American Baptists, many of whose churches already had deaconesses, began to change from deaconesses, typically not on a par with male deacons, to women deacons, who were on a par with men. American Baptists generally did not ordain male or female deacons. Most black Baptists continued to use nonordained deaconesses throughout this period.

Major opposition to ordained women deacons emerged among Southern Baptists in 1973 with the formation of the Baptist Faith and Message Fellowship and the launching that same year of two publications, *The Southern Baptist Journal* and *Baptists United News*. This organization and these publications made it their goal to seek out and destroy alleged liberalism in Southern Baptist life; among others, "liberals" included women ordained as deacons and the churches that ordained them.

In 1998, historian Wayne Flynt claimed that "Not even racial integration drew as much fire during the 1970s as the shifting roles of women. Every incident created a controversy."[1] Battles over women's ordination, conflict resulting from the Equal Rights Amendment and the Women's Liberation Movement, and other factors kept Baptist life stirred up not only in Alabama but in many other states as well. Southern Baptists simply could not agree on the propriety of ordaining women to the diaconate or ministry.

This chapter will describe patterns of transition and progress relating to women deacons and deaconesses, with sections featuring developments within local churches and, more broadly, developments among American

---

[1]Wayne Flynt, *Alabama Baptists: Southern Baptists in the Heart of Dixie* (Tuscaloosa: University of Alabama Press, 1998) 538.

Baptists and Southern Baptists. A description of mounting opposition to ordained women deacons will then follow.

Transition and Progress

Transition and progress characterized developments relating to women deacons and deaconesses in the 1960s–1970s. Articles in the four volumes of the *Encyclopedia of Southern Baptists*, published between 1958 and 1982, illustrate the changes. Volumes 1–2, released in 1958, included articles on deacons and ordination; neither mentioned women. Volume 3, published in 1971, treated the 1960s and did not include articles on deacons or ordination. However, volume 4, published in 1982, treated the 1970s and included several pertinent articles on women deacons, women's ordination, women in ministry, women in church-related vocations, women's movements among Southern Baptists, and women in the New Testament.

On an international basis, the World Council of Churches published *The Ministry of Deacons* in 1965. This book featured discussions of deacons in the New Testament, reflections on the ministry of deacons in the church, and assessments of the diaconate in the Orthodox Church, the Anglican Communion, the Lutheran Church, Reformed Churches, American Presbyterianism, and Baptist churches. George R. Beasley-Murray, a minister of the Baptist Union of Great Britain and principal of Spurgeon's College in London, wrote the essay, "The Diaconate in Baptist Churches." This essay made no references to Baptist women deacons or deaconesses in British Baptist history except to quote from confessions written by John Smyth and Thomas Helwys in the early 1600s that mentioned deacons, men and women.[2] This essay failed to capture the rich history of women in the diaconate of British Baptist life. Women deacons would soon begin to get more respect, especially among Baptists in the United States.

Local-Church Developments. On the local-church level, many churches with deaconesses began to shift to women deacons. In 1960, The First Baptist Church of Washington, D.C., created a board of deaconesses, which by 1961 had thirty-five members. In 1974, the church combined its board of deacons and board of deaconesses into one deacon board.[3] The church began to ordain many women to the diaconate. In September 1984, follow-

---

[2]George R. Beasley-Murray, "The Diaconate in Baptist Churches," in *The Ministry of Deacons*, World Council of Churches Studies no. 2 (Geneva, Switzerland: World Council of Churches, 1965) 72-81.

[3]Deborah Cochran, e-mail to author, 6 May 2004.

ing the June 1984 resolution adopted by the Southern Baptist Convention opposing women's ordination, Washington's First Baptist Church would issue its own resolution defending women's ordination and local-church autonomy. (See a copy of the resolution in chapter 8.)

Many firsts began to take place regarding women in the diaconate. In 1969, Faith Baptist Church in Georgetown, Kentucky, ordained two women deacons, apparently making it the first Southern Baptist church in Kentucky to do so. The entire congregation participated in the laying on of hands.[4] In 1971, the St. Charles Avenue Baptist Church in New Orleans, Louisiana, became the first Southern Baptist church in Louisiana to ordain women deacons.[5] In February 1974, the University Baptist Church in Austin, Texas, became the first Southern Baptist church in Texas to ordain women deacons,[6] followed in June of that same year by the First Baptist Church of Austin.[7] In 1975, *The Deacon* published an article on women deacons in the University Baptist Church in Austin. Gerald E. Mann, the church's pastor and writer of the article, claimed that "our congregation concluded that the Scripture must be interpreted in light of changing cultural conditions as well as the *central principles* taught by Jesus Christ: the principles of human equality, the Golden Rule, and man in the image of God."[8]

Examples of other churches electing women deacons in the 1960s for the first time, all in North Carolina, included Wendell Baptist Church, Wendell (1962); First Baptist Church, Sylva (1963); Mars Hill Baptist Church, Mars Hill (1964); Memorial Baptist Church, Williamston (1964); and Watts Street Baptist Church, Durham (1966). In 1964, Watts Street had ordained Addie Davis as the first woman minister in Southern Baptist life. That event received wide coverage in Baptist news media and helped stimulate new interest in the ordination of women in general.

Following are examples of twenty-three churches in five states in the 1970s electing women deacons for the first time:

---

[4]Bob Terry, "Two Women Ordained by Faith Baptist, Georgetown," *Western Recorder* (6 February 1969): 9.

[5]"St. Charles Avenue Baptist Church: About Us—History." <www.scabc.org/history.htm>, accessed 9 November 2004.

[6]Gerald E. Mann, "How We Got Women Deacons," *The Deacon* 5/3 (April-June 1975): 47.

[7]Jane Archer Feinstein, letter to author, 3 September 2004.

[8]Mann, "How We Got Women Deacons," 47.

Virginia
  Vienna Baptist Church, Vienna (1971)
  First Baptist Church, Petersburg (1973)
  University Baptist Church, Charlottesville (1974)
  Hampton Baptist Church, Hampton (1975)
  Cedar Run Baptist Church, Culpeper (1976)
  Ginter Park Baptist Church, Richmond (1978)
  Westhunt Baptist Church, Richmond (1978)
  First Baptist Church, Bristol (1979)
  West Main Baptist Church, Danville (1979).
North Carolina
  First Baptist Church, Sanford (1973)
  First Baptist Church, Statesville (1973)
  First Baptist Church, Elkin (1974)
  First Baptist Church, North Wilkesboro (1976)
  Rowland Baptist Church, Rowland (1978)
  First Baptist Church, Lenoir (1979)
  Park View Baptist Church, Durham (1979).
South Carolina
  First Baptist Church, Barnwell (1973)
  Boulevard Baptist Church, Anderson, (1975)
  First Baptist Church, Pendleton (1975).
Tennessee
  First Baptist Church, Oak Ridge (1971)
  Glendale Baptist Church, Nashville (1974).
Texas
  Second Baptist Church, Lubbock (1976)
  Royal Lane Baptist Church, Dallas (1977).

Another new development began to take place in several states, especially North Carolina and Virginia. Deacon bodies with female members began to elect women to serve as chairs of those bodies. In 1977, the North Carolina Baptist newspaper, the *Biblical Recorder*, published an article by Marian Grant (wife of the editor Marse Grant) reporting the results of her attempts to identify North Carolina Baptist churches in which women had been chosen to serve as deacon chairs. Grant listed eleven such churches and the years those churches first chose women deacon chairs:

  First Baptist Church, Spring Hope (1962)
  Pullen Memorial Baptist Church, Raleigh (1972)
  Myers Park Baptist Church, Charlotte (1974)
  Grace Baptist Church, Statesville (1975)

Mars Hill Baptist Church, Mars Hill (1976)
Warsaw Baptist Church, Warsaw (1976)
Watts Street Baptist Church, Durham (1976)
First Baptist Church, Rockingham (1977)
Spilman Memorial Baptist Church, Kinston (1977)
Wake Forest Baptist Church, Winston-Salem (1977).[9]

During the same general period, women deacon chairs also appeared, for example, in such churches as the Louisburg Baptist Church, Louisburg, North Carolina (1968); Vienna Baptist Church, Vienna, Virginia (1973); Faith Baptist Church, Georgetown, Kentucky (1978); Fellowship Baptist Church, Americus, Georgia (1978); First Baptist Church, Gaithersville, Maryland (1979); and the Main Street Baptist Church, Emporia, Virginia (1979). Undoubtedly, there were others.

Church Administration magazine reported in August 1971 that the Manhattan Baptist Church in New York City had ordained two deaconesses in 1970. The article included a photograph of the two women, Ann Hurt and Carolyn Simons, having hands laid upon them "with the congregation participating."[10] Between 1970 and 1995, in the Metropolitan (New York) Baptist Association, churches would ordain seventeen women deacons, of whom seven would serve as deacon chairs.[11]

American Baptist Developments. Everett C. Goodwin, described by noted American Baptist historian Edwin Gaustad as "a keen student of ABC [American Baptist Churches] practices,"[12] has provided some insightful comments regarding the transition from deaconesses to women deacons in American Baptist churches. Goodwin, pastor of the Scarsdale Community Baptist Church in Scarsdale, New York, claimed in 2004 that

> Many American Baptist churches have had merged or single boards of deacons for several decades. In the "old days" the deacons handled communion, worship leadership, and other "public" roles, while the deaconesses were more focused on social and hospitality issues but probably would assist the deacons in hospital visitation or care-giving. In more

---

[9]Marian Grant, "A Number of Women Chairing Boards of Deacons," *Biblical Recorder* (19 November 1977): 7.

[10]Melvin Hawthorne, "Deaconesses Ordained in Manhattan Baptist Church," *Church Administration* 13/11 (August 1971): 39.

[11]DeLane M. Ryals, "Southern Baptist Women Ministering in Metro New York, 1970–1995," *Baptist History and Heritage* 39/2 (Spring 2004): 91.

[12]Edwin Gaustad, e-mail to author, 25 August 2004.

conservative regions of American Baptist churches, that still may be the case, at least in some situations.

However, many (I am guessing the majority) American Baptist churches merged separate boards or reconstituted into a single Diaconate by the late 1960s or 1970s. In a few cases, they had always had a single board.[13]

In 1960, Donald F. Thomas prepared a significant manuscript titled "The Deacons and Deaconesses: A Study in Backgrounds and Present Practice among American Baptist Churches." His study included sending 500 questionnaires to American Baptist churches, of which 281 were completed and returned. Of the reporting churches, 127 included deaconesses as a part of the boards of deacons, and 122 listed separate boards of deaconesses. The survey revealed that 147 churches installed deaconesses using a recognition service, eighty-one using an installation service, and the rest by other means. By comparison, twenty-eight churches affirmed deacons by ordaining them, 109 by installing them, 152 by recognizing them, and the rest by other means.[14] One possible reason for the high level of acceptability of deaconesses in American Baptist life may relate to the fact that their churches generally tended not to ordain deacons or deaconesses, thus eliminating the barrier of ordination. In addition, American Baptists typically held to more progressive views of women in church leadership than did Southern Baptists.

Churches responding to Thomas's survey identified many different functions for boards of deaconesses and for boards of deacons (in some churches, deaconesses were part of the board of deacons).[15] Duties receiving the top ten votes (in descending order) for boards of deaconesses included assisting at baptism, preparing Communion elements, calling on the sick and shut-ins, calling on nonmembers for the church, participating on pulpit committees, interviewing candidates for church membership, coordinating evangelistic programs, administering the deacon's fund, serving on the watch-care committee, and taking a lead in church discipline. Other duties included leading prayer services, making certain the pulpit

---

[13]Everett C. Goodwin, e-mail to author, 8 May 2004.

[14]Donald F. Thomas, "The Deacons and Deaconesses: A Study in Backgrounds and Present Practice among American Baptist Churches" (prepared for the Division of Evangelism, American Baptist Home Mission Society, September 1960) 33, 37, 38.

[15]Ibid., 39-40.

ministry was provided, instructing new members, leading church services, taking Communion to the shut-ins, serving as the pulpit committee, giving leadership in social action, assisting at the Communion service, serving on a board of missions, and serving on a board of education.

Subcommittees of boards of deaconesses listed on the survey results included (from the highest number of churches to the lowest) Communion, Baptism, Visitation, Membership, Evangelism, Floral and Welfare, Nursery, Shut-ins, Worship, Music, and Fellowship.[16]

A 1963 Baptist church manual simply observed that "There should be some women members on the Board of Deacons, although that point has been debated among Baptists." While acknowledging that Baptists' long reluctance to let women speak in church services had kept them from serving as deacons, the writers concluded: "There seems to be no good reason why women should not be deacons, and there are good reasons why they should be. Besides taking part in the regular duties of the office, there are some services which they can render better than men."[17]

Judson Press issued an influential book in 1964, *The Work of the Deacon and Deaconess*, by Harold Nichols. This writing treated male and female deacons alike in discussing qualifications, duties, and relationships. It observed that "There are two main streams of thought regarding the status of the deaconess today. One of these holds that the deaconess is a deacon. As such, she possesses all the requisites, qualifications, and training, and carries on all of the functions of a deacon. The second view is that the status of a deaconess is different from that of a deacon. Under this view, her duties vary from those of the deacon, and, like the duties of those in the early centuries, are concentrated upon the needs of the women in the church."[18] The book strongly urged churches to consider electing women to the diaconate: "Churches that do not have a board of deaconesses or a board of deacons made up of both men and women should give thoughtful, prayer consideration to a change of policy so that they may take advantage of the contributions women can make in this important area of the church's work and witness."[19] Nichols summarized his chapter on

---

[16]Ibid., 41.

[17]Norman H. Maring and Winthrop S. Hudson, *A Baptist Manual of Polity and Practice* (Valley Forge PA: Judson Press, 1963) 114.

[18]Harold Nichols, *The Work of the Deacon and Deaconess* (Valley Forge PA: Judson Press, 1964) 88.

[19]Ibid., 89.

deaconesses by claiming that "the deacon and the deaconess should be considered as equals." Therefore, "Every local church should fully describe the place of the deaconess in the organization of the church."[20]

Because of the popularity and importance of Nichols's book, Judson Press released a revised edition in 1984. Whereas the chapter, "The Deaconess," appeared as chapter 11 near the end of the 1964 edition, the revised edition made two major changes. First, it moved "The Deaconess" chapter to the front of the book as chapter 2. Second, it indicated that throughout the book the words "deacons" applied to both men and women in the diaconate.[21]

In 1965, the American Baptist Convention (ABC), meeting in San Francisco, adopted a resolution on the status of women. Asserting that "We believe there should be no differential treatment of men and women in the church, family, or society and that there should be equal opportunity for full participation in the work of our God," the resolution further urged "full participation of women in the life and work of the church (including the pastorate) in all countries."[22] This was a powerful statement in defense of women's rights to serve as deacons and churches' duties to help make it happen. In sharp contrast, the Southern Baptist Convention (SBC) has apparently never, since 1845, adopted a resolution advocating full equality for women in all leadership positions of the church.

In 1969, Judson Press published Donald F. Thomas's book, *The Deacon in a Changing Church*. Appendix 1, "The Deaconess," concluded by stating: "An increasing number of churches have the deacons and deaconesses meet in joint sessions with some regularity. This proves enriching to the life of the church. A small, but growing trend is to assign to the deaconesses the same functions as the deacons in all of their duties."[23]

In 1977, Judson Press released the revised edition of a manual for church officers. A brief section on deaconesses noted that "More and more churches have come to the point of making up the board of deacons of both men and women with no distinction of function or privilege." However, in churches which still have two boards—deacons and deaconesses—the deaconesses should typically engage in "parish visitation, the preparation

---

[20]Ibid., 94.

[21]Ibid., rev. ed., 14.

[22]*Year Book*, American Baptist Convention, 1965–1966, 74.

[23]Donald F. Thomas, *The Deacon in a Changing Church* (Valley Forge PA: Judson Press, 1969) 114.

of the Communion materials, washing the Communion cups, assisting candidates at the time of baptism, helping individuals in need." A separate board of deaconesses should meet separately; occasionally, there may be joint meetings with the board of deacons.[24]

Southern Baptist Developments. In 1968, the Southern Baptist Sunday School Board's Convention Press published *The Ministry of the Deacon*, by Howard B. Foshee, secretary of the board's Church Administration Department. Widely used in Southern Baptist churches, with 350,000 copies distributed by 1990,[25] this book included only a few paragraphs on deaconesses and concluded by opposing deaconesses on a programmatic basis. Although acknowledging that "women are equipped by temperament to serve in a pastoral ministry," Foshee believed that "there seems small need for electing deaconesses today" because "of the unparalleled service opportunities in the mission action program of Woman's Missionary Union." To add deaconesses into local-church life "could only add overlapping organizational structure that might actually lead to a decrease in service."[26]

Foshee's 1975 Broadman Press book, *Now That You're a Deacon*, asked, "Should a church elect deaconesses?" Foshee noted that "a significant number" of churches in the ABC had elected deaconesses and that "only a very few" churches in the SBC had elected "women to serve as deacons." Then he presented the same programmatic opposition to deaconesses that had appeared in his 1968 book.[27]

James W. Cox, associate professor of preaching at the Southern Baptist Theological Seminary, adapted for use in America in 1969 the 1960 British edition of the *Minister's Worship Manual: Orders and Prayers for Worship*, compiled by Ernest A. Payne and Stephen F. Winward, both British Baptists. This 1969 manual contained a four-page worship service titled "The Commissioning of a Deaconess." This was not a formal ordination with the laying on of hands. Instead, the presiding minister declared, "In the name of the Lord Jesus Christ, the Head of the Church, we declare you to

---

[24]Glenn H. Asquith, *Church Officers at Work*, rev. ed. (Valley Forge PA: Judson Press, 1977) 56-57; originally published in 1951.

[25]Robert Sheffield, *The Ministry of Baptist Deacons* (Nashville: Convention Press, 1990) 4.

[26]Howard B. Foshee, *The Ministry of the Deacon* (Nashville: Convention Press, 1968) 8.

[27]Howard B. Foshee, *Now That You're a Deacon* (Nashville: Broadman Press, 1975) 128.

be set apart and commissioned for the work of a deaconess, and to be duly called and inducted to that service in this church."[28]

In the 1970s, many important writings relating to deaconesses, women deacons, women's ordination, and women's issues in general were published and widely distributed among Southern Baptists. Writings described, advocated, and attacked women's roles in church and denominational life, including the diaconate.

Deaconesses had existed among Southern Baptists for decades, but the deaconess concept began to expand in Southern Baptist life in the early 1970s. Three factors likely contributed to this development. First, the Church Administration Department of the Southern Baptist Sunday School Board introduced *The Deacon* magazine in 1970. During the 1970s that publication included many articles on deaconesses and women deacons. Second, in 1972, the Church Administration Department introduced the Deacon Family Ministry Plan, which represented a serious effort to move deacon functions more into spiritual ministries, with less focus on administrative concerns and business matters. Third, in 1970 and 1971, Broadman Press published two volumes in *The Broadman Bible Commentary* favoring use of the word "deaconess" in Romans 16:1 and "slightly" favoring it in 1 Timothy 3:11.[29]

The discussion of women deacons gained major impetus when E. Glenn Hinson, associate professor of Church History at the Southern Baptist Theological Seminary, courageously jumpstarted it by publishing his article, "On the Ordination of Women as Deacons." The article first appeared in the 1 April 1972 issue of *Western Recorder*, state newspaper for Kentucky Baptists.[30] The same article later appeared in other publications, for example, the *Baptist Standard*, state newspaper for Texas Baptists; the *Capital Baptist*, newspaper of the District of Columbia Baptist Convention; and *The Deacon*, a publication of the SBC Sunday School Board. The *Capital Baptist* retained the original title; the *Baptist Standard* changed the article to "Early Christian Practices Give Support to Ordina-

---

[28]Ernest A. Payne, Stephen F. Winward, and James W. Cox, *Minister's Worship Manual: Orders and Prayers for Worship*, American edition (New York: World Publishing Co., 1969) 236.

[29]Dale Moody, "Romans," *The Broadman Bible Commentary*, vol. 10 (Nashville: Broadman Press, 1970) 279; and E. Glenn Hinson, "1-2 Timothy and Titus," *The Broadman Bible Commentary*, vol. 11 (Nashville: Broadman Press, 1971) 320.

[30]E. Glenn Hinson, "On the Ordination of Women As Deacons," *Western Recorder* (1 April 1972): 3, 15.

tion of Baptist Deaconesses"; and *The Deacon* cautiously deleted the word "Ordination" from the original title and assigned it a new title, "On the Election of Women as Deacons."[31]

Hinson used the bulk of his article to review the diaconate of women in the New Testament and early Christian centuries and to address the status of women in contemporary churches, but his introduction summarized his basic position. He noted that women's liberation had caused "a sizable number of Southern Baptist churches" to ponder "whether to ordain women as deacons or deaconesses." Then in two pivotal paragraphs, he made his case:

> The factors which deter many churches from giving *de jure* acknowledgement of the *de facto* role of women in our church life are doubtless weighted more heavily on the side of tradition or prejudice than on that of the Bible and theology. Western society has been paternalistic from the beginnings of the Christian era on. Accordingly, women have not received official recognition in the way men have, despite the fact that they have performed a signal service in the churches. Scriptures, taken out of context and applied as hard and fast rules, and history have been used as sticks to prop up typical prejudices in this regard.
>
> Anyone who has investigated the evidence will discern quickly that he cannot construct an ironclad case either for or against the ordination of women as deacons from a study of early Christian customs. However, by taking into account not only the data regarding the development of the office of women deacons or deaconesses but also the early Christian principle of equality within the church, one can give a positive approval of the practice.[32]

Hinson also indicated that 1 Timothy 5:10, which focuses on widows, may "supply a clue to the origin of the office of women deacons." This verse "strongly suggests that widows performed diaconal functions. . . . But it is not likely that all widows did so."[33]

Published reactions to the Hinson article were swift and often negative. For example, the (Texas) *Baptist Standard* published four letters to the

---

[31]"Early Christian Practices Give Support to Ordination of Baptist Deaconesses," *Baptist Standard* (29 March 1972): 8-9; "On the Ordination of Women as Deacons," *Capital Baptist* (8 February 1973): 3, 6; "On the Election of Women as Deacons," *The Deacon* 3/3 (April-June, 1973): 5-7.

[32]Hinson, "On the Ordination of Women as Deacons," 3.

[33]Ibid.

editor relating to the article—all negative—in its 26 April 1972 issue, and even titled the letters-to-the-editor page "Reject Idea of Deaconesses." Richard O. Pierce of Corpus Christi claimed that Hinson's article "is heavy with conjecture, and the tone of the article indicates he is considerably tilted towards the 'liberal' end of the religious spectrum." S. H. Walton of Longview wrote that "Hinson needs to study much more. He cannot convince true Bible-believers, for he goes 'outside' of God's word for so-called 'evidence.' " Sheila Rodgers of Texarkana stated that "in reading the scripture E. Glenn Hinson gave, I can find no authorization to ordain women as deacons." J. N. Hoover of Odessa admonished "how easy it is to let our intellectual logic lead us to conclusions which are not in accordance with God's sure word!"[34]

The Deacon reprinted excerpts from letters to editors of Baptist state newspapers, all reacting to the Hinson article. Without identifying the letter writers or the publications in which the letters appeared, these reprints typically hit women's ordination hard. The editor of *The Deacon* even titled the article containing the reprints "Many Southern Baptists Opposed to 'Women Deacons.' " Among the comments were these:

> "It is completely disgusting to me how our denomination has gone so far from the Bible."

> "Women as deacons in the church is contrary to Bible teaching, as found in 1 Timothy 3:11. . . . I can only view your [Glenn Hinson's] agreement with this as a continuance of the liberal movement and point out that Baptist churches have ceased to use the Bible as a guide."

> "I would like to know how any church that believes the Bible is true can have women deacons. When my church gets women deacons, I am ready for another church."[35]

Several complete issues of Southern Baptist periodicals focused on topics relating to women's issues, including women in the diaconate. *Home Missions* magazine, published by the Home Mission Board under the editorship of Walker L. Knight, distinguished itself as a publication willing to deal in honest fashion with difficult and sensitive issues in Baptist life. Topics about women dominated the May 1972 issue on "Woman's Changing Role in the Church." Knight's lead article noted that Southern

---

[34]"Reject Idea of Deaconesses," *Baptist Standard* (26 April 1972): 2.

[35]"Many Southern Baptists Opposed to 'Women Deacons,' " *The Deacon* 3/3 (April-June 1973): 8, 9.

Baptists had recently ordained a second and third woman to the ministry, that other churches were busy studying the Bible and considering ordaining women, and that "many churches have women serving as deacons, and this practice appears to be on a sharp increase in many areas, especially the Eastern states."[36]

Knight pointed out why Southern Baptists had always had trouble granting equality to women and allowing them leadership roles, which, by implication, included women deacons, in the church and denomination:

> Baptists of the South share the Southerners' idealized picture of woman, wanting her to be soft, feminine, and beautiful, a "lady" for whom intellectual accomplishments are secondary to the graces of entertaining, motherhood, and serving her family. If she is inclined to be intellectual, she has to make it appear to be almost an accident. Her strength must come in the form of weakness, and she must ever be careful of the male ego, lest she wound it beyond repair and bring harm to herself in the process.[37]

Knight concluded his article by suggesting that the SBC elect a female president in 1972 "not in tokenism, but in recognition of her service and her role of equality in the Southern Baptist Convention."[38] (Through 2004, the convention has never elected a female president. The likelihood that it will elect one in the near future is zero. Southern Baptist fundamentalism, which has controlled the convention presidency since 1979, tends to say no to placing women, particularly ordained women, in top positions of leadership in the church and denomination.)

The Deacon devoted its April-June 1973 issue to "The Rise of Women Deacons." Although a breakthrough for the publication, caution characterized the approach. The editor wrote that

> *The Deacon* is not crusading for the election of women to this office; we are simply recognizing that the question is being raised. We are sharing information on all sides of the debate in an attempt to help churches answer for themselves whether women should be elected to this office.[39]

---

[36]Walker L. Knight, "Equality and Stained Glass: A Look at Woman's Changing Role in the Church," *Home Missions* 43/5 (May 1972): 2.

[37]Ibid., 5.

[38]Ibid., 6.

[39]The editor, "The Issue of 'Women Deacons,'" *The Deacon* 3/3 (April-June 1973): 4.

At no point did the editor use the word "ordination" in talking about women deacons; he used the word election.

Three successive articles then presented *pro, con,* and *perhaps* views on whether churches should elect women as deacons.[40] The *pro* article consisted of Glenn Hinson's article that had appeared in several Baptist state papers in 1972 and 1973. The *con* article reprinted several letters to editors of state papers which had reacted negatively to Hinson's article. The *perhaps* article took a neutral stance toward women deacons.

A fourth article reflected the results of a telephone survey, conducted by *The Deacon*'s staff, of churches known to have women deacons. Some of the churches reported having had women in the deaconship forty or fifty years, and, in one case, even longer. The editor issued a word of caution:

> Don't assume because of this report that electing women to the deaconship is a widespread practice among Southern Baptists. When this survey was taken in September of 1972, we had definite proof that women had been elected as deacons in about twenty Southern Baptist churches. . . . Even if you assume that two or three hundred churches have women deacons, that's still an infinitesimal percentage of the thirty-four thousand churches in the Southern Baptist Convention.[41]

The report gave detailed information on seven churches: Crescent Hill Baptist Church in Louisville, Kentucky; Rivermont Avenue Baptist Church in Lynchburg, Virginia; Tacoma Park Baptist Church in Washington, D.C.; Oakhurst Baptist Church in Decatur, Georgia; Third Baptist Church in St. Louis, Missouri; Myers Park Baptist Church in Charlotte, North Carolina; and Baptist Temple Church in Alexandria, Virginia.

Two of these churches had separate organizations of "deaconesses": Rivermont Avenue had had deaconesses since 1928, did not ordain them, and did not allow them to share in serving the Lord's Supper. Third Baptist had chosen its first deaconesses more than forty years earlier. They did not collect the offering or participate in the Lord's Supper. This church did not ordain deaconesses, but neither did it ordain deacons.

---

[40]Hinson, "On the Election of Women as Deacons," *The Deacon* 3/3 (April-June 1973): 5-7; "Many Southern Baptists Opposed to 'Women Deacons,' " *The Deacon* 3/3 (April-June 1973): 8-9; Carlton L. Myers, "Deaconesses, Women Deacons, or Deacons' Wives," *The Deacon* 3/3 (April-June 1973): 10-12.

[41]"Women in the Deaconship: A Survey of Selected Southern Baptist Churches," *The Deacon* 3/3 (April-June 1973): 13-14.

Four of these churches elected their first "women deacons" in the early 1970s: Myers Park (1970), Baptist Temple Church (1970), Crescent Hill (1972), and Oakhurst (1972). All four churches ordained women deacons and gave them the same privileges and duties as male deacons. They were all part of one deacon body in each church.

Takoma Park had had women in the diaconate for more than fifty years. For the first time, however, in 1972, women deacons were allowed to serve the Lord's Supper. The women were ordained. The church's bylaws required an equal number of men and women on the deacon body.

The report listed several other churches known to have women serving in the diaconate as of September 1972: "First Baptist Church, South Boston, Virginia; Faith Baptist Church, Georgetown, Kentucky; Manhattan Baptist Church, New York City; First Baptist Church, Lynchburg, Virginia; Norway Baptist Church, Norway, South Carolina; University Baptist Church, Watts Street Baptist Church, Cedar Fork Baptist Church, and Plainview Baptist Church, all in Durham, North Carolina; Menokin Baptist Church, Warsaw, Virginia; and First Baptist Church, Oak Ridge, Tennessee."[42]

The special issue of *The Deacon* concluded by printing an article on Betty Galloway, who had been ordained as a deacon in September 1971 in the First Baptist Church of Oak Ridge, Tennessee. The policy adopted by the church allowing for women deacons had resulted in some criticism from sources outside the congregation.[43]

In 1975, following a typically cautious pattern, the editor of *The Deacon* introduced an article on women deacons in the University Baptist Church in Austin, Texas, by stating that "printing the article should not be taken as an endorsement of women deacons by your editor or by the Sunday School Board."[44] Then in 1979, a new editor of *The Deacon* wrote an editorial under the title "What about Women Deacons?" While acknowledging that the publication had published several articles on women deacons in the 1970s, he commented on the fact that "Occasionally we are asked why we consistently depict deacons as men and thus are now acknowledging the existence of women deacons in some of our Southern

---

[42]Ibid.

[43]Yvonne H. Callahan, "Mrs. Betty Galloway: Portrait of a Woman in the Deaconship," *The Deacon* 3/3 (April-June 1973): 16-18.

[44]Mann, "How We Got Women Deacons," 46.

Baptist churches." Then he noted that as readers "the men deacons are a predominant audience. Thus a male orientation is bound to emerge."[45]

In addition to articles in the 1970s in *Home Missions* and *The Deacon*, at least two other Baptist journals dedicated entire issues to matters relating to women. *Review and Expositor*, a publication of the faculty of Southern Baptist Theological Seminary, themed its Winter 1975 issue "Women and the Church."[46] Although the issue did not focus directly on women deacons, it certainly helped raise the consciousness of readers to issues relating to women in all phases of Baptist life. The editor of the issue related women's developments in the mid-1970s to the work of the Holy Spirit: "The awakening of conscience with respect to the personhood of woman, with increasingly active concern for her identity, dignity, freedom, and rights, may well be an indication of the moving of the Spirit in the Church and in the world today."[47]

Baptist History and Heritage, published by the Southern Baptist Historical Commission, centered its January 1977 issue around "The Role of Women in Baptist History." Along with articles on women in missions, women's right to vote, the role of women in Baptist history, and the status of women in the SBC, this issue included Charles Deweese's article, "Deaconesses in Baptist History: A Preliminary Study." Deweese's article presented basic information on the history of Baptist deaconesses and Baptist attitudes toward deaconesses.[48]

In 1977, of some consequence, the spring issue of the *Southwestern Journal of Theology*, published by Southwestern Baptist Theological Seminary, focused on the theme, "Baptists Deal with Controversial Issues." Along with articles on such controversial issues as liberation theology, the educational crisis, Christian faith and human sexuality, the pastor and the tongues movement, and the meaning of the folk song movement, the issue included an article titled "The Role of Women in the Church," by Ralph H. Langley, pastor of Willow Meadows Baptist Church in Houston, Texas. His first sentence read, "Women are welcome in the church—but are not welcome yet into the leadership levels of the church." Then to prove his

---

[45]Henry Webb, "What about Women Deacons?" *The Deacon* 9/3 (April-June 1979): 3.

[46]"Women and the Church," *Review and Expositor* 72/1 (Winter 1975) 3-69.

[47]Ibid., 3.

[48]"The Role of Women in Baptist History," *Baptist History and Heritage* 12/1 (January 1977): 1-57.

point, he put forward eight questions, the first of which asked, "How many churches do you know that have women deacons?"[49]

Langley used most of his article to detail events surrounding his church's decision to ordain Susan Sprague to the ministry. He ended his article by printing several letters sent to him by individuals in five states and the District of Columbia, all reacting to Sprague's ordination. Three affirmed the ordination; three opposed it.[50] At times, other Southern Baptist churches ordaining women deacons found themselves caught up in the same kind of controversy described by Langley.

Other Southern Baptist publications and even Baptist state conventions also dealt with women's issues in the 1970s. In 1974, *The Baptist Program*, published by the SBC Executive Committee, published an article by Nell Magee, a consultant in the Sunday School Board's National Student Ministries. Describing women and their rights as "one of the most provocative topics today," Magee aggressively pushed for increased roles for women in church leadership by focusing on biblical teachings. For her, Genesis 1 and 2 showed that "the creation of persons was an act of equality," and Jesus viewed it as a part of his Messiahship "to bring woman to full personhood, to give her equality of being." Magee acknowledged verses in Paul's writings that seem to suggest that women should be silent in church and subordinate to men (1 Cor. 11:3-9; 1 Cor. 14:33-35; Eph. 5:22-24; Col. 3:18-19; and 1 Tim. 2:11-14). However, she insisted that "the real basis for Paul's concept of personhood is found in Galatians 3:28." Magee concluded by offering some suggestions for Southern Baptists based on the precepts of scripture. One simply stated that "we need to encourage churches to consider ordaining women as deacons."[51]

Above the title for Magee's article, the editor of *The Baptist Program* inserted two statements: "A super sensitive topic Southern Baptists are discussing. Reader response invited." Reaction was apparently heavy. The January 1975 issue included two pages of pro and con responses from Southern Baptists around the country.[52]

---

[49]Ralph H. Langley, "The Role of Women in the Church," *Southwestern Journal of Theology* 19/2 (Spring 1977): 60.

[50]Ibid., 71-72.

[51]Nell Magee, "One Woman Speaks," *The Baptist Program* (August 1974): 8, 22.

[52]"More on the 'SBC and Women,' " *The Baptist Program* (January 1975): 22-23.

The Baptist State Convention of North Carolina adopted a resolution on women in 1975 but only after vigorous and extended discussion. Because of its significance for the mid-1970s, and because it contributed to the fact that, by 2005, North Carolina would have more women deacons than any state in the South, with the possible exception of Virginia, the resolution is reproduced here in full.

> *Whereas,* "There is neither Jew nor Greek, there is neither bond nor free, there is neither male nor female; for ye are all one in Jesus Christ." (Gal. 3:28);
> *Whereas,* it is the right and responsibility of all Christians to witness in God's name through proclaiming the Word, offering physical and spiritual comfort to those in need, and engaging in constructive participation in a Christian church;
> *Whereas,* the New Testament cites several examples . . . of women who responded to God's call with devoted service;
> *Whereas,* women today are still dedicating their lives to the Lord;
> THEREFORE BE IT RESOLVED that the Baptist State Convention in annual session, November 10-12, 1975, recognizing the freedom of conscience of the believer, affirms the right of all Christian women to follow God's will in their lives, including those whose call leads to ordination and professional ministry.[53]

In 1976, woman deacons received attention in Baptist Press releases (the news service operated by the SBC Executive Committee since 1946), thus illustrating how important and sensitive the issue was. In January, Baptist Press reported that Temple Baptist Church in Champaign, Illinois, had ordained two women deacons (Watha Anderson and Cheryl Rascoe), believed to be the first Southern Baptist church in Illinois to do that.[54] In October 1976, the Resolutions Committee of the Illinois Baptist State Association chose not to recommend to the state association a proposed resolution opposing "women's ordination as deacons and preachers."[55] In February 1976, Baptist Press reported that the deacon body of the Mars Hill Baptist Church in Mars Hill, North Carolina, had elected Evelyn Underwood

---

[53]*Annual,* Baptist State Convention of North Carolina, 1975, 73.

[54]"Illinois Church Ordains Two Women Deacons," Baptist Press, 23 January 1976.

[55]*Book of Reports,* Illinois Baptist State Association, 26-28 October 1976, C-7.

as deacon chair.[56] A few churches had elected women chairs earlier; many would do it later.

Also in 1976, the Baptist General Association of Virginia adopted the report of its Christian Life Committee on "Women in the Church." The report began by claiming that "the awakening of conscience with respect to the personhood of women, including their identity, dignity, freedom, and rights, may well be a work of the Holy Spirit in our time. The challenge to Southern Baptist churches, where women comprise an estimated fifty percent of church membership, is acute now that women seek official recognition as deacons or deaconesses and as ordained ministers."[57]

The report noted that a survey done of churches in the Baptist General Association revealed 520 deaconesses and female deacons in fifty-seven churches and that in some instances, the role of deaconess was subordinate to that of male deacons. The Christian Life Committee concluded its report by commending, among others, "those churches which have elected women to serve as deaconesses or deacons, giving them the same responsibilities as men in similar positions."[58]

The Theological Educator, published by New Orleans Baptist Theological Seminary, included in a 1977 issue an appraisal of the ordination of Baptist women. J. Terry Young, associate professor of theology at the seminary, acknowledged in his opening sentence that "one of the hottest topics to hit the discussion circuit among Baptists in a long time is the subject of the ordination of women." Young claimed that the discussion of ordination centered around two topics: the meaning of ordination (and he stated that Baptists had not developed a theology of ordination) and the role and status of Baptist women that the Women's Liberation Movement had brought to the forefront of attention (and he asserted that Baptists had done a poor job of articulating the meaning of the Christian doctrine of creation of man in God's image "as male and female without distinction in God's sight").[59]

Young appealed to the New Testament, citing Jesus' own positive attitudes toward women, quoting Galatians 3:28, and affirming that "the New Testament itself set in motion the forces that finally overthrew human

---

[56]"Mars Hill Baptist Church Elects Woman Deacon Chairman," Baptist Press, 2 February 1976.

[57]*Annual*, Baptist General Association of Virginia, 1976, 139.

[58]Ibid.

[59]J. Terry Young, "Baptists and the Ordination of Women," *The Theological Educator* 7/2 (Spring 1977): 7-8.

slavery and are now giving woman her rightful place in society unhindered by male chauvinism." After indicating that most people who oppose women's ordination base their opposition on 1 Timothy 3:12—which calls for deacons to be "the husband/s of one wife" (KJV, RSV), Young put forward his view that "this was probably Paul's prohibition of ordination for the polygamous" and that "even a superficial reading suggests that it is hardly a definitive prohibition of the ordination of women."[60] (Compare now the NRSV's politically correct paraphrase "married only once.")

The late 1970s witnessed some major Southern Baptist developments relating to women's issues, all with implications for women deacons. In 1978, the Southern Baptist Sunday School Board hosted the Consultation on Women in Church-Related Vocations. The consultation was sponsored by three SBC boards, four commissions, and two seminaries; by the Baptist Joint Committee; and by Woman's Missionary Union. Although this meeting did not zero in on women deacons, its general discussions of women's issues affected women at all levels. Typical presentations included "Women in Biblical Perspective" by Evelyn and Frank Stagg; "Analysis of Southern Baptist Literature and Women" by Kay Shurden; and "Personal Experiences in Church-Related Vocations" by Lynda Weaver-Williams, Rachel Richardson Smith, Helen E. Falls, and Sue Fitzgerald. Among other notable consultation leaders were Carolyn Weatherford, Jimmy Allen, Roy Honeycutt, Randall Lolley, and Baker James Cauthen.[61] This consultation had the dual effect of promoting healthy discussions of women's issues and of serving as a lightning rod to opponents of women's ordination and women pastors. Catherine B. Allen, of national Woman's Missionary Union, chaired the steering committee for the consultation.

Called and Committed, a publication of Southern Baptist Women in Ministry, published two pertinent articles in 1979 relating to women deacons and deaconesses. One article talked about the strategy for electing women deacons. Although claiming that many Southern Baptist churches had ordained women deacons, it pointed out that "efforts to elect women to the board of deacons have failed in some churches. It seems failure comes most often in churches which vote on the issue of women deacons rather than on specific women." The article used as a positive example the

---

[60]Ibid., 8-9.

[61]"Consultation on Women in Church-Related Vocations, 1978," located in Women in Baptist Life Collection, AR 160, box 1, folder 1-10, Southern Baptist Historical Library and Archives, Nashville.

First Baptist Church of Bristol, Virginia, which had ordained its first woman deacon in early 1979. Several years earlier, that church had deleted sexist language from its constitution without taking a vote on the issue of women deacons per se.[62]

In its May 1979 issue, *Called and Committed* printed some results of a survey of selected Southern Baptist churches conducted in 1978 by Clay L. Price of the Missions Surveys and Special Studies Department of the SBC Home Mission Board. When asked if they approved of women ministers, seventeen percent said yes and eighty percent said no. Thirty-four percent favored women deaconesses; sixty-three percent did not.[63]

The year 1979 was the best year in the Sunday School Board's history in terms of releasing important information about women deacons. Ironically, that was the same year in which the SBC elected its first fundamentalist president, a pattern which to date has continued without interruption. That development, coupled with the SBC's 1984 adoption of a resolution opposing women's ordination (described in chapter 5), would result in a decline in discussions of women deacons in Sunday School Board publications.

In 1979, the Sunday School Board released three important items relating to women deacons. First, *Search* published an eighteen-page article by Charles H. Chandler titled "What about Women Deacons?" Second, Broadman Press released Leon McBeth's book, *Women in Baptist Life*, which included a fourteen-page chapter titled "Women Deacons." Third, Broadman Press also released Charles Deweese's book, *The Emerging Role of Deacons*, a history of Baptist deacons, which is still in print in 2005. This book did not include a separate chapter on women deacons and deaconesses; instead, it integrated a discussion of them throughout the chapters.

The *Search* article examined biblical, historical, and practical issues. While claiming that "an ironclad case cannot be constructed either for or against the ordination of women as deacons based on a study of the New Testament," the article did assert that by affirming "the early Christian principle of equality within the church, however, one can give a positive

---

[62]"FBC Ordains Woman Deacon . . . Not a New Story," *Called and Committed* 2/1 (February 1979): 4.

[63]"Ordination of Women, a Survey," *Called and Committed* 2/2 (May 1979): 2. See also Clay L. Price, "A Survey of Southern Baptist Attitudes toward Women in Church and Society" (Master's thesis, West Georgia College, 1978).

approval to the practice."[64] Chandler listed advantages and disadvantages of including women as deacons. Possible advantages included giving "worth and personhood to women, recognizing women as equally created in the image of God"; making creative use of women's gifts and time for ministry; latching onto receptive attitudes in American culture to women's roles in leadership; the healthy experiences of churches with women deacons; increasing the number of persons available for deacon ministry; and giving women the opportunity for spiritual growth through service. Possible disadvantages included disrupted church fellowship, marital conflict, male abdication of leadership roles, rejection by a majority of women in the church, pressure from sister churches, and conflict over traditional preferences for male deacons. The article concluded with a question and an answer: "What about women deacons? The power of ordination is vested in the local church. Your church must make its own decision!"[65]

Sections on deaconesses and women deacons in the two 1979 books by McBeth and Deweese focused specifically on the role of both in Baptist history. Each used a wide array of resources to present basic trends relating to women in the diaconate across four centuries of Baptist life.[66]

Mounting Opposition

The 1970s witnessed the launching of a series of calculated attacks against women's ordination to the diaconate and the ministry. A pivotal starting point was the formation of the Baptist Faith and Message Fellowship in Georgia in 1973, with M. O. Owens of North Carolina as the first president. The purpose of the Fellowship focused on identifying and attacking Southern Baptist "liberals," including ordained women and their churches, since the practice of women's ordination meant that the subscribers did not believe in biblical inerrancy. That same year, the new Fellowship began to publish *The Southern Baptist Journal*, with William A. Powell as editor, as a medium for publicly attacking liberals. Also in 1973, Baptists United for Spiritual Revival, a North Carolina organization, began to publish *Baptists*

---

[64]Charles H. Chandler, "What about Women Deacons?" *Search* 8/3 (Spring 1979): 29.

[65]Ibid., 40.

[66]Leon McBeth, *Women in Baptist Life* (Nashville: Broadman Press, 1979) 139-52; Charles W. Deweese, *The Emerging Role of Deacons* (Nashville: Broadman Press, 1979) passim.

United News, with Robert M. Tenery as editor. Its purpose was similar to that of *The Southern Baptist Journal*.

An early evidence of the importance of women's issues to *The Southern Baptist Journal* was the publication in its January 1974 issue of the article, "God's Chief Assignment to Women," by Joyce Rogers, wife of Adrian Rogers (who would become perhaps the most influential Southern Baptist in the last quarter of the twentieth century). Following a common pattern used by fundamentalist writers in dealing with the role and status of women in Baptist life, this article made no references to the life and teachings of Christ and did not appeal to the four Gospels; rather, all scriptures cited came from the Old Testament and selected writings of the apostle Paul.

Joyce Rogers set the tone for themes about women that would characterize Southern Baptist fundamentalism into the 2000s. She claimed that "the Bible says that a woman is not to teach or usurp authority over the man" and that "a woman is not only to be submissive to her husband, but to the male leadership in the church." She cited two scriptures to prove her point that women should keep silent in church and not exercise authority over man: 1 Corinthians 14:34-35 and 1 Timothy 2:11-12. According to Rogers, woman's submission all started because Eve sinned first in the creation accounts in Genesis. Quite simply, from Genesis 3:16 forward, "the man would lead; the woman was to be submissive." Countering the claims of some that because of Christ's life and teachings, Galatians 3:28 abolished distinctions between male and female, Rogers simply responded: "How we have misinterpreted God's Word!" Stating that "those who take this text as a proof text for equal authority for women have not studied the rest of the related Scriptures," she then appealed to 1 Corinthians 11:3 and Ephesians 5:22-24 as passages that, for her, locked in women's submission to men for eternity.[67]

In December 1975, Robert M. Tenery's editorial in *Baptists United News* was titled "The Ordination of Women." The purpose of Tenery's editorial was to attack the resolution favoring women's ordination that the Baptist State Convention of North Carolina had adopted in November 1975. Tenery viewed this action as "unfortunate" for four key reasons. First, "the only clear teachings on ordination in the New Testament make it clear that ordination was for men." Second, it "was passed on the crest

---

[67]Joyce Rogers, "God's Chief Assignment to Women," *The Southern Baptist Journal* 2/1 (January 1974): 3, 9.

of a modern fad known as the 'Women's Liberation Movement.' " Third, he questioned the motives of the "liberal pastors" who voted for it: "We have a sneaking suspicion that some liberal pastors who were wanting to inject the practice of ordaining women into the life of their local churches were having trouble with Deacon Bodies. Convention endorsement of the practice would serve to make it much more palatable to balky deacons." Fourth, he questioned the ability of churches to think for themselves:

> If the Convention were to vote to paint their steeples fire engine red they would do it. Convention actions are more authoritative to them than the New Testament. . . . The procedure is simple. A liberal pastor can persuade to blindly embrace any action of the Convention and then maneuver the Convention to endorse liberal ideas.[68]

As the 1970s-1990s would progress, Southern Baptist fundamentalists would, ironically, incorporate this exact strategy into their patterns of operation.

The topic of ordination of women to the diaconate and ministry appeared often in fundamentalist Baptist publications in the late 1970s. In January 1977, *The Southern Baptist Journal* cited several prominent Southern Baptist leaders who had "recently given encouragement to overlooking the Bible doctrine of ordaining men only": James L. Sullivan, SBC president; Duke K. McCall, president of the Southern Baptist Theological Seminary; Wayne Ward, professor of theology at Southern Seminary; and Charles Ashcraft, executive secretary of the Arkansas Baptist Convention. The list even included a female division director at the Home Mission Board who was an ordained deacon at the First Baptist Church of Decatur, Georgia.[69]

What was the primary reason why *The Southern Baptist Journal* objected to affirmations of women's ordination? The answer was straightforward: "The issue has nothing to do with the ability of the women to serve. The entire issue is whether or not a person believes in the Verbal Inspiration of the entire Bible as the infallible Word of God." The publication took the position that "liberalism, apostasy, and modernism" always take over when people lose faith in biblical inerrancy and let their own opinions

---

[68]Robert M. Tenery, "The Ordination of Women," *Baptists United News* 3/10 (29 December 1975): 4.

[69]"Some SBC Leaders on Ordaining Women," *The Southern Baptist Journal* 5/1 (January 1977): 11.

guide them. "One evidence of this in recent years in the Southern Baptist Convention is the rapidly expanding new movement of ordaining women."[70]

This attitude filtered out into many churches. In March 1977, James R. Gray, pastor of the Unity Baptist Church in Starr, South Carolina, described the ordination of women as "a controversial issue in Christian circles." Claiming that the scriptures support ordination for men only, he stated that persons who favor women's ordination deny that "God's word is infallible." In fact, "when the trend of human thinking opposes the Word of God, that thinking must be in error."[71]

In April 1977, while still serving as SBC president, James L. Sullivan, in an interview with Baptist Press, acknowledged the negative criticisms being leveled against women's ordination; then he ventured his own view on the matter: "In the SBC, we have quite a few women ordained as deacons, but it's still a matter of controversy and differences of interpreting scriptures." However, when the day comes that women have more positions in Baptist life, "we'll be logical and accept it."[72] Sullivan's own church, First Baptist Church of Nashville, Tennessee, would ordain women deacons beginning in 1986 and would ordain a woman to a chaplaincy ministry in 2000.

Conclusion

Dynamic factors—religious, political, and cultural—affected Baptist life in the 1960s-1970s, all impacting the roles of women in church life, including women in the diaconate. Such factors included the Women's Liberation Movement, the adoption of the Civil Rights Act in 1964, discussions in the 1970s regarding the Equal Rights Amendment, the American Bicentennial Celebration in 1976, and President Jimmy Carter's human rights initiatives. Simultaneously, Baptists witnessed the ordination to the ministry in 1964 of Addie Davis, the first Southern Baptist woman so ordained; adoption of human rights resolutions by the Baptist World Alliance, the ABC, and the SBC; the establishment of the American Baptist Women in Ministry organization in 1974; the holding of the Southern

---

[70]Ibid.

[71]James R. Gray, "Ordination: Male or Female," *The Southern Baptist Journal* 5/2 (March 1977): 9.

[72]James Lee Young, "Sullivan—Could Not Have Predicted Pressures," Baptist Press (27 April 1977): 2.

Baptist Consultation on Women in Church-Related Vocations in 1978; and the expansion of Baptist publications willing to discuss women deacons and deaconesses. Consequently, the number of women deacons and women serving as chairs of deacon bodies began to grow.

Simultaneously, stiff resistance to women's ordination erupted in Southern Baptist life, due primarily to the rise of the Baptist Faith and Message Fellowship in 1973. This organization, its leaders, and its publica tions ardently and persistently attacked women's ordination for several reasons: it lacked a biblical basis; it resulted from a failure to view biblical inerrancy as the keystone of the Baptist faith; it represented a form of yielding to modernism, liberalism, and apostasy; and it countered the masculine dominance of the fundamentalist movement. Opposition would intensify in the 1980s, as would the expansion of ordained women deacons.

Chapter 5

Women Deacon
Ordination Crisis, 1980s

Southern Baptists railroaded down two different sets of tracks in the 1980s, traveling in opposite directions. By 1990, "the Southern Baptist Convention . . . was torn apart by the most serious controversy in the history of the denomination."[1] Conflicting attitudes toward women's roles and ordination lay at the center of the crisis.

Women deacons received accelerated attention. Numerous local churches, many for the first time, elected and ordained them. Increasing numbers of churches with women deacons began to elect women as chairs. Simultaneously, opposition to women's ordination expanded and intensified. Baptist associations and conventions adopted resolutions both opposing and supporting women's ordination. Seminary students prepared Doctor of Ministry theses and research papers relating to women's issues.[2]

For Southern Baptists, the 1980s was a defining decade. Fundamentalist presidents presided over every annual session of the Southern Baptist Convention (SBC). The convention's 1984 adoption of a resolution opposing women's ordination spelled trouble for churches choosing to ordain women deacons and ministers. In 1987, the convention adopted the fundamentalist-oriented, creed-based Peace Committee Report. In 1988, the convention adopted a resolution on the priesthood of believers that

---

[1] Walter B. Shurden, introduction to *The Struggle for the Soul of the SBC: Moderate Responses to the Fundamentalist Movement*, ed. Walter B. Shurden (Macon GA: Mercer University Press, 1993) ix.

[2] See, e.g., Dale D. Burton, Jr., "The Northeast Baptist Church Considering the Ordination of Women as Deacons" (D.Min. thesis, New Orleans Baptist Theological Seminary, 1980); Joseph Allen Brown, "Ordination of Women to the Diaconate at the First Baptist Church of Shawnee, Oklahoma" (D.Min. thesis, Southern Baptist Theological Seminary, 1984); Glen Schmucker, "A Survey of the Central Issues in the Current Debate over the Ordination of Women among Southern Baptists" (D.Min. seminar paper, Southwestern Baptist Theological Seminary, 1984); Floyd Elias Patterson, "An Issues Approach to the Closure of Conflict over the Ordination of Women as Deacons" (D.Min. thesis, Southern Baptist Theological Seminary, 1985).

reflected a strong emphasis on pastoral authority, thus diminishing women's leadership roles in churches.

September 1980 was a pivotal month: fundamentalist leader Paul Pressler announced that fundamentalists were going to take over the denomination; within two weeks, the Moderate Movement was launched in Gatlinburg, Tennessee, through the coordinating efforts of Cecil Sherman, to counter attacks on the convention. Moderate Baptists began to organize in defense of women's ordination and other causes. In 1983, *SBC Today* was launched, and Women in Ministry, SBC (later Southern Baptist Women in Ministry, and still later Baptist Women in Ministry) was organized and released the first issue of its publication, *FOLIO*. In 1984, the SBC Forum, a national gathering of moderate Baptists, held its first meeting. In 1986, moderate Baptists organized the Southern Baptist Alliance (later Alliance of Baptists). In 1989, they launched the Baptist Theological Seminary at Richmond.

Local-church developments, publications of SBC agencies, release of a new fundamentalist publication, reactions of Baptist associations to churches with women deacons, and the 1984 SBC resolution opposing women's ordination and reactions to it—these developments comprised the arenas within which much of the action took place.

Local-Church Developments

In the 1980s, Baptist churches across the United States began to take new initiatives relating to women deacons. Developments in four churches in Texas, Georgia, and North Carolina illustrate some of these initiatives. After reviewing events in these churches, this chapter will present detailed listings of selected other churches nationwide that elected women deacons and deacon chairs for the first time.

Two prominent churches, Seventh and James Baptist Church in Waco, Texas, and First Baptist Church in Asheville, North Carolina, adopted women deacons in the early 1980s. The story of women deacons in the Seventh and James Baptist Church received lengthy treatment in a 1998 article by Carol Crawford Holcomb in *Texas Baptist History: The Journal of the Texas Baptist Historical Society*.[3] Holcombe noted that the new emphasis on women's roles in Southern Baptist life had "coincided with the

---

[3]Carol Crawford Holcomb, "'Coming into a New Awareness': Women Deacons at Seventh and James Baptist Church," *Texas Baptist History: The Journal of the Texas Baptist Historical Society* 18 (1998): 1-25.

calls for social justice in American culture during the 1960s such as civil rights for African Americans and the emerging women's liberation movement."[4] The Seventh and James Baptist Church worked during the 1970s to change the concept of its deacons from a board directing church business to a pastoral-care model. Further, the church discussed throughout the 1970s the idea and possibility of ordaining women deacons. The church then ordained its first five women deacons on 22 June 1980: Katherine Cooper, Mary Ila Colvin, Laverne Mosley, Frances Newland, and Kathleen Underwood. The church's "formidable shift in attitudes" toward women deacons resulted because church members "talked to one another and they listened intently—to the words of their own faith, to each other, and to the world around them."[5]

In 1975, the board of deacons of First Baptist Church in Asheville, North Carolina, with the support of the church's pastor, Cecil Sherman, recommended a church policy that would allow women to be elected as deacons or deaconesses. The recommendation failed. In 1980, the church did change its policy to allow for women deacons. The church elected its first three women deacons in November 1981: Bunah Clark, Mary Eisenhauer, and Madeline Pennell. They were ordained, along with other new deacons, in January 1982.[6]

The First Baptist Church of Christ at Macon, Georgia, voted in March 1985 to change church policy to provide for the possibility of ordaining women deacons. The church ordained its first three women deacons, Deigie Andrews, Carolyn Martin, and Beverly Penley, in January 1986.[7] Prior to those developments, the church's Committee to Study Ordination of Women as Deacons had recommended to the church in January 1985 that the church retain the practice of having male deacons only. In response, committee member John H. Jones, Jr., read a lengthy minority report that favored women deacons. Titled "My Reasons for Believing That Women Can Be Spiritual Leaders in Our Church," Jones's report defended his position by including sections on scripture, the nature of God, the attitude of Christ, the stance of seminaries and their leaders, the negative effect of

---

[4]Ibid., 6.

[5]Ibid., 20.

[6]Charles W. Deweese, *The Power of Freedom: First Baptist Church, Asheville, North Carolina, 1829–1997* (Franklin TN: Providence House Publishers, 1997) 236-37.

[7]Connie Jones, e-mail to author, 30 August 2004.

the 1984 SBC resolution opposing women's ordination, positions of leading Baptist theologians, and the reality that other Baptist churches in Georgia and elsewhere were approving women deacons.[8] Most insightful, the report noted, for example, that the 1984 SBC resolution referenced forty-two scripture verses: "Not one comes from Jesus' teachings or the Gospels. And no distinction is made between the eternal considerations and cultural codes."[9] Partly because of Jones's report and the ensuing disagreement in the church, the committee's report was tabled until March 1985, when women deacons were approved.

Established in 1945, Forest Hills Baptist Church in Raleigh, North Carolina, made clear in a document adopted in 1956 that all deacons would be male. The church's Rules of Procedure Committee recommended women deacons in 1977, but the recommendation failed because it did not receive the required two-thirds vote. In March 1985, a special committee urged deleting the word "male" from the qualifications for deacons, and when the vote was taken, eighty percent of those voting approved it. In 1986, the church elected its first two women deacons, Jessie Edwards and Jerry Hester.[10]

Other churches in several states also adopted women deacons in the 1980s. Nine examples in six states included the First Baptist Church of Clarendon, Arlington, Virginia (1980); Hominy Baptist Church, Candler, North Carolina (1981); Northside Baptist Church, Jackson, Mississippi (1982); Snyder Memorial Baptist Church, Fayetteville, North Carolina (1984); Trinity Baptist Church, Norfolk, Virginia (1984); First Baptist Church, Nashville, Tennessee (1986); University Baptist Church, Baton Rouge, Louisiana (1987); Masonboro Baptist Church, Wilmington, North Carolina (1989); and Shades Crest Baptist Church, Birmingham, Alabama (1989).

Many churches elected women to serve as chairs of deacon bodies, especially in North Carolina. Seventeen examples from eight states follow:

North Carolina
    First Baptist Church, Elkin (1980)
    First Baptist Church, Lenoir (1982)

---

[8]John H. Jones, Jr., "My Reasons for Believing That Women Can Be Spiritual Leaders in Our Church" (30 January 1985): 1-15; document faxed to author by Connie Jones, 30 August 2004.

[9]Ibid., 9.

[10]Jack Porter, letter to author, 28 August 2004.

First Baptist Church, Raleigh (1982)
Rowland Baptist Church, Rowland (1982)
Wendell Baptist Church, Wendell (1982)
First Baptist Church, Wadesboro (1983)
Hominy Baptist Church, Candler (1983)
Zebulon Baptist Church, Zebulon (1986).
Virginia
West Main Baptist Church, Danville (1982)
River Road Baptist Church, Richmond (1985)
Chatham Baptist Church, Chatham (1988).
Churches in six other states included
Tennessee: First Baptist Church, Oak Ridge (1981)
Georgia: Oakhurst Baptist Church, Decatur (1983)
Kentucky: Central Baptist Church, Lexington (1986)
South Carolina: First Baptist Church, Clemson (1986)
Texas: Royal Lane Baptist Church, Dallas (1986)
Mississippi: Northside Baptist Church, Jackson (1989).

Publications of Southern Baptist Convention Agencies

Important Broadman Press books and denominational journals and other periodicals, such as those published by the Southern Baptist Historical Commission, Southern Baptist Theological Seminary, and the Sunday School Board, focused on women deacons in the 1980s. Leon McBeth, professor of Church History at Southwestern Baptist Theological Seminary, was perhaps the major writer of the decade regarding Baptist women's issues.

In 1980, the Sunday School Board published *Deacons: Servant Models in the Church*, a book by Henry Webb, then editor of the board's magazine, *The Deacon*. Webb's book would exert a strong impact on deacon developments among Southern Baptists throughout the 1980s. In discussing "The Deacon's Wife," Webb claimed that 1 Timothy 3:11 "seems to favor application to deacons' wives." He stated that "most churches have decided to elect only men as deacons" but that "each church must come to its own decision whether to elect women as deacons."[11]

Leon McBeth's book, *The Baptist Heritage: Four Centuries of Baptist Witness* (1987), acknowledged the growth of women deacons and observed

---

[11]Henry Webb, *Deacons: Servant Models in the Church* (Nashville: Broadman Press, 1980) 45-46.

that "Women emphasize that their role is that of *deacons*, not *deaconesses*, because the latter term has often designated a subordinate role." Then McBeth identified three sets of factors that "helped lead to changing roles, and in some cases the recovery of ancient roles, for Baptist women." The first set of factors included changes in society that propelled women into the workplace and into leadership positions in business, education, and government; increased education for women; and brought about the "liberation" of women in American culture. Second, changes in biblical understanding in which Baptists rediscovered "an emphasis upon human equality" advanced the cause of women in the church. Third, the use of ordination for nonpreaching ministries encouraged the ordination of women.[12]

McBeth published two important articles in the 1980s: "The Ordination of Women" in the fall 1981 issue of *Review and Expositor* and "Perspectives on Women in Baptist Life" in the July 1987 issue of *Baptist History and Heritage*. The former article appeared in an issue devoted to the theme of ordination; the latter in an issue devoted to women in Southern Baptist history. Neither article focused solely on women deacons, but each had obvious implications for them.

McBeth noted that the ordination of women, particularly to the ministry, was a relatively new trend in Baptist life and that Addie Davis's ordination to the ministry in 1964 "ushered in a new era in the history of Southern Baptist ministry." In fact, women's ordination had become "both troublesome and controversial. Opponents and proponents have scrambled for biblical, theological, and practical arguments to buttress their viewpoints."[13]

After describing ordination in Southern Baptist history, McBeth suggested six factors that may have contributed to the profound changes taking place in Southern Baptists' conceptions of women in religion: the presence of women educationally prepared for church service, the reality of women responding to spiritual needs, the impact of the Women's Liberation Movement, awareness of women's ordination in other denominations, fresh interpretations of scripture, and expanded views of ministry.[14]

---

[12]H. Leon McBeth, *The Baptist Heritage: Four Centuries of Baptist Witness* (Nashville: Broadman Press, 1987) 691-92.

[13]H. Leon McBeth, "The Ordination of Women," *Review and Expositor* 78/4 (Fall 1981): 515.

[14]Ibid., 519-21.

Then, after detailing some Baptist reactions to women's ordination, McBeth presented three implications for Baptists: the need to come to terms with who has the authority to ordain, the need to define the basic meaning of ordination, and the need to explore the nature and call to Christian ministry.[15]

In categorizing perspectives on women in Baptist life, McBeth creatively presented six angles: "From the angle of service, we depend on you." "From the angle of ministry, we fear you." "From the angle of missions, we follow you." "From the angle of scripture, we puzzle over you." "From the angle of history, we ignore you." "From the angle of the future, we must loose you."[16] Regarding this last item, McBeth commented that for generations men had defined women's roles; interpreted their place in history; determined what they could "do, say, wear, or own"; pronounced verdicts on whether God could call them and, if so, to what; had decided whether they could serve as "deacons, teachers, or ministers"; and had "jello-molded" them into what men thought they should be. As a response to men's control of women's affairs, McBeth concluded, "I feel very deeply that the time has come for a moratorium of men making authoritative pronouncements about women"; he urged women to take up their own mantle as biblical scholars, students of Baptist history, and definers of their own roles.[17]

Sunday School Board periodicals also contributed to the debate regarding women deacons. In 1984, *The Deacon* published a lengthy article, "What about Women Deacons?" prepared by Charles H. Chandler, pastor of the Pennsylvania Avenue Baptist Church in Urbana, Illinois. Chandler began by acknowledging that in some churches the question about women deacons was "an explosive issue," while in others it was "an honest search for truth." He reviewed appropriate New Testament passages and concluded that an ironclad case could not be made for or against women deacons. He reviewed church history and decided that women deacons had existed in certain periods and not in others but that a renewed interest in recent years was clear. He reviewed current practices and some special areas of concern and determined both that women deacons themselves found their ministries to be rewarding and that churches must make their

---

[15]Ibid., 525-27.

[16]H. Leon McBeth, "Perspectives on Women in Baptist Life," *Baptist History and Heritage* 22/3 (July 1987): 4-10.

[17]Ibid., 10.

own decisions regarding electing women to the diaconate since the power of ordination resides in the local church.[18]

In 1985, Ron Sisk, director of program development for the Southern Baptist Christian Life Commission, published a brief article, "Women in the SBC: A Status Report," in *The Student*, a Sunday School Board publication. Although he pointed out some continuing areas of difficulty for women in all types of leadership positions, he concluded that "more and more Southern Baptists are interpreting the Bible and the leadership of the Holy Spirit in ways leading to significant new opportunities of Christian service for Southern Baptist women."[19]

In the 1980s, the Sunday School Board had in place an appraisal process for evaluating manuscripts to be published. Appraisal readers were asked to evaluate manuscripts according to their biblical accuracy, theological soundness, and denominational acceptability. On 7 March 1985, Bob Dean, the board's editorial and curriculum specialist, sent a letter to appraisal readers with copies to Sunday School Board President Lloyd Elder and four other board administrators, Morton Rose, Gary Cook, Howard Foshee, and Ralph McIntyre. The letter included a document titled "Guidelines for Dealing with the Ordination of Women" with the notation that board trustees had approved it on 6 February 1985.[20]

The document first expressed two general guidelines: "(a) to give clear support to basic Christian and Baptist beliefs and (b) to deal factually and fairly with differing points of view among Southern Baptists."[21] The first subpoint under the first general guideline stated explicitly: "The Sunday School Board will continue to emphasize that the ordination of deacons and ministers is a matter completely under the authority of the local congregation." The second subpoint then stated that

> The Sunday School Board will continue to affirm and encourage the biblical and historic contribution of women to the cause of Christ. The

---

[18]Charles H. Chandler, "What about Women Deacons?" *The Deacon* 14/3 (April-June 1984): 45-50.

[19]Ron Sisk, "Women in the SBC: A Status Report," *The Student* 64/8 (February 1985): 45.

[20]Bob Dean, letter to Sunday School Board appraisal readers, 7 March 1985; located in AR160, Women in Baptist Life Collection, box 2, folder 2-6 titled "Ordination of Women—Clippings," Southern Baptist Historical Library and Archives, Nashville.

[21]Ibid.

worth and dignity of all persons in the church and in places of service to the Lord are established by the authority of the Scriptures, by the liberating power of the gospel, by the lordship of Christ, by the gifts and calling of the Holy Spirit, and by the examples of devout persons in biblical times and Baptist heritage.[22]

Subpoints under the second general guideline urged board editors to treat women's ordination "factually and fairly with neither point of view being ignored or disparaged" to ensure "that all writers do not represent only one perspective on the subject of the ordination of women." Further, editors were to enlist writers who represented various views on women's ordination (and other controversial topics). No writer was to give the impression to readers that his/her work presented "an official Baptist or Sunday School Board view." While the board acknowledged the need to recognize differences of opinion among Southern Baptists regarding women's ordination, it also urged "the wisdom of not making such differences a test of faith, fellowship, or biblical authority."[23] After the forced retirement of President Lloyd Elder in 1991 by fundamentalist trustees, many Southern Baptist leaders would most definitely make women's ordination a test of faith, fellowship, and biblical authority. In fact, the process was already in motion in certain sectors.

Women's Issues and the *Southern Baptist Advocate*

In 1980, the *Southern Baptist Advocate* emerged in Dallas, Texas, as a new fundamentalist publication. Russell Kaemmerling, the first editor, wished to distinguish the *Advocate* from the *Southern Baptist Journal*, launched in 1973, which had become a *"National Enquirer* type of publication." Kaemmerling regarded "inerrancy as a crucial starting point for theological discussion" but claimed that the *Advocate* would address other issues as well.[24] Throughout the 1980s, the publication would use rigid views of biblical inerrancy to hammer against women's ordination to the diaconate and ministry. The *Advocate* differed little from the *Southern Baptist Journal* in the way it incessantly attacked women's leadership roles in Baptist life. Several examples between 1981 and 1985 will make the point.

---

[22]Ibid.

[23]Ibid.

[24]Tammi Ledbetter, *"Advocate* Offers New Voice," *Southern Baptist Advocate* 1/1 (August 1980): 1.

The *Advocate* staff devoted an entire 1981 issue to the Religious RoundTable and its founder and president, Ed McAteer, and mailed it to all 34,000 Southern Baptist churches. The RoundTable was described as

> a Washington-based coalition of business, political, and religious leaders. The objective of the RoundTable is primarily to favorably impact federal policy by activating the potential influence of millions of Americans who adhere to traditional, family-based moral principles.[25]

This objective apparently did not include women who sought liberation from masculine dominance. After asking, "How does the RoundTable feel about the 'Equal Rights Amendment,' feminist activism, and women's liberation in general?" the *Advocate* responded with explicit clarity: "The radical so-called 'liberationist' movements among women today are for the most part anti-God, immoral, and degrading to womanhood."[26] Baptist women could draw little consolation from that assessment.

In subsequent issues, the *Advocate* printed articles such as the following:

> "SBC Vice President's Church Okays Women Deacons," referring to Gene Garrison, pastor of First Baptist Church in Oklahoma City;
>
> "Oklahoma City Association Opposes Action by Garrison," a reprint of a Baptist Press article regarding an action of the Capital Baptist Association;
>
> "Chafin Ordains Female Divorcee," citing the ordination of Rosemary Crenshaw to the diaconate of the South Main Baptist Church in Houston, Texas, where her daughter, Sherry Melton, already served as a deacon;
>
> "SBC Feminists Launch Organization," describing the formation of the Women in Ministry, SBC organization and the unveiling of its newsletter, *FOLIO*;
>
> "The Ministry of Women," by Johanna L. Wilson, a free-lance writer in Orlando, Florida, who discredited both the ordination of women as nonbiblical and the right of women to exercise authority in the church or leadership over man; and
>
> "Sunday School Board Publication Contradicts Resolution on Women," claiming that T. B. Maston's article, "The Bible and Women," published

---

[25]"Introducing the RoundTable," *Southern Baptist Advocate* 2/2 (March-April 1981): 3.

[26]"Answers to Your Questions about the Religious RoundTable," *Southern Baptist Advocate* 2/2 (March-April 1981): 5.

in the February 1985 issue of *The Student*, contradicted the SBC's 1984 adopted resolution that opposed the ordination of women.[27]

The cumulative impressions made upon the reader by these articles was that fundamentalists viewed women's issues as central to the crisis facing Southern Baptists and that churches, associations, state conventions, and the SBC should not tolerate progressive developments relating to the ordination of women to the diaconate and the ministry.

Reactions of Baptist Associations to Women Deacons

Southern Baptist associations in the 1980s actively involved themselves in dealing with churches that ordained women as deacons or ministers. In 1982, James E. Carter, pastor of the University Baptist Church in Fort Worth, Texas, published an article on "Dealing with Doctrinal Conflict in Associational History." He claimed that since 1960, instances had grown in which associations refused to seat messengers from churches and withdrew fellowship from them. The three key issues causing such action included baptism, especially alien immersion; charismatic practices, notably glossolalia or speaking in tongues; and the ordination of women, particularly ordination to the ministry. Regarding women's ordination, Carter cited as an example the South District Association of Baptists in Kentucky which in 1977 had withdrawn fellowship from the Beech Fork Baptist Church in Gravel Switch because it had ordained Suzanne Coyle to the gospel ministry.[28]

Actions of three Southern Baptist associations in California, Oklahoma, and Alabama will suffice to demonstrate the trend within some associations to work against churches that ordained women deacons (and pastors). Major developments in the California and Oklahoma associations took place within seven days of one another in October 1983. For at least two reasons, these two developments may have contributed to the writing and adoption of the SBC's resolution in June 1984 opposing the ordination of women. First, both events received wide coverage in the Baptist news. Coverage of both by Baptist Press led some Baptist newspapers to carry the stories. Second, *The Southern Baptist Journal*, a fundamentalist Baptist

---

[27] *Southern Baptist Advocate* 4/2 (March-April 1983): 1, 6, 7; 4/3 (May 1983): 12; 4/5 (September 1983): 1, 6; 5/5 (June 1984): 8-9; 6/2 (February 1985): 2, 16.

[28] James E. Carter, "Dealing with Doctrinal Conflict in Associational History," *Baptist History and Heritage* 17/2 (April 1982): 38, 40-41.

publication of the Baptist Faith and Message Fellowship, and the *Southern Baptist Advocate* carried news about these events and included negative editorial attacks on women's ordination.

Redwood Empire Baptist Association in California. This association voted 83-54 on 10 October 1983 to adopt the recommendation of its Credentials Committee not to seat messengers from three churches: Redwood Baptist Church in Napa, the First Baptist Church of Sonoma, and the Tiburon Baptist Church in Tiburon. Defending its recommendation, the Credentials Committee cited several "letters of complaint" about these churches and "their practice of ordaining women, and the breach of fellowship it is causing." The second part of the adopted recommendation put the three churches on a one-year probation "in the hope that fellowship can be restored between all of our churches as they stop this practice that is unscriptural to most Baptists."[29]

Later that same day, the association passed a motion asking its Constitution and Bylaws Committee to prepare for consideration an amendment "to provide that any church that ordinates [ordains] women to Deaconship or Pastor positions can/cannot be members" of the association.[30] This process dragged on for a few years until the association's constitution in 1987 included a new article II on Authority. The last paragraph of this new article noted that "the Association has no authority over any church, but may determine the propriety of retaining in its union any church which has become unscriptural in its doctrines and practices . . . and may withdraw fellowship, at the Annual Meeting, by a three-fourths (3/4) vote of the voting messengers."[31] These actions illustrate how and why a Baptist association used the issue of ordaining women deacons and pastors as a tool for changing its constitutional procedures in order to deal with allegedly unscriptural churches.

In early 1984, soon after the Redwood Empire Association had made its decisions regarding three churches, *The Southern Baptist Journal* published a Baptist Press article focusing especially on the Tiburon Baptist Church. The article noted that Fred Grissom, interim pastor at Tiburon, was assistant professor of Church History at Golden Gate Baptist Theological Seminary in Mill Valley, and that Bonnie Chappel, one of Tiburon's

---

[29]*Annual*, Redwood Empire Baptist Association (CA), 10 October 1983, 21, 22.
[30]Ibid., 25.
[31]*Annual*, Redwood Empire Baptist Association (CA), 17 October 1987, 16.

women deacons, had previously served as secretary to Harold Graves when he was president of Golden Gate.[32]

Then the editor of *The Southern Baptist Journal*, in commenting on women's ordination, attributed such ordination to the liberalism in Baptist higher and theological education:

> The closer a church is to one of the 71 schools, colleges, universities, seminaries, and the other SBC agencies—the more the churches are influenced by the professors and the employees of the agencies. As the years go by, these churches become more liberal and fail to follow the Word of God. Not only that—but most of these churches do not baptize very many people each year. Liberals usually cause the churches to decline in everything except the spread of the deadly liberalism.[33]

Capital Baptist Association in Oklahoma. On 17 October 1983, seven days after the Redwood Empire Baptist Association's actions against three churches with ordained women, the Capital Baptist Association in Oklahoma, by a vote of 209-100, adopted a motion "to bar the seating of the messengers from the First Baptist Church of Oklahoma City." This action resulted from the announcement of the association's Credentials Committee that it had received a letter of protest from another church in the association upset over the fact that First Baptist Church of Oklahoma City had ordained women as deacons. This led the committee to "recommend that messengers from our sister church which has ordained women as deacons shall not be seated."[34] First Baptist had ordained three women in September.

First Baptist Church had voted 232-167 on 16 January 1983, to change its bylaws to allow for women deacons. The association reacted immediately. As early as 14 February 1983, the association's executive board adopted a resolution, "Concerning the Ordination of Women," which read as follows:

> WHEREAS the action of a church affiliated with Capital Baptist Association in voting to permit the ordination of women has been widely publicized, BE IT THEREFORE RESOLVED that the following statement be circulated to the churches of Capital Baptist Association:

---

[32]"Ordaining Women," *The Southern Baptist Journal* 12/1 (January-February 1984): 3.

[33]Ibid., editorial comments.

[34]*Annual*, Capital Baptist Association (OK), 17 October 1983, 33.

a. The doctrinal position of Southern Baptist churches of Capital Baptist Association does not agree with the position of ordaining women, and that, b. We do not know of any other churches affiliated with the Capital Baptist Association practicing or contemplating the practice of ordaining women, and that, c. We ask the present Constitutional Committee of the Associate [Association] to make the above matter of study and that a report be given to the board by June 15, 1983.[35]

The association did not wait until June. On April 18, the executive board voted to go on record affirming that "We believe that the Bible does not authorize the ordination of women" and "that any church that is a member of our association that ordains women be informed that such action is not true to the scriptures and does not agree with our doctrinal position."[36]

The matter softened somewhat during the association's annual meeting in October 1984. By a vote of 392-90, messengers adopted a motion by Bailey Smith, a recent SBC president, that "we as an association express our continuing belief in the role of men as deacons and pastors but in the spirit of harmony in Christ we seat the messengers of the First Baptist Church of Oklahoma City."[37] At this same meeting, the association adopted a "Resolution on the Ordination of Women"; it stated that "no further necessity remains for a continuing discussion of the issue of women's ordination"; and it resolved that "we have adequately discussed the matter and return instead to the major business of cooperative ministry in evangelism and missions."[38]

The Southern Baptist Journal entered this discussion when it printed in its January-February 1984 issue a Baptist Press story on First Baptist Church's ordination of three women deacons. *The Southern Baptist Journal* inserted a cartoon into the article ridiculing the ordination process. The editor of the journal attacked Herschel Hobbs, then retired but longtime pastor of First Baptist Church: "Some wondered why Dr. Hobbs did not speak up to uphold the clear Word of God and explain why their church could not ordain women because of what the Bible said when they had the two-hour discussion on Jan. 16, 1983. One answer is that Dr. Hobbs did not attend that very important business meeting. There may be other reasons

---

[35]Ibid., 38.
[36]Ibid., 40.
[37]*Annual*, Capital Baptist Association (OK), 14 October 1984, 36.
[38]Ibid., 52.

Dr. Hobbs did not stand true for the Bible and his church at such a crucial turning point."[39]

Hobbs had served two terms as SBC president in the early 1960s; had served for eighteen years (1958-1976) as preacher for the Southern Baptist Radio and Television Commission's flagship radio program, *The Baptist Hour*, which was carried on hundreds of stations; and had for years written Sunday School lesson materials for teachers for the SBC Sunday School Board. Respected nationwide as a convincing advocate of traditional Southern Baptist principles, Hobbs may well have been the single most influential Southern Baptist in the third quarter of the twentieth century. *The Southern Baptist Journal* thus interpreted the Capital Baptist Association's actions as its willingness to risk its relationship with its oldest church and Herschel Hobbs himself over the issue of the ordination of women deacons.

Gene Garrison, pastor of First Baptist Church, Oklahoma City, during the 1981-1983 developments relating to women deacons, and an SBC vice president at the time of their ordination, delivered a sermon to his congregation on 1 July 1984, titled "Why the First Baptist Church of Oklahoma City Ordained Women as Deacons (Or, Putting a Controversy in Proper Perspective)." At the outset, he claimed that "without the slightest exaggeration, it would be safe to say that nothing in the entire, illustrious history of this congregation has been so well publicized nationally, nor has anything provoked more controversy than has the decision to ordain women [deacons]." He noted that the controversy had come from sources outside his church rather than within. Even though 167 church members had voted against allowing women deacons, "I have not known one single, unkind, harsh, critical act or attitude to characterize any subsequent discussion of this issue in the church. This, I say, is a mark of spiritual maturity."[40]

Garrison cited some factors that caused a negative reaction among conservative Oklahoma Baptists to the church's 16 January 1983 decision to allow women deacons, but one stood out. He wrote that "I could not believe my eyes the next morning when I opened *The Daily Oklahoman* and saw an 8-column banner headline stretching all the way across the top of

---

[39]"First Baptist Church of Oklahoma City, Okla., Ordained Three Women Deacons," *The Southern Baptist Journal* 12/1 (January-February 1984) 25-26.

[40]Gene Garrison, "Why the First Baptist Church of Oklahoma City Ordained Women as Deacons, or, Putting a Controversy in Proper Perspective," *Echoes from the Pulpit* (1 July 1984): 1.

the front page, reading 'CITY'S FIRST BAPTIST CHURCH VOTES TO OK WOMEN AS DEACONS.' " Although acknowledging that the story was well written and that the church had not asked for any coverage, Garrison continued:

> Unfortunately, on that exact same day the annual Oklahoma Baptist Evangelism Conference opened in Del City, and literally hundreds of pastors came to attend the sessions. They saw the headline and the story, of course. And unbelievably, many of them actually thought we had timed this entire matter and orchestrated the whole event in order to coincide with the evangelism conference. That accusation has been heard more than once.[41]

The result was that some of the more conservative pastors erroneously interpreted the events in our church as flaunting our decision and challenging those with contrary views to make their positions public. "And so, they have done it. And done it. And done it. And done it again. Believe me, everyone knows the ordination of women as deacons is not popular among Oklahoma Baptists."[42]

Garrison summarized the chief point of his sermon in one sentence:

> The First Baptist Church of Oklahoma City ordained women as deacons because a majority of the members in the congregation who participated in the decision-making process came to believe the New Testament teaches that, in some churches, the practice is not only permissible but also an expression of the intention of Jesus Christ in his offer of abundant life to everyone.[43]

Garrison concluded by asserting that

> at the risk of sounding defensive, I must place the blame for the public disagreements, the judgmental disavowals, and the denominational discord on the doorstep of those who have refused to allow this church to be what it is: an independent, self-governing, democratic body, responsible only to God for an accurate understanding of His Word and His mission in the world; and who have, instead, understood their role to be that of self-appointed critics, judges, determiners, and protectors of orthodoxy.[44]

---

[41]Ibid., 2.
[42]Ibid.
[43]Ibid.
[44]Ibid., 5.

Garrison admitted that he would never say that every church should do what First Baptist Church did regarding women deacons, "but I would say that under the circumstances, as painful as some of the results have been, we absolutely could do nothing else than what we have done."[45]

Calhoun Baptist Association in Alabama. In 1988 and 1989, this association also took actions against a church because it had ordained women deacons. Barry Howard was pastor of the First Baptist Church of Williams in Jacksonville, Alabama, in September 1988 when the church elected its first women deacons. The ordination created an apparent dilemma for G. Harold Chandler, director of missions for the Calhoun Baptist Association, and illustrated how sensitive the issue was for the association. Chandler gave a lengthy report to the 17 October 1988 meeting of the association explaining his participation in the ordination service of women at First Williams, especially in view of "an erroneous statement in today's *Anniston Star*." The pastor had invited Chandler to share in the ordination of deacons, and he agreed to do so. Later, Chandler learned that two women would be ordained. He explained to the association: "Realizing that this was a new thing for churches in our area to ordain women deacons, and realizing that most churches in our association would not choose to do what this local autonomous church had decided to do, I declined the invitation to have the ordination prayer." Still, he agreed to attend the service at the request of the pastor after consulting with his father, a former director of missions, and with the Calhoun Association's moderator.[46]

Following the ordination service, Chandler accepted the pastor's request to give the prayer of benediction. But, Chandler stated, "I did not participate in the ordination service itself as was falsely stated in today's issue of *The Anniston Star*." He invited the association's executive committee, if it wished, "to provide him with clear guidelines or suggestions as to which invitations that I should accept or not accept into member churches in the future."[47]

During this same annual meeting in October 1988, the Calhoun Association voted to instruct its Credentials and Petitionary Letters Committee to "look into the recent action of the First Baptist Church of Williams, in ordaining women to serve in the office of deacon, as it involves the 'harmonious working together of the churches' as stipulated

---

[45]Ibid., 6.
[46]*Annual*, Calhoun Baptist Association (AL), 17 October 1988, 21, 22.
[47]Ibid., 22.

in article VI of the Associational Constitution" and to report back to the association "with a recommendation of appropriate action."[48]

When the association met in October 1989, its clerk moved "that those messengers elected by the churches constitute the official body of this Ninety Eighth Annual Session." Then the Credentials and Petitionary Letters Committee presented the following amendment to the motion: "That the messengers of First Baptist Church, Williams, not be seated at the 1989 session of Calhoun Baptist Association." A ballot vote was taken on the amendment, which was later reported to have passed 349-273. Still later, another ballot vote was taken on the original motion "relative to withdrawing fellowship from Williams First Baptist Church." With 601 votes cast, the association voted 331 to 269, with one abstention, not to seat the messengers of Williams First.[49]

1984 SBC Resolution
Opposing Women's Ordination Plus Reactions

Women's ordination to the diaconate and pastoral ministry, and other leadership roles for women took a big hit in June 1984 when the SBC adopted a resolution "On Ordination and the Role of Women in Ministry." That resolution was a clear attempt to squash patterns of progress churches were making in ordaining women. The resolution served notice that the fundamentalist mindset dominating the convention intended to make women's ordination a key feature of its attacks on alleged liberalism and disbelief in inerrancy.

Three consecutive "whereas" statements in the resolution projected a negative view of women's ordination:

> WHEREAS, The Scriptures attest to God's delegated order of authority (God the head of Christ, Christ the head of man, man the head of woman, man and woman dependent one upon the other to the glory of God) distinguishing the roles of men and women in public prayer and prophecy (1 Cor. 11:2-5); and
>
> WHEREAS, The Scriptures teach that women are not in public worship to assume a role of authority over men lest confusion reign in the local church (1 Cor. 14:33-36); and

---

[48]Ibid., 23.

[49]*Annual*, Calhoun Baptist Association (AL), 16 October 1989, 25, 26, 27, 28.

WHEREAS, While Paul commends men and women alike in other roles of ministry and service (Titus 2:1-10), he excludes women from pastoral leadership (1 Tim. 2:12) to preserve a submission God requires because the man was first in creation and the woman was first in the Edenic fall (1 Tim. 2:13ff.).

The resolution's final paragraph resolved

That we not decide concerns of Christian doctrine and practice by modern cultural, sociological, and ecclesiastical trends or by emotional factors; that we remind ourselves of the dearly bought Baptist principle of the final authority of Scripture in matters of faith and conduct; and that we encourage the service of women in all aspects of church life and work other than pastoral functions and leadership roles entailing ordination.[50]

Reaction to this resolution was swift, strong, and extensive. The reaction took many shapes. Two types of reaction included letters to the SBC president and actions of Baptist state conventions. All these reactions took place in 1984.

Letters to Charles F. Stanley. Charles F. Stanley, pastor of the First Baptist Church of Atlanta, Georgia, was elected SBC president during the convention meeting in which this resolution was adopted. The Charles Stanley Papers in the Southern Baptist Historical Library and Archives include letters to him from many individuals, a church, a deacon body, and an associational executive committee, all registering intense opposition to the resolution. Other letter writers, some supporting and some opposing women's ordination, questioned the rationale behind the resolution.

Sue Walters wrote Stanley on 16 June 1984 and asked, "How long will it take the religious leaders of our Southern Baptist denomination to recognize that you cannot dictate God's will in the lives of people"? Her daughter had graduated with a Master of Divinity degree in March 1984 and felt called to a preaching ministry. Now her own denomination was telling her that she should be denied ordination. Walters continued, "It is hard to understand people who confess to love God and to follow his leadership not to recognize this call in the lives of others whether they are male, female, black or white or whatever the difference may be."[51]

---

[50]*Annual*, Southern Baptist Convention, 1984, 65.

[51]Sue Walters, letter to Charles Stanley, 16 June 1984 (city and state not included in letter).

142   *400 Years of Baptist Service*

Paris L. Owens, of St. Louis, Missouri, had read about the adoption of the resolution in the June 15 issue of the St. Louis *Globe-Democrat*. On June 19, she responded by sending a letter to Charles Stanley, stating:

> I am very dismayed. . . . I am a young black woman and also a member of a Baptist church which is under the leadership of the Southern Baptist Conference [Convention]. I do not agree with the reasoning for the opposition of the ordination of women to the ministry. In my opinion, I feel this is a setback for women. I was taught that all human beings are equal. But according to the latest resolution, we have some exceptions. . . .
> It is depressing that as far as we have strived for greater expectations, there are still a great number of people who want to keep the barrier up and say "No Women Allowed." . . . If a woman can become a doctor, lawyer, judge, and even an astronaut, then why not a minister?[52]

Several letters to Stanley attacked the denomination's rationale for adopting the resolution. On June 24, Deborah Stephenson, member of the First Baptist Church of Decatur, Georgia, acknowledged that she "was not surprised that the ordination of women was not supported" but claimed that she "was appalled at the reasoning behind the stand. Women as the originators of Edenic fall—of sin?! The text used to support this is 1 Timothy 2:11-15. But what about Romans 5:12 where Adam is named as being the origin of sinful beings?" Stephenson concluded that "the SBC has gravely damaged the worth of women with this resolution and I for one must loudly oppose it!"[53]

On July 3, Susan D. Parker, of Hartselle, Alabama, reacted to the resolution by sending a letter to "Brother Brooks Barkley" at First Baptist Church in Hartselle, which she copied to Hudson Baggett, executive director of the Alabama Baptist Convention, and to Charles Stanley. She indicated that she was "very proud of our Southern Baptist Convention" for taking a stand against "women entering the pastoral ministry." However, even she questioned the basis for the decision: "Why then with so much good scriptural basis for the decision did the membership even bring up an archaic, ridiculous basis as part of their decision as woman committing the original sin? If any man in our church is without sin—original or other—then let him cast the first stone."[54]

---

[52]Paris L. Owens, letter to Charles Stanley, 19 June 1984.
[53]Deborah Stephenson, letter to Charles Stanley, 24 June 1984.
[54]Susan D. Parker, letter to Brooks Barkley (copied to Charles Stanley), 3 July 1984.

Mary B. Parker, of Valdosta, Georgia, in an undated letter, claimed to be "upset" over the adopted resolution

> not to ordain women as ministers or deacons because women were responsible for bringing sin into the world. Come on now, who twisted Adam's arm? We preach to our children today to determine for themselves the path they will follow; not to give in to peer pressure; that they must accept responsibility for their own actions. Now isn't it time that man accepted responsibility for *his* actions? My conscience would never allow me to live with myself if I did not raise my voice in protest in this matter.[55]

On July 12, Andrew M. Manis, pastor of the Richland Baptist Church in Falmouth, Kentucky, wrote Stanley a letter stating that his church viewed the SBC resolution to be "an embarrassment before the world and a disgrace before God." Therefore, on July 8 his church had "adopted a resolution repudiating the SBC's 1984 resolution on women in ministry and went on record as supporting the right of women to serve in any capacity in the Body of Christ that is open to men." Manis compared the opposition to women's ordination to Southern Baptist views of slavery and racism. He stated that the Southern Baptist Convention had come into existence in 1845

> because of its refusal to acknowledge the equality of all persons in Christ. Thus we built a rationale for slavery on a foundation of biblical texts. We did the same with the issue of racial segregation in the 1950s and 1960s. It is long past time that Southern Baptists got on the right side of history for a change. We believe sexism is no more acceptable to the Gospel of Jesus Christ than racism.[56]

On September 13, Michael J. Clingenpeel, pastor of Franklin Baptist Church in Franklin, Virginia, wrote Stanley on behalf of the church's deacon body, which had voted unanimously on September 10 both to adopt a statement expressing concern about the SBC's 1984 resolution and to send the statement to convention officers. The deacon statement described the convention resolution as "spurious" and repudiated its "unbiblical implication" that "women have a greater responsibility than men for the advent of human sin and the present human condition. We affirm the

------

[55]Mary B. Parker, letter to Charles Stanley, no date.
[56]Andrew M. Manis, letter to Charles Stanley (resolution attached), 12 July 1984.

biblical truth that 'all have sinned and come short of the glory of God' (Romans 3:23)." The statement affirmed that "any person, regardless of gender, has the opportunity and obligation to respond to the call of God upon his or her life."[57]

On October 1, Charles B. Nunn, Jr., executive director of the Richmond Baptist Association in Richmond, Virginia, wrote Stanley on behalf of the association's executive committee. Citing Galatians 3:28 as a biblical affirmation of the dignity and worth of every person, Nunn shared that his executive committee viewed the 1984 convention resolution as one that "gives us concern." He observed that in the Richmond Association sixty percent of the churches had "ordained women to serve as deacons; eight RBA churches have ordained women to the Gospel ministry." He then indicated that the association's executive committee "affirms the action and practice of its member churches in ordaining men and women. Our diversity has not been divisive."[58]

Actions of Baptist State Conventions. In their fall 1984 meetings, Baptist state conventions reacted variously to the SBC's June 1984 resolution that opposed women's ordination. At least three conventions, Arkansas, Louisiana, and Texas, considered resolutions of appreciation for women without mentioning ordination.

The Arkansas Baptist State Convention considered a resolution titled "Concerning the Equality of Men and Women before God." The fourth paragraph read: "BE IT FINALLY RESOLVED that we affirm that men and women share equally in carrying out the Great Commission of our Lord." An amendment to delete that paragraph was precluded by a motion to table the entire resolution; the motion to table carried.[59]

The Louisiana Baptist Convention objected to the Southern Baptist resolution and its implication "that womankind is responsible for the 'Edenic Fall,' thus placing the burden upon women, even Christian women, for the fall of man." The state convention messengers resolved to "reaffirm their confidence in our dedicated Christian women, assure them that we believe that every believer is equal at the foot of the cross and commend them for their inspired and loving service to our Lord and His church."[60]

---

[57]Michael J. Clingenpeel, letter to Charles Stanley (resolution attached), 13 September 1984.

[58]Charles B. Nunn, Jr., letter to Charles Stanley, 1 October 1984.

[59]*Annual*, Arkansas Baptist State Convention, 1984, 46, 50.

[60]*Annual*, Louisiana Baptist Convention, 1984, 201.

The Baptist General Convention of Texas adopted a positive resolution, with no negative connotations or attacks on the SBC resolution. It affirmed "that men and women share in the dignity of creation" and that "Jesus Christ by his attitude and actions affirmed the worth and dignity of women." It resolved to affirm women "in places of special service to which God has called them," and it encouraged "all Texas Baptists to continue to explore further opportunities of service for Baptist women, to ensure maximum utilization of all God-called servants of our Lord Jesus Christ."[61]

At least five other state conventions—District of Columbia, Georgia, Kentucky, North Carolina, and South Carolina—plus the Baptist General Association of Virginia, focused directly on the women's ordination issue. All six of these state bodies emphasized that the ordination of women was a decision to be made by the local church. The Georgia Baptist Convention stated its adopted resolution in one sentence: "We affirm the historic Baptist position that ordination is at the discretion of the local church under the leadership of God's spirit."[62] The other states reacted to the resolution in more detail.

A "whereas" statement in the District of Columbia Baptist Convention's adopted "Resolution on Ordination and Local Church Autonomy" expressed concern that "Application of pressure by other Baptist bodies with local church ordination is divisive and an encroachment upon this historic principle of Baptist polity [local-church autonomy]." Then it urged all Baptist bodies not to interfere in this function of the local church. More specifically, it called upon "all Baptist bodies to refrain from making ordination a test of fellowship or a factor in seating of delegates or messengers to associational, state, or national convention meetings."[63]

The Kentucky Baptist Convention's adopted resolution titled "Resolution on the Autonomy of the Local Church Regarding the Ordination of Women" simply affirmed "the complete autonomy of the local church." Later, the convention adopted a supplementary statement that read: "We affirm the role of women in the total service of the Kingdom of God."[64]

The Baptist State Convention of North Carolina reaffirmed previous resolutions on the same subject which it had adopted in 1975 and reaffirmed in 1983. The Committee on Resolutions acknowledged "the good

---

[61]*Annual*, Baptist General Convention of Texas, 1984, 74.
[62]*Annual*, Georgia Baptist Convention, 1984, 35.
[63]*Minutes*, District of Columbia Baptist Convention, 1984, 31.
[64]*Annual*, Kentucky Baptist Convention, 1984, 80, 98.

intentions of people on both sides of this issue." The resolution quoted Galatians 3:28, noted the dedicated service of women in Christian service, asserted that "the right of ordination lies within the jurisdiction of the local church," and resolved that "recognizing the freedom of conscience of the believer, affirms the right of the local church to ordain all persons who are called to a church-related ministry."[65]

The South Carolina Baptist Convention focused more heavily on local-church responsibility for ordination than the other conventions. After presenting its position in five "whereas" statements, the South Carolina resolution summarized its major thrust in its resolve that

> the matter of ordination affirming the calling of God of persons to specific places of service for and to the church, be left to the local church congregation; and that the leadership and messengers to the South Carolina Baptist Convention, remembering the purpose of the Convention is to promote missions at home and abroad for furtherance of the Kingdom of God, refrain from the temptation to seek to instruct local churches in matters of faith and practice.[66]

The Resolutions Committee of the Baptist General Association of Virginia adopted an untitled resolution that expressed firm belief "in the equality of privilege and responsibility of all believers in God and in His continuing call today to whomsoever He chooses to do His work, without regard for race, nationality or gender"; in the biblical claim that all have sinned; in soul competency; and in local-church autonomy. An amendment adopted as part of the resolution asserted "That we affirm the right and responsibility of women to engage in any ministry to which God has called them; and that any ordination in regard to the performance of these ministries be regarded as a matter of local church practice, not denominational policy."[67]

Conclusion

Many writers, such as Wayne Flynt and David Morgan, have carefully assessed women's issues in Baptist life in the 1980s and have reached similar conclusions. Flynt, in his definitive history of Southern Baptists in Alabama, detailed some affirmations of women's ordination as deacons and

---

[65]*Annual*, Baptist State Convention of North Carolina, 1984, 93.
[66]*Annual*, South Carolina Baptist Convention, 1984, 50.
[67]*Annual*, Baptist General Association of Virginia, 1984, 150-51.

ministers and some fundamentalist reactions to such ordination. He concluded that

> Such [fundamentalist] attitudes clashed with the predominant American cultural pattern of enlarging opportunity for women as well as the autonomy of local Baptist churches. With the SBC defining women's opportunities in ever diminishing ways . . . at the same time that churches were ordaining unprecedented numbers of women deacons and ministers, conflicts became inevitable.[68]

Morgan wrote in his book on Southern Baptist women's search for status that "Ordaining women as deacons was unacceptable to fundamentalists and other biblical literalists because [for them] ordination symbolized a bestowal of authority and because, they believed, the scriptures forbade women to exercise authority over men."[69]

As a result of these attitudes, women's issues became hotly contested topics in Baptist churches, associations, and conventions in the 1980s. Women's ordination lay at the center of the discussions. Using such ordination as a reason to separate from alleged liberals, Southern Baptist fundamentalists countered progressive cultural developments, which favored women's rights, by holding tightly to restrictive views of Genesis and the writings of the apostle Paul (to the neglect of the teachings of Jesus), applied biblical inerrancy in a fashion guaranteed to hurt women's opportunities as deacons and ministers, held firmly to masculine leadership in church life, created new organizations and publications to advance their cause, and set a standard of opposition for future Southern Baptist attitudes toward women.

Simultaneously, moderate Baptists listened to the calls for freedom by women in American culture, read the Bible through lenses of freedom, paid increasing attention to the views of Christ toward women, read the apostle Paul in more contextual fashion, advocated women's ordination, offered women new positions of leadership in church life, formed new structures and publishing outlets to support women's rights in the Christian life, created a new seminary to train women and men, and made it clear that

---

[68]Wayne Flynt, *Alabama Baptists: Southern Baptists in the Heart of Dixie* (Tuscaloosa: University of Alabama Press, 1998) 584.

[69]David T. Morgan, *Southern Baptist Sisters: In Search of Status, 1845-2000* (Macon GA: Mercer University Press, 2003) 167.

biblical Baptists might have to move into the future without the word "Southern."

These sharp contrasts and battles would characterize Southern Baptists as they moved into the 1990s. Meanwhile, Bold Mission Thrust, the SBC's effort to share the gospel to the whole world, was being shoved to the back of the denominational shelf. Besides, why would non-Christians want to listen to representatives of a denomination that exhibited so much discord?

Chapter 6

Women Deacon/Deaconess Trends, 1990–2005

During the period 1990–2005, rapid growth and continuing conflict characterized trends relating to women deacons. Women deacons expanded significantly in congregations related to the American Baptist Churches (ABC). To illustrate, the ABC of Massachusetts alone reported seventy-three churches with women deacon chairs in 2004.[1] In 2005, hundreds of churches in North Carolina and Virginia had women deacons. Many other states experienced numerical expansion as well, especially Georgia, South Carolina, and Texas.

In this chapter we will examine seven topics: increases in women deacons and chairs in 1990–2005; special advancements among Virginia Baptists; continuing opposition among most Southern Baptists; new resources advancing women's causes; the openness of American Baptist churches to women deacons; the black Baptist preference for deaconesses; and, briefly, patterns among the Seventh Day Baptists.

Two sets of contrasts set the tone for where this chapter is headed. First, a 1999 edition of the Texas Baptist Forum, a website of the *Baptist Standard*, Texas Baptists' largest newspaper, printed two contrasting letters to the editor relating to women deacons. Paul B. Taylor of Orange, Texas, wrote, "If a church is ordaining women as deacons, then it should repent and return again to the true faith, which the Holy Scriptures clearly teach." In contrast, Carey Moore of Waxahachie, Texas, wrote, "It is disgraceful that we, in our churches at the end of the 20th century, are still unable to extend to the woman the wide range of ministry those deserving women, such as Phoebe, were granted in Paul's day."[2]

Second, Baptists in other states contributed their own pros and cons. Mike L. McKinney, senior pastor of Leawood Baptist Church in Leawood, Kansas, wrote a pamphlet in 1998 titled "Why Women Deacons?" in which he presented a biblical and historical rationale for women deacons in

---

[1]Robert B. Wallace, letter to author, 5 October 2004.

[2]Texas Baptist Forum. <www.baptiststandard.com/1999/7_28/pages/letters.html>, accessed 27 August 2004.

Baptist churches. He concluded: "When deacons are truly servants, with Jesus as the model, then males and females share in the ministry. Each brings to the 'servant' ministry the uniqueness of his or her God-given gender and applies that uniqueness to the needs of the people whom he or she serves."[3] In contrast, Joda L. Collins, pastor of Kingwood Baptist Church in East Ridge, Tennessee, published *The Biblical Role of Women in the Church* (revised edition, 2001). Collins claimed that his book clarified "the biblical basis for male pastors and male leadership in the church," and he concluded that "women are not called of God (though congregations might hire them, against the will of God) to serve the church in any capacity that includes preaching, supervising men or teaching men."[4] Collins plainly excluded women deacons from church life.

Increase in Women Deacons/Chairs

The period from 1990 to 1995 witnessed an explosion in the number of women deacons and deacon chairs, especially in North Carolina and Virginia, and to a lesser degree in a few other states. Many Southern Baptist churches that aligned with the Cooperative Baptist Fellowship (CBF) showed significant interest in women deacons. The following presents evidences of these developments in several states.

Many churches elected and ordained women deacons for the first time. Twenty-one selected examples in ten states follow:

Georgia
    Tabernacle Baptist Church, Carrollton (1990)
    Briarcliff Baptist Church, Atlanta (early 1990s).
North Carolina
    Shiloh Baptist Church, Shiloh (1990)
    North Chapel Hill Baptist Church, Chapel Hill (1991).
South Carolina
    Shaws Fork Baptist Church, Aiken (1991)
    The Baptist Church of Beaufort, Beaufort (1998).
Texas
    First Baptist Church, Arlington (1991)
    Wilshire Baptist Church, Dallas (1991)
    Trinity Baptist Church, San Antonio (1994)

---

[3]Mike L. McKinney, "Why Women Deacons? A Biblical and Historical Rationale for Women Serving as Deacons in Baptist Churches," 1998.

[4]Joda L. Collins, e-mail to author, 10 September 2001.

First Baptist Church, Waco (1996)
First Baptist Church, Abilene (1997).
Virginia
Walnut Grove Baptist Church, Mechanicsville (1990)
Bon Air Baptist Church, Richmond (early 1990s)
First Baptist Church of City Point, Hopewell (1994)
Alum Spring Baptist Church, Culpeper (1999)
Angel's Rest Baptist Fellowship, Pearisburg (2001).
Churches in other states included
Oklahoma: Spring Creek Baptist Church, Oklahoma City (1993)
Tennessee: First Baptist Church, Memphis (1993)
Washington: Martin Luther King Jr. Memorial Baptist Church, Renton (1994)
Missouri: University Heights Baptist Church, Springfield (1995)
Florida: First Baptist Church, St. Petersburg (1999).

The most positive sign that Baptist churches with women deacons were willing to give them major positions of leadership focused on the election of numerous women deacons to serve as chairs of their deacon bodies. The appendix at the end of this book provides the names, cities/towns, and states of selected Baptist churches that either have or have had women to serve as chairs or cochairs of deacon bodies since the early 1960s. This representative list includes 292 churches in twenty-five states, the District of Columbia, and Nova Scotia. The leading states are North Carolina with seventy-eight, Virginia with sixty-six, and Georgia with thirty-one. The actual number of such churches is unknown because of the difficulty involved in securing this information. Undoubtedly, hundreds more churches have or have had women deacon chairs. Since the number of churches with women deacons that have not yet had a female chair is much larger than the number that have, it is likely that thousands of Baptist churches, nationwide and worldwide, have women deacons.

North Carolina and Virginia led the way in electing women deacon chairs, but a few other states began to join the forward progress. Because of the significance of this development, sixty-two examples follow from eleven states, including twenty-three in North Carolina, eighteen in Virginia, eight in Georgia, three each in South Carolina and Texas, two in Missouri, and one each in Kansas, Louisiana, Maryland, Oklahoma, and Washington. Churches who chose their first woman deacon chairs during 1990–2005 included

North Carolina
    First Baptist Church, Greensboro (1990)
    Knightdale Baptist Church, Knightdale (1990)
    Masonboro Baptist Church, Wilmington (1990)
    First Baptist Church, Sanford (1992)
    Immanuel Baptist Church, Greenville (1993)
    Park View Baptist Church, Durham (1993)
    First Baptist Church, Mt. Gilead (1996)
    First Baptist Church, Gastonia (1997)
    First Baptist Church, Sylva (1997)
    North Chapel Hill Baptist Church, Chapel Hill (1997)
    College Park Baptist Church, Winston-Salem (1998)
    First Baptist Church, Winston-Salem (1998)
    Forest Hills Baptist Church, Raleigh (1998)
    First Baptist Church, Morganton (1999)
    Weldon Baptist Church, Weldon (1999)
    Warrenton Baptist Church, Warrenton (2000)
    Shiloh Baptist Church, Shiloh (2001)
    First Baptist Church, Hickory (2002)
    Arlington Boulevard Baptist Church, Greenville (2003)
    First Baptist Church, Marion (2003)
    First Baptist Church, Kannapolis (2004)
    Roxboro Baptist Church, Roxboro (2004)
    Warsaw Baptist Church, Warsaw (2004)
Virginia
    Trinity Baptist Church, Norfolk (1990)
    University Baptist Church, Charlottesville (1990)
    Bon Air Baptist Church, Richmond (1994)
    Cedar Run Baptist Church, Culpeper (1995)
    Effort Baptist Church, Palmyra (1995)
    Walnut Grove Baptist Church, Mechanicsville (1995)
    Hampton Baptist Church, Hampton (1996)
    Parkwood Baptist Church, Annandale (1996)
    First Baptist Church of Clarendon, Arlington (1998)
    Richland Baptist Church, Hartwood (1999)
    Westhunt Baptist Church, Richmond (2000)
    Abingdon Baptist Church, Abingdon (2001)
    Ginter Park Baptist Church, Richmond (2001)
    Alum Spring Baptist Church, Culpeper (2002)
    Calvary Baptist Church, Fairfax (2002)
    Angel's Rest Baptist Fellowship, Pearisburg (2003)
    Marlow Heights Baptist Church, Front Royal (2004)

Rivermont Baptist Church, Danville (2004)
Georgia
    First Baptist Church, Roswell (2001)
    Smoke Rise Baptist Church, Stone Mountain (2001)
    Carlton Baptist Church, Carlton (2002)
    Tabernacle Baptist Church, Carrollton (2002)
    Briarcliff Baptist Church, Atlanta (2003)
    First Baptist Church, Forsyth (2003)
    First Baptist Church of Christ at Macon (2003)
    First Baptist Church, Gainesville (2004)
Texas
    First Baptist Church, Austin (1992)
    Wilshire Baptist Church, Dallas (1994)
    First Baptist Church, Arlington (1999)
South Carolina
    Shaws Fork Baptist Church, Aiken (1996)
    First Baptist Church, Pendleton (1998)
    Boulevard Baptist Church, Anderson (2000)
Missouri
    First Baptist Church, Jefferson City (1997)
    University Heights Baptist Church, Springfield (1998)
Oklahoma: Spring Creek Baptist Church, Oklahoma City (1994)
Louisiana: University Baptist Church, Baton Rouge (1995)
Washington: Martin Luther King Memorial Baptist Church, Renton (1997)
Kansas: Leawood Baptist Church, Leawood (2004)
Maryland: First Baptist Church, Wheaton (2004)

A remarkable story emerged in the Southern Baptist-related Metropolitan New York Baptist Association. Between 1970 and 1995, seven women served as deacon chairs in this association.[5]

Many churches elected women as deacon chairs on more than one occasion. Each of the following nineteen selected churches in eight states and one Canadian province has elected women to serve as deacon chairs five or more times, including six in North Carolina, five in Virginia, two in Texas, and one each in Georgia, Kentucky, Massachusetts, Mississippi, Tennessee, and Nova Scotia, namely,

North Carolina
    College Park Baptist Church, Greensboro

---

[5]DeLane M. Ryals, "Southern Baptist Women Ministering in Metro New York, 1970-1995," *Baptist History and Heritage* 39/2 (Spring 2004): 91.

First Baptist Church, Elkin
First Baptist Church, Raleigh
Louisburg Baptist Church, Louisburg
Park View Baptist Church, Durham
Pullen Memorial Baptist Church, Raleigh
Virginia
      Berea Baptist Church, Rockville
      First Baptist Church, Winchester
      Franklin Baptist Church, Franklin
      River Road Baptist Church, Richmond
      University Baptist Church, Charlottesville
Texas
      First Baptist Church, Austin
      Second Baptist Church, Lubbock
Georgia: Fellowship Baptist Church, Americus
Kentucky: Faith Baptist Church, Georgetown
Massachusetts: West Acton Baptist Church, Acton
Mississippi: Northside Baptist Church, Jackson
Tennessee: First Baptist Church, Jefferson City
Nova Scotia: First Baptist Church, Halifax

Pertinent facts emerged concerning women deacon chairs, church policies relating to women deacons, and women deacons in general. Five relate to Texas churches. Calvary Baptist Church in Waco, by unwritten policy, alternates male and female chairs every other year.[6] In 2000, a husband-wife team served as cochairs of the deacon body of the Second Baptist Church in Lubbock. By 2004, eight women had served as chair or cochair of the deacon body.[7] The First Baptist Church of Austin ordained its first women deacons in 1974, elected thirty-six women deacons by 2001, elected its first female deacon chair in 1992,[8] and elected five more female chairs by 2004.[9] Jane Archer Feinstein, deacon chair in 2004, reported that sixteen of the church's fifty deacons in 2004 were women. Feinstein

---

[6]Sharyn E. Dowd, e-mail to author, 23 April 2004.

[7]Michelle Doss, e-mail to author, 23 April 2004 and 24 August 2004; Stephanie Nash, e-mail to Philip Wise, 7 September 2004 (forwarded by Philip Wise to author, 8 September 2004).

[8]*Into His Marvelous Light: 150 Year History of First Baptist Church, Austin, Texas* (Austin: First Baptist Church, 2001) 84, 97, 177-78.

[9]Jane Archer Feinstein, letter to author, 3 September 2004.

dreamed about 2005: "For our next year I'd like to make the roster one-half women and one-half men. It's doable."[10]

In November 1990, the First Baptist Church in Arlington, Texas, adopted, via five separate votes, five recommendations from its Deacon Qualification Study Committee. The third recommendation read: "We recommend that the opportunity to serve as deacons be open to those men and women who best meet the church-approved Guidelines for Deacons." This recommendation was adopted by a vote of 800 to 239, and was the church's first time to approve women deacons. Then in March 1991, the Deacon Ordination Committee reported to the deacons that eleven new deacons would serve that year, including women. In April, Pastor Charles Wade welcomed Sondra Adair, Ellen Bunkley, and Carma McCollum to their first deacons meeting.[11]

First Baptist Church in Waco, Texas, ordained its first women deacons in 1996. "The church, once seen as socially conservative, has moved rapidly to elect many more women to this leadership position."[12] Anita Rolf served as a deacon, and in 2000 she served on the Deacon Selection Committee and was delighted to be a part of the process that elected not only women deacons but also the church's first black and Hispanic deacons. Roth stated that "That was important to me. Empowering women has paved the way to empowering others."[13]

Other findings related to six North Carolina churches. Pullen Memorial Baptist Church in Raleigh has had women deacons, not deaconesses, since 1927.[14] Between 1972 and 2003, ten women served thirteen terms as deacon chair.[15] Rita Blackmon served as deacon chair at Knightdale Baptist Church for three terms: 1999–2000, 2002–2003, and 2003–2004.[16] The deacon body of Ridge Road Baptist Church in Raleigh, during a two-year period of the current pastorate of Mack Thompson, elected women to

---

[10]Ibid.

[11]George Watson, "A Case Study of the Decision by First Baptist Church, Arlington, Texas, to Elect Women Deacons" (D.Min. thesis project, Bethel Theological Seminary, 2000) 175-77.

[12]William Pitts, " 'We Need You to Serve': Establishing Women Deacons at First Baptist Church, Waco, 1996" (unpublished manuscript, 2001) 1. (The manuscript will be published by Paternoster in 2005.)

[13]Ibid., 12.

[14]Roger H. Crook, e-mail to author, 25 August 2004.

[15]Roger H. Crook, e-mail to author, 8 September, 2004.

[16]Rita Blackmon, e-mail to author, 5 May 2004.

occupy all three offices: chair, vice-chair, and secretary.[17] First Baptist Church in Lenoir has three women deacons classified as Life Deacons.[18] The bylaws of First Baptist Church in Mount Airy specify that the deacon body should consist of eighteen men and eighteen women.[19]

While serving several years ago as a deacon in the Boiling Springs Baptist Church in Boiling Springs, North Carolina, Kathryn Hamrick gave birth to her fourth son. Her pastor, T. Max Linnens, commented that it was the first time he had ever visited one of his deacons in a maternity ward. Hamrick later served as deacon chair. Then in the 1990s, she served three terms as president of the general board and chairman of the executive committee of the Baptist State Convention of North Carolina—the only woman ever to do so. She later served two years as first vice president of the state convention.[20] Hamrick typified many women deacons who exerted heavy influence in the larger Baptist community.

Second Baptist Church in Petersburg, Virginia, first ordained women to the diaconate in 1950 (they were known as deaconesses until 2001). They met in plenary session with the deacons but had their own assignments and officers. Since a merger of the two bodies in 2001, three women have served as chair. The church's bylaws stipulate that an equal number of men and women serve in the active deacon body.[21] In the fall of 1997, First Baptist Church, Greenville, South Carolina, ordained a woman deacon whose mother had been ordained a deacon twelve years earlier and whose grandmother had been ordained in 1975 as one of the church's first three women deacons.[22]

In 2004, Frank Broome, director of the CBF of Georgia, provided a list of twelve selected churches in Georgia that either had or had had female deacon chairs: Carlton Baptist Church, Carlton; Cave Springs Baptist Church, Cave Springs; Fellowship Baptist Church, Americus; First Baptist Churches of Gainesville, Macon, Morrow, and Savannah; Highland Hills Baptist Church, Macon; Memorial Baptist Church, Savannah; North River

---

[17]Mack Thompson, e-mail to author, 5 May 2004.
[18]David Smith, e-mail to author, 12 October 2004.
[19]Roger Gilbert, e-mail to author, 27 April 2004.
[20]Kathryn Hamrick, e-mail to author, 5 May 2004.
[21]Joe Lewis, e-mail to author, 27 October 2004.
[22]"Deacon Generations," *Fellowship!* (March 1998), 13.

Baptist Church, Alpharetta; Northside Drive Baptist Church, Atlanta; and Oakhurst Baptist Church, Decatur.[23]

Virginia Baptists: A Case Study in Forward Progress

Virginia, like North Carolina, has a long history of giving women more opportunities as deacons and deaconesses than other states in the South. This special look at women deacons in Virginia begins with an examination of an article on women deacons and leadership written by Mike Clingenpeel, distinguished editor of the *Religious Herald*, followed by a review of attacks on that article by T. C. Pinckney, a prominent Virginia Baptist fundamentalist. This section will continue by sharing brief information about a statement on the dignity of women adopted by the Woman's Missionary Union of Virginia. It will conclude with a detailed look at the forward progress of women deacons in Virginia as represented in one key church and eleven Baptist associations.

In the 23 March 2000 issue of the *Religious Herald*, Virginia Baptists' leading newspaper, Editor Mike Clingenpeel titled his editorial "The Changing Face of Leadership." Citing a study by Rolen Bailey, a Virginia Baptist leader, Clingenpeel observed that the number of Virginia Baptist churches with women deacons had doubled since 1984. Whereas 150 churches had women deacons in 1984, 363 had them in 1999. Further, thirty-seven more churches had approved having women deacons, but none had active women deacons at the time. Churches with women deacons existed in all but five Virginia Baptist district associations. These churches included all membership sizes and geographic locations.[24]

Clingenpeel noted that a majority of Virginia Baptists had not ordained women deacons, but he pointed out that "as the 21st century opens . . . the trend in Virginia Baptist churches is moving steadily toward inclusion of women in the diaconate." Further, "Virginia Baptists wisely have not allowed ordination of women as deacons to become a test of fellowship."[25]

T. C. Pinckney used Clingenpeel's comments about women deacons to establish a critical difference between churches related to the Baptist General Association of Virginia (BGAV) and the more recent fundamentalist convention, Southern Baptist Conservatives of Virginia (SBCV). For

---

[23]Frank Broome, e-mail to author, 8 May 2004.

[24]Mike Clingenpeel, "The Changing Face of Leadership," *Religious Herald* (23 March 2000): 8.

[25]Ibid.

Pinckney, the growing presence of women deacons in the BGAV and the absence of them in the SBCV represented a distinction "springing from different understandings of the Bible." Therefore, he admonished that "if your church has or intends to have women deacons, stay with the BGAV, for you would not be accepted in the SBCV or happy if accepted." In a final salvo, Pinckney accused Clingenpeel of placing "human impressions or judgment ahead of biblical guidance, and he buys into the current post-modern approach that there is no absolute standard except the absolute standard of accepting anything."[26]

On 11 September 2004, the Trustee and Advisory Board of the Woman's Missionary Union of Virginia adopted a "Declaration of the Dignity of Women." This statement declared that "women *are* leaders in the church, called by God, commissioned by Christ, led by the Holy Spirit, with a strong, noble heritage," and "that we reject any devaluation of women worldwide." The document observed that women comprised the core of the earliest New Testament churches, even serving as deacons.[27]

A fascinating case study and story of women deacon developments in one Virginia Baptist church centers in the University Baptist Church in Charlottesville. Howard Newlon, historian of this church, provided a detailed account of such developments. By 2004, the church had elected thirty women deacons, the first ones having been chosen in 1974. These women had served as deacons for a total of eighty-four years, since twenty of them had served between two and seven three-year terms. Between 1974 and 2004, forty-one percent of all deacons elected were women; that increased to forty-eight percent in 1999–2004. The deacons elected their first female deacon chair in 1990. "Since then six women have served [as chair], one having served twice. Four of the last five chairs have been women. In addition, two women have been elected 'Deacon Emeritus.' " Newlon observed that women had served as deacons for thirty years "on an equal basis with men and in many other traditionally 'male' roles."[28]

In addition to electing women deacons, University Baptist Church also ordained four women for the pastoral ministry, in 1982, 1983, 1992, and

---

[26]T. C. Pinckney, "BGAV Direction," *The Baptist Banner* (May 2000). <www.thebaptistbanner.com/archive/500%20BGAV%20Direction.htm>, accessed 14 November 2004.

[27]"Declaration of the Dignity of Women," *Religious Herald* (23 September 2004): 8.

[28]Howard Newlon, Jr., letter to author, 8 September 2004.

1996. One of the factors causing the church to relate to the CBF was the church's negative reaction to the SBC's 1984 adoption of a resolution opposing the ordination of women. On the Sunday following that SBC action, the church used only women deacons to receive the offering. Newlon asserted with pride that "Clearly with regard to deacons UBC is an 'equal opportunity employer' and I'm convinced that because of that we are greatly blessed."[29]

Thirteen directors of missions or other staff members of Virginia Baptist associations shared valuable information regarding women deacons, or the absence of them. Directors of two associations, the Blue Ridge Association and the Clinch Valley Association, indicated that none of their churches had women deacons.[30] Directors of missions of eleven other associations provided names of churches that to their knowledge had women deacons, female deacon chairs, and deaconesses in the present or past. Some shared the names of churches with women deacons but did not tell whether any of them had female chairs; others shared only the names of churches they knew to have female chairs. In certain cases, some churches not listed as having female chairs actually had or had had one or more; they are listed in the appendix.

Reporting associations included the following: Blackwater (thirteen churches with women deacons; four with female chairs); Highlands (seven churches with women deacons); Lebanon (four churches with women deacons; one with a female chair); Mid-Tidewater (three churches with women deacon chairs); Peninsula (seven churches with women deacons; three with female chairs); Petersburg (eight churches with women deacons); Portsmouth (five churches with women deacons; one with a female chair); Richmond (provided six examples of churches with women deacons or deaconesses but stated that "Most of our churches have women deacons. Some may call them deacons or deaconesses but they all fill the same role in our churches." These deaconesses "are ordained and participate in the work of the Board of Deacons and serve the Lord's Supper"); Shiloh (eight churches with women deacons); Strawberry (five churches with women deacons; one with a female chair); and Wise (three churches with women deacons).[31] This list included sixty-nine churches with women

---

[29]Ibid.

[30]Wayne Hannah (Blue Ridge), telephone call to author, 14 October 2004; Jerry Hall (Clinch Valley), e-mail to author, 13 October 2004.

[31]Nancy C. Greene (Blackwater), e-mail to author, 23 November 2004; David

deacons plus the Richmond Association's claim that most of its churches had women deacons or deaconesses, even though it provided only six examples. This sampling of Virginia associations proves that numerous Virginia Baptist churches include women in the diaconate.

Continuing Opposition among Most Southern Baptists

Between 1990 and 2005, the SBC essentially declared war against churches with women deacons through a constant flow of actions supporting its 1984 resolution opposing women's ordination. The 1998 edition of the Baptist Faith and Message added a new section on "The Family." One sentence in that new section read: "A wife is to submit herself graciously to the servant leadership of her husband."[32] The concept of submission, critical to the fundamentalist mindset, both further retarded Southern Baptist views of women and resulted in significant opposition from Baptists who prefer to treat women with more dignity. Then the SBC's adopted revision of the Baptist Faith and Message in 2000 added a new sentence to the original 1963 article on "The Church": "While both men and women are gifted for service in the church, the office of pastor is limited to men as qualified by Scripture."[33] That assertion included continuing implications for ordained women deacons.

The North American Mission Board took two key actions affecting women. In 2002, NAMB decided that it would no longer endorse as chaplains women who had been ordained,[34] and in 2004, NAMB adopted a document that both attacked ordained women deacons and implied that

---

Plott (Highlands), letter to author, 12 May 2004; Dave Stancil (Lebanon), e-mail to author, 12 October 2004; John Patterson (Mid-Tidewater), telephone call to author, 19 October 2004; Donna Williams (Peninsula), e-mail to author, 2 November 2004; G. C. Harbuck (Petersburg); e-mail to author, 22 October 2004; Lue English (Portsmouth), e-mail to author, 29 October 2004; Norman Burnes (Richmond), e-mails to author, 15 October 2004 and 19 October 2004; Lanny Horton (Shiloh), fax to author, 12 November 2004; Esther O. Woodford (Strawberry), 7 October 2004; and Lee Kidd (Wise), e-mail to author, 27 October 2004.

[32]*Annual*, Southern Baptist Convention, 1998, 78.

[33]"Report of the Baptist Faith and Message Study Committee to the Southern Baptist Convention, Adopted June 14th, 2000." <www.sbc.net/2000-bf_m.html>, accessed 2 April 2002.

[34]James Dotson, "NAMB will no longer endorse ordained female chaplains," Baptist Press (8 February 2002).

churches with women deacons would no longer be eligible to receive NAMB funds to use in starting new churches.[35] The Fall 2004 issue of *The Whitsitt Journal* printed a cartoon relating to the latter action in which a woman said, "Hey Doc! Did you hear that the SBC is not going to allow their new churches to have women deacons?" Doc responded, "That's okay. Women can still be deacons in biblically based churches."[36]

Since the early 1900s, the Southern Baptist Sunday School Board (now LifeWay Christian Resources) has consciously excluded explicit support for ordained women deacons in its published pastor and church manuals[37] and in key books on deacons,[38] of which millions of copies have sold. LifeWay handbooks, resource books, training kits, planning guides, audiotapes, videotapes, CDs, and DVDs on deacon ministries have typically refused to promote women deacons.

To illustrate how women deacons began to be squelched in Sunday School Board literature, *Search* published an article in 1990 by Robert Sheffield, the board's national deacon consultant, titled "A Historical Look at Deacon Ministry"; the article did not mention women deacons. Earlier articles on deacons in *Search* had mentioned them.

In 1990, the Sunday School Board also published Sheffield's book, *The Ministry of Baptist Deacons*. In evaluating 1 Timothy 3:11, Sheffield asserted that "this verse refers to the wives of deacons." He stated that

---

[35]Martin King, "NAMB trustees meet, approve guidelines for church starts." <www.baptistpress.com> (7 October 2004), accessed 20 October 2004. See also Stan Norman, "Ecclesiological Guidelines to Inform Southern Baptist Church Planters." <www.namb.net/news/guidelines> (28 September 2004), accessed 20 October 2004.

[36]Weaver/Yarber, "Hey Doc!!" *The Whitsitt Journal* 12/2 (Fall 2004): 24.

[37]See, e.g., J. R. Hobbs, *The Pastor's Manual* (Nashville: Broadman Press, 1934; 17th printing, 1947); Franklin M. Segler, *The Broadman Minister's Manual* (Nashville: Broadman Press, 1969); and Howard B. Foshee, *Broadman Church Manual* (Nashville: Broadman Press, 1973).

[38]See, e.g., P. E. Burroughs, *Honoring the Deaconship* (Nashville: Sunday School Board of the Southern Baptist Convention, 1929; rev. ed. 1936); Robert E. Naylor, *The Baptist Deacon* (Nashville: Broadman Press, 1955); Howard B. Foshee, *The Ministry of the Deacon* (Nashville: Convention Press, 1968); idem, *Now That You're a Deacon* (Nashville: Broadman Press, 1975); Henry Webb, *Deacons: Servant Models in the Church* (Nashville: Convention Press, 1980); and Robert Sheffield, *The Ministry of Baptist Deacons*, ed. Gary Hardin (Nashville: Convention Press, 1990; repr. 1993).

"Many churches in the Southern Baptist Convention have women serving as deacons. Most do not." He concluded that "the decision whether to elect women as deacons is a local church decision."[39] Like all the major books published on deacons in the twentieth century by the Sunday School Board, Sheffield's book did not explicitly advocate women deacons.

Attitudes of selected Southern Baptist state convention executive directors and others provide insights into Southern Baptist approaches to women deacons. Jim Wideman, executive director of the Baptist Convention of New England, noted in 2004 that he knew of three Baptist churches in New England with women deacons. However, the topic of women deacons "is not an issue in New England churches. Most of our churches do not have women deacons, but if they did, in 5 of our 7 associations, it would not become an issue."[40] Writing for David Waltz, executive director of the Baptist Convention of Pennsylvania/New Jersey, Glenna Hegenbart indicated an awareness of two convention churches with women deacons. Generally, "Most churches don't have women as deacons and would not consider them for that job. But there is a tolerance for those churches that may choose to have women deacons."[41]

Leaders of a Baptist general association and of two state conventions in some midwestern states observed that Southern Baptists typically exhibited reluctance to use women deacons in those areas. William L. Weedman, senior associate executive director of the Illinois Baptist State Association, shared that in the Illinois Baptist General Association "I can convey with certainty that women deacons in our Anglo churches are a non-issue. I do not know of any Anglo churches that have women deacons. However, there may be some African-American churches in our state that have women deacons."[42] Jimmy L. Ballentine, executive director of the Baptist Convention of Iowa, knew of only one church in his convention with women deacons, although he indicated that "Iowa has strong advocates for both women's rights and for the autonomy of the local church."[43] R. Rex Lindsay, executive director of the Kansas-Nebraska Convention of

---

[39]Sheffield, *The Ministry of Baptist Deacons*, 43-44.
[40]Jim Wideman, e-mail to author, 27 September 2004.
[41]Glenna Hegenbart (for David Waltz), e-mail to author, 29 September 2004.
[42]William L. Weedman, letter to author, 28 October 2004.
[43]Jimmy L. Ballentine, e-mail to author, 11 October 2004.

Southern Baptists, knew of two churches in his convention with women deacons but claimed: "Status of women as deacons—not very receptive."[44]

Women deacons are few in number in western states; however, several Oklahoma churches and even more Texas churches elect and ordain them. In an article titled "Should We Have Women Deacons?" published in a 1975 issue of the *Baptist New Mexican*, R. A. Long, said no.[45] In a similar article in 1981, J. B. Fowler, editor of the *Baptist New Mexican*, wrote that deaconesses were acceptable as long as they were not ordained.[46] An official history of New Mexico Southern Baptists, released in 2002, pointed out that "some Baptist churches in New Mexico have had deaconesses";[47] however, the writer did not mention ordained women deacons.

In several states, Baptist associations continued to get agitated over churches with women deacons. In 1997, in the Tuckaseigee Association in North Carolina, associational unity was threatened over several issues, including churches with women deacons. The association appointed a committee that year to study the issues and make recommendations. After many meetings, the committee recommended to the association in 1999 that it remain unified, affirm local-church autonomy, and cultivate respect for diverse views on sensitive issues. Thus, the association adopted a "peace plan."[48]

Similarly, in February 2004, the executive council of the Concord Baptist Association in Missouri voted unanimously not to take action against the First Baptist Church of Jefferson City, which had ordained women deacons for many years. The special meeting and vote resulted from the fact that Roy Dameron, a member of the Concord Baptist Church in Jefferson City (but not a member of the executive council), had asked permission to speak during the council's regular January 2004 meeting during which he had asked the association to take a stand against women's ordination.[49]

---

[44]R. Rex Lindsay, e-mail to author, 7 October 2004.

[45]R. A. Long, "Should We Have Women Deacons?" *Baptist New Mexican* (26 June 1975): 6.

[46]J. B. Fowler, "As I See It," *Baptist New Mexican* (12 September 1981): 2.

[47]Daniel R. Carnett, *Contending for the Faith: Southern Baptists in New Mexico, 1938-1995* (Albuquerque: University of New Mexico Press, 2002) 142.

[48]Tony W. Cartledge, "Tuckaseigee Association Adopts Peace Plan," *Biblical Recorder News* (29 October 1999). <www.biblicalrecorder.org/news/10_29_99/ tuckaseigee.html>, accessed 27 August 2004.

[49]Doyle Sager, "Concord Baptist Association." <www.missouribaptists.org/

New Resources Advancing Women's Causes

To advance the cause of Baptist women, including the ordination of women deacons and ministers, and to counter growing Southern Baptist opposition, Baptists have produced many valuable publications. Several examples follow.

First, in 1990, Samford University Press released a book with an international perspective containing the papers of the Study and Research Division of the Baptist World Alliance for 1986–1990. This volume contained several papers on Baptist women presented to the BWA commissions on Baptist Heritage, Christian Ethics, and Human Rights.[50]

Second, in 1993, Mercer University Press released *The Struggle for the Soul of the SBC: Moderate Responses to the Fundamentalist Controversy*, edited by Walter B. Shurden. This book detailed many developments relating to women. Two items had special significance. One was the essay by Libby Bellinger, "The History of Southern Baptist Women in Ministry." The other was "An Address to the Public from the Interim Steering Committee of the Cooperative Baptist Fellowship," adopted on 9 May 1991 and prepared by Cecil E. Sherman and Walter B. Shurden. This document detailed differences between the CBF and the SBC by focusing on six topics: the Bible, education, mission, pastor, women, and church. The discussion of women ended with the simple statement: "Our model for the role of women in matters of faith is the Lord Jesus."[51]

Third, in 2000, *Christian Ethics Today* published an article titled "Women in the Southern Baptist Convention," by William E. Hull, research professor at Samford University. This profound article contained some of the same biblical material that had appeared in his earlier article, "Woman

---

content/ConcordAssociation02292004.htm>, accessed 27 August 2004.

[50]William H. Brackney, ed., *Faith, Life, and Witness: The Papers of the Study and Research Division of the Baptist World Alliance, 1986–1990* (Birmingham AL: Samford University Press, 1990). See the following essays: "The Ministry of Women in the Baptist Churches of the USSR," by Heather Vose, 129-38; "Women of the Southern Baptist Convention," by Eljee Bentley, 138-46; "Women's Issues," by Beth H. MacClaren, 215-27; and "Baptists and 'Freedom of Expression without Distinction as to . . . Sex,' " by Shirley F. Bentall, 275-86.

[51]Walter B. Shurden, ed., *The Struggle for the Soul of the SBC: Moderate Responses to the Fundamentalist Movement* (Macon GA: Mercer University Press, 1993) 266. These two items appear in complete form on 129-50 and 309-14.

in Her Place: Biblical Perspectives," published twenty-five years earlier in the Winter 1975 issue of *Review and Expositor*. (In chapter 1, this earlier article is described in some detail.) However, two major additions included Hull's initial section on the implications of the 1998 and 2000 SBC actions relating to women, and his final section on gender equality in church life. Hull concluded his revised article with a challenge:

> Traditions die hard in the Deep South, none more so than stereotypes regarding the role of women. But remember that women such as Lydia and Priscilla and Phoebe came into their own and furnished crucial leadership to the early church in ways that would have been impossible in the Jewish, Greek, or Roman religions of that day. How ironic! The first-century church, despite all of the *limitations* placed on women by its culture, was *ahead* of its time whereas the twenty-first century church, despite all of the *opportunities* offered to women by its culture, is in danger of falling *behind* its time. Let us resolve to change provincial Southern traditions at least as much as the early church changed provincial Palestinian traditions in the spirit of the Christ who offers spiritual freedom and equality to all who follow him.[52]

Fourth, *Putting Women in Their Place: Moving Beyond Gender Stereotypes in Church and Home*, edited by Audra Trull and Joe Trull, was published in 2003. Hull's article, which had appeared in *Christian Ethics Today* in 2000, also appeared as the first essay in this book. The book contained twelve essays by Baptist men and women, including an Old Testament scholar, a New Testament scholar, a theologian, a Baptist historian, pastors, and others.[53]

Examples of other books supporting rights for Baptist women included *What the Bible Really Says about Women* (Smyth and Helwys Publishing, 1994) by Sheri Adams; *Women's Place in Baptist Life* (Baptist History and Heritage Society, 2003) by Carolyn D. Blevins; and *Southern Baptist Sisters: In Search of Status, 1845–2000* (Mercer University Press, 2003) by David T. Morgan.

---

[52]William E. Hull, "Women and the Southern Baptist Convention," *Christian Ethics Today* 6/4 (August 2000). <www.christianethicstoday.com/Issue/029/Issue%20029_August_2000.htm>, accessed 27 August 2004.

[53]Audra and Joe Trull, eds., *Putting Women in Their Place: Moving beyond Gender Stereotypes in Church and Home* (Macon GA: Smyth and Helwys, 2003).

American Baptist Openness

Historically, American Baptists have generally been more open than Southern Baptists to deaconesses, women deacons, and women in ministry. As one significant illustration, the American Baptist Historical Society devoted the December 1994 issue of its journal, *American Baptist Quarterly*, to a series of articles on women in ministry among American Baptists and Freewill Baptists.

More recent observations of two key American Baptist pastors add specific understanding to the deacon practices of American Baptist churches. Everett C. Goodwin, pastor of the Scarsdale Community Baptist Church in Scarsdale, New York, claimed in 2004 that his present deacon chair was a woman, as was her predecessor. He added, "It is my sense that a great many American Baptist Churches have had female [deacon] chairs, especially in the last fifteen years." Further,

> By now, in churches where there is a single board, roles are essentially undifferentiated. Many Diaconates are subdivided into working committees to organize communion, worship, care-giving, hospitality, etc., etc. From my perspective, those placed on such committees or serving as chairs of them are usually selected for their interest or ability—a kind of "service by gift" rather than by gender selection.
>
> In my present church, for example, one woman who has a real interest, combined with a very nurturing personality, requested the opportunity to serve on the membership care committee. Likewise, a woman is chair of the missions committee because of both interest and administrative ability. Generally speaking, I believe that most American Baptist churches which have male/female combined boards generally select both board leadership and specific committee leadership according to talent, experience, and availability. Availability is very important, of course, since most American Baptist churches have a larger number of women as active members than men.
>
> Regarding the serving of communion or ushering for worship, men and women are scheduled equally. Very often in my present church a combination of men and women service the communion elements. Sometimes it might be all women. Other times (though more rarely!) it might be all men. I think this is becoming more frequent and typical.[54]

---

[54]Everett Goodwin, e-mail to author, 8 May 2004.

Ron Freyer Nicholas, who has served since 1984 as senior pastor of several American Baptist churches in Massachusetts, Iowa, Utah, California, Wisconsin, and Michigan, offered the following assessment of American Baptist practices, concluding with a special focus on his current church, the Michigan Avenue Baptist Church in Saginaw, Michigan, where he and his wife Inga serve as copastors.

Having grown up in Virginia as a Southern Baptist, then becoming American Baptist in 1974 at age 26, I had a difficult couple of years relearning what it meant to "be Baptist" the ABC way. It was a time that ABCUSA had just changed its national and regional structures and that many local churches were also rethinking many ways of living as "Christians of the American Baptist persuasion." As 1980 approached, the ABC church I had joined (and many other ABC churches as well) rewrote their church constitutions to include . . . [a] huge advance [regarding deaconesses]. . . .

They abolished the office of "deaconess." Afterward, there were only deacons, male and female, serving together in one Diaconate, with one chair. The chair could be either gender, without prejudice. ABC churches, generally, do not ordain deacons, so there are precious few ordaining/commissioning services extant, I suppose. In many, if not most, ABC churches, "deacons" are a board of the church but not THE board, and are elected to fixed terms of two or three years, just as any other board in the church. In this model the Diaconate are the "caring committee" working as pastoral assistants, rather than the governing board of a church, and definitely NOT as supervisors of the pastor's work. . . .

Many ABC churches have language in their constitutions/by-laws respecting nondiscrimination. This one [Michigan Avenue Baptist Church] does. Ours is in the by-laws and says: "It is the policy of this church not to discriminate in any manner (race, gender, marital status, etc.) in the hiring, election, appointment, call, or retaining, of any person to any position of leadership or service except as membership or legal age conditions specified in these By-Laws may apply. The only criteria shall be an individual's availability, ability, and competency to do a specified job."

Of course this policy applies to the election and call of pastors and deacons, as well as all elected/appointed positions in the life of this church. Many, if not most, ABC churches operate with an IMPLICIT policy of nondiscrimination, even if they don't have one stated EXPLICITLY in their governance documents.

Over the years, as I have consulted with many constitution/bylaws revision committees, I have advocated (usually successfully) for inclusion an EXPLICIT statement of these two positions.[55]

In 2004, the executive ministers of five regions in the ABC provided valuable information regarding the status of women deacons in their respective geographical areas. Robert B. Wallace, interim executive minister of the ABC of Massachusetts, stated: "Generally our churches welcome women deacons." An annual report from sixty-five percent of the 290 churches in the ABC of Massachusetts "revealed 175 deacon chairpersons, of whom 102 were men and 73 were women." Wallace indicated that both of the region's Native American churches had women deacon chairs: The Gay Head Community Baptist Church in Vineyard Haven, Massachusetts, and the Mashpee Baptist Church in Mashpee, Massachusetts.[56]

Two churches in the ABC of Massachusetts supplied information as well. Heather Hawkins, deacon chair in First Baptist Church of Jamaica Plain, reported in 2004 that deacons in her church were not ordained. Further, her pastor was a woman.[57] Jeff Long-Middleton, pastor of the West Acton Baptist Church in Acton, reported that his church voted in April 1946 to include three deaconesses on the deacon board.[58] However, the church has "never 'ordained' either women or men deacons." Further, "Our church has had several female chairpersons of the Board of Deacons. Indeed, over the past 14 years, I think they have all been female." He added that women serving as deacons is "largely a nonissue within the American Baptist circles that I frequent."[59]

Alan G. Newton, executive minister of the ABC Rochester/Genesee Region, centered in Rochester, New York, stated that of the thirty-five congregations affiliated with his region, "at least 27 would have women deacons on par with male deacons. Three others would have deaconesses

---

[55]Ron Freyer Nicholas, e-mail to author, April 23, 2004.

[56]Robert B. Wallace, letter to author, 5 October 2004.

[57]Heather Hawkins, telephone call to author, 11 November 2004.

[58]Jeff Long-Middleton, e-mail to author, 12 November 2004. A copy of the church's minutes for 7 April 1946 provided by Long-Middleton verified the church's policy change of "adding Deaconesses to the Board of Deacons" (letter to author, 29 November 2004).

[59]Jeff Long-Middleton, e-mail to author, 1 November 2004.

with a separate role different from that of the male deacons." Further, "Generally our churches do not ordain deacons or deaconesses."[60]

Arlo R. Reichter, executive minister of the ABC of Wisconsin, wrote that the Wisconsin ABC had sixty-five churches, of which forty-five had women deacons and thirty had women deacon chairs. He added that "30% of our congregations are pastored by women. The highest percentage of the 35 ABC/USA regions."[61] Sandra Cope, clerk-historian of the First Baptist Church of Waukesha, Wisconsin, shared that the church elected its first woman deacon in 1915, that many women had served as chair of the deacon board, and that "Women and men are considered equal in our church."[62]

Marcia J. Patton, executive minister of the Evergreen Association of ABC in Kent, Washington, claimed that thirty churches in the association had women in the diaconate. Twenty churches had women deacons on a par with men; ten had deaconesses. Most of the churches with women deacons have had one or more women serve as chair.[63] Paul D. Aita, pastor of the Japanese Baptist Church in the Evergreen Association, claimed that the church had its first female deacon chair, June Yabuki, in the late 1960s.[64] Further, he wrote, "At the present time, this church makes no distinction whatever between men and women in terms of what roles they can hold in the church." More specifically, "Our Diaconate Board is made up of men and women, with no requirement that specific positions be filled by one sex or the other, nor any quotas for how many of each there should be."[65]

Riley Walker, executive minister of the ABC of the Dakotas, with offices in Sioux Falls, South Dakota, wrote that twenty-four of his region's fifty-four churches had women serving in the diaconate, either as deacons or deaconesses.[66] He solicited specific information from several of those churches and then supplied e-mail replies (made either to him or to staff member Kim Aalberg) for this research from eleven churches, five in North Dakota and six in South Dakota. The five North Dakota churches included Bethel Baptist Church, Powers Lake; First Baptist Church, Bismarck; First Baptist Church, Fargo; Immanuel Baptist Church, Minot; and Killdeer Bap-

---

[60]Alan G. Newton, letter to author, 1 October 2004.
[61]Arlo R. Reichter, e-mail to author, 7 October 2004.
[62]Sandra Cope, e-mail to author, 19 October 2004.
[63]Marcia J. Patton, e-mail to author, 29 September 2004.
[64]Paul D. Aita, e-mail to author, 18 October 2004.
[65]Paul D. Aita, e-mail to author, 12 October 2004.
[66]Riley Walker, letter to author, 12 October 2004.

tist Church, Killdeer. The six South Dakota churches were First Baptist Church, Pierre; First Baptist Church, Sioux Falls; First Baptist Church, Vermillion; First Baptist Church, Whitten; First Baptist Church, Winner; and Trent Baptist Church, Trent. Nine of the churches had women deacons equal in status to men, and two had deaconesses who had lesser duties (Whitten and Winner). In one church, deaconesses met separately from deacons (Witten); in another, they met with the deacons (Winner). At least seven of the churches have had women to chair their respective deacon bodies (Bismarck, Fargo, Minot, Pierre, Powers Lake, Sioux Falls, and Vermillion).

Pastors and others in some of the churches provided valuable insights into attitudes and practices. At Bethel, the diaconate had six men and six women, with Kari Enget serving as current chairperson. Pastor Gary Cole observed, "We still have women deacons who are reluctant to serve communion. They can; they choose not to."[67] At Bismarck, Steve Wisthoff stated, "Currently, our chairperson is Annette Pickard who not only chairs the deacons but also shares the pulpit in my absence."[68] At Fargo, Dixie Potratz Lehman wrote, "The moderator serves as chair of the deacons and currently is a woman. To us gifts are more important than gender."[69] At Pierre, Theadora Boolin replied that in addition to women deacons, "We also have a woman pastor, ordained, seminary trained. We have had women moderators of First Baptist Church."[70] At Trent, Dave Knutson stated that the church had women deacons, but women preferred not to serve as chair for two reasons: the "lightning rod" nature of the position, especially when issues get tense, and the belief that "the men would tend to take a background position on the Diaconate, as well as other boards of the church."[71] At Vermillion, Shelly Aakre wrote concisely, "We have four male deacons

---

[67]Gary Cole, e-mail to Kim Aalberg, 30 September 2004 (forwarded to author, 12 October 2004).

[68]Steve Wisthoff, e-mail to Kim Aalberg, 11 October 2004 (forwarded to author, 12 October 2004).

[69]Dixie Potratz Lehman, e-mail to Riley Walker, 30 September 2004 (forwarded to author, 12 October 2004).

[70]Theadora Boolin, e-mail to Riley Walker, 5 October 2004 (forwarded to author 12 October 2004).

[71]Dave Knutson, e-mail to Kim Aalberg 1 October 2004 (forwarded to author 12 October 2004).

and four women deacons. They have equal status. Our current chair is female. We are blessed with wonderful deacons."[72]

In addition to information provided by executive ministers of five regions in the ABC, the Website of the ABC of the Pacific Southwest, headquartered in Covina, California, included a "Suggested Constitution and By-Laws—Single Board" for local churches. Article 5 on church officers stated: "The Board of Deacons shall consist of elected deacons and deacons ex-officio. (It should be noted that the term 'deacon' is not restrictive, but includes women as well.)" Specifically, "The elected deacons shall number at least six and not more than twenty-one, and shall be chosen from the men and women members of the church."[73]

The First Baptist Church of San Francisco, dually aligned with the ABC (since 1974) and the SBC (since 1984), adopted a new constitution and bylaws in 2003. The bylaws described the Deacon Ministry Team as "a group of lay men and women called forth from the active membership of the congregation who are not serving as full-time First Baptist Church staff members."[74]

Black Baptist Preference for Deaconesses

During the period 1990–2005, most, but not all, black Baptists preferred deaconesses. The National Baptist Publishing Board published a revised edition of *A Deaconess Guide* in 1986 and a reprint in 1997. The intent of the guide was to "help many churches in perfecting the function of Deaconesses." Describing deaconesses as "female assistants to deacons," the guide affirmed that they have their basis in the New Testament, that they "are necessary and have a definite place in every Baptist Church," that "they are not ordained as are the deacons," that they should be "selected by the pastor and officers of the church," although their selection should be "subject to the approval of the church," and that they should "visit the sick, those in prison, and those who are helpless and miserable."[75]

---

[72]Shelly Aakre, e-mail to Kim Aalberg, 2 October 2004 (forwarded to author 12 October 2004).

[73]"Local Church: Suggested Constitution and By-Laws—Single Board," American Baptist Churches of the Pacific Southwest. <www.abcpsw.com/chblsb.html>, accessed 8 November 2004.

[74]"First Baptist Church [San Francisco] Constitution and By-laws." <www.fbcsf.org/about/conlaw.htm>, accessed 8 November 2004.

[75]*A Deaconess Guide: Designed for the Organizing of the Consecrated Women*

Deaconesses were especially to "perform other duties in the interests of the female members of the church." These included such duties as "bathing a sick sister," "laundering the clothing used by the sick sister," "counselling young women," and "attending the candidates for baptism."[76]

T. DeWitt Smith, Jr., pastor of the West Hunter Street Baptist Church in Atlanta, Georgia, wrote two books relating to deacons in black churches. Titled *The Deacon in the Black Baptist Church* (third printing, 1993), the first book noted that

> In the Black Baptist Church it is not an uncommon practice for the deacon's wife to be a member of the deaconess board. It then becomes her duty to assist the candidate in preparation for baptismal services. She also is a valuable asset in preparing the Lord's Table for holy communion. Her presence is a symbol of humility and dignity. She is often thought of by the younger generation as a special person with a very special work.[77]

Smith then presented a model ordination service for deacons in which deaconesses had several roles. They participated in the processional along with the pastor, deacons, and choir. One deaconess read a New Testament passage. The deaconess wife of the deacon being ordained was asked by the pastor: "Do you accept the will of the congregation and promise to fulfill your duties as a deaconess of the . . . Church and walk by your husband's side in office and at home, keeping reverent the name of Jesus Christ in your life?" The deaconess then replied: "With God's help I accept the will of the Lord as expressed through this congregation and will do my best to walk worthy of the vocation to which I am being called." Along with the pastor and deacons, the deaconesses participated in the laying on of hands and finally, with the pastor, deacons, and congregation, the deaconesses extended the right hand of fellowship to the newly ordained deacon.[78]

DeWitt's second book, *New Testament Deacon Ministry in African-American Churches* (1994), said less about deaconesses, but did highlight two important ministry functions for them. Deacons and deaconesses, DeWitt wrote, should help "screen each individual applicant, who comes

---

of the Church, Classic Series (Nashville: National Baptist Publishing Board, 1997) 6, 9, 11, 16.

[76]Ibid., 6, 7.

[77]T. DeWitt Smith, Jr., *The Deacon in the Black Baptist Church* (Atlanta: Church/Home Productions, 1983; 3rd printing, Atlanta: Hope Publishing House, 1993) 38.

[78]Ibid., 78-81.

for help; to investigate their claims; see if they really need the church's assistance, as they claim." In addition, deaconesses should be part of family ministry teams along with their deacon husbands to visit church families.[79]

The Deaconess: Walking in the Newness of Life, released in a revised edition in 1993, was written by Maurice Riley, a deaconess for forty years in the Mount Calvary Baptist Church in Newark, New Jersey. The back cover featured a strong endorsement by Deaconess Helen V. Tate, president of the Women's Auxiliary of the National Baptist Deacon's Convention of America, Inc.

Riley noted that some black Baptist churches have a Deacons' Wives Committee; others have a Board of Deaconesses that includes deacon's wives and selected other women. She claimed that deaconesses have a biblical basis, that the pastor always either appoints or approves women to be deaconesses, that all deacons' wives do not automatically get appointed as deaconesses, that some deaconess boards present deaconess-of-the-year awards for outstanding services, and that "the deaconess, being a female servant, assists the pastor and deacons in carrying out the ministries of the church."[80]

Riley observed that deaconess duties, which vary according to churches, include preparing Communion elements, caring for the Communion glasses and linen, preparing candidates for baptism, following up with new converts, counseling young women, comforting those in mourning or distress, and visiting the sick and poor and providing needed services to them. If the deaconess is a deacon's wife, "she is a colaborer with him, not to dictate to or interfere with his assigned responsibilities, but to encourage him with compassion and understanding of his duties."[81]

Riley observed that deaconess committees in various churches, associations, conferences, and conventions engage in outreach ministries. Examples of such ministries are soup kitchens for the elderly and homeless; home-cooked dinners for elderly, sick, and shut-in members; support groups for AIDS victims; door-to-door canvassing; counseling, Bible study, and training for young people; hospital and nursing home ministries; evangelistic outreach; birthday parties at nursing homes; assistance to flood

---

[79]T. DeWitt Smith, Jr., *New Testament Deacon Ministry in African-American Churches* (Atlanta: Hope Publishing House, 1994) 45, 49.

[80]Maurice Riley, *The Deaconess: Walking in the Newness of Life*, rev. ed. (Newark NJ: Christian Associates Publications, 1993) 3, 123, 137-38.

[81]Ibid., 140.

and hurricane victims; jail and halfway-house ministries; a ministry to unwed mothers; clothes closets; making dolls for the Salvation Army to deliver to needy children; and working with blind students.[82]

A 1998 manual for black Baptist pastors claimed that Phoebe in Romans 16:1 was the first deaconess. The writing assumed that deaconesses are wives of deacons and should not be ordained. It asserted that both deacons and deaconesses "must be committed to give of themselves beyond the call of duty."[83]

A 2003 book on church administration in the black Baptist experience was written by Floyd Massey, Jr., pastor emeritus of the Macedonia Baptist Church in Los Angeles, California, and by Samuel Berry McKinney, pastor emeritus of the Mt. Zion Baptist Church in Seattle, Washington. Chapter 2 on "Traditional Patterns of Power in Black Baptist Churches" claimed that "in the average black Baptist church, the deacon board is the power board." Although that board typically does not include women, "in the average black church, there is a women's block of power that functions as a prime mover. In some churches it might be the women's society; in others the deaconesses or mothers' board or young matrons."[84]

A 2004 website titled "Deaconess Training Guides and Course Inspiring Deaconesses to Achieve Excellence" featured the writing and workshop ministries of Frances "Fran" A. Jones, a deaconess in the African-American Word of God Baptist Church in Washington, D.C. The thrust of her whole ministry promoted deaconess bodies as being separate from deacon bodies. Considered an expert on deaconess ministry, Jones traveled throughout the nation conducting conferences and workshops helping deaconesses and deaconess boards do their ministries well. Deaconess spouses, pastors, and deacons also attended the meetings. For example, in September 2004, she led a two-day Deaconess Conference and Renewal Retreat at the Marriott Gaithersburg Washington Center in Gaithersburg, Maryland.

Jones's five published books include: *The Making of a Deaconess*, *The Making of a Deaconess Workbook*, *The Making of a Deaconess Journal*, *Deaconesses Going beyond the Communion Table*, and *Called Out to Step*

---

[82]Ibid., 127-28.

[83]Marcel Kellar, *Boyd's Pastor's Manual for the Pastor, Preacher and Parish* (Nashville: Boyd Publications, 1998) 249-51.

[84]Floyd Massey, Jr., and Samuel Berry McKinney, *Church Administration in the Black Perspective*, rev. ed. (Valley Forge PA: Judson Press, 2003) 31, 35.

Up to a Deaconess Ministry: A 12 Step Program from Observation to Consecration. Jones's writings have received positive reviews from representatives of various African-American Baptist organizations, such as Deaconess Joan Hill, president of the Women's Auxiliary, National Baptist Deacon's Convention of America, Inc.; C. H. Johnson, a Maryland pastor and president of the Eastern Region of the Progressive National Baptist Convention; and Frank D. Tucker, past president of the Baptist Convention of D.C. and Vicinity. Tucker described Jones as "rapidly becoming this country's foremost authority on deaconesses in the African-American church."[85]

Robert B. Wallace, interim executive minister of the ABC of Massachusetts, provided information on black Baptists in his organization. In 2004, he claimed that "The African American churches tend to have separate boards with the deaconesses filling lesser roles (deaconesses preparing communion and deacons serving and the like). National Baptists ordain deacons and dedicate deaconesses so churches that are dually aligned would follow this practice."[86]

In contrast to the concept of separate boards for deacons and deaconesses in the African-American tradition, some African-American churches have only one board consisting of men and women treated equally. To illustrate, the 2004 bylaws of the First Baptist Church of Fairmont, West Virginia, read as follows: "The Board of Deacons shall consist of six men and six women. One-third of the men and one-third of the women shall be elected each year at the Annual Meeting to serve a term of three years."[87] This church was affiliated with the ABC, West Virginia Baptist Convention, and Fairmont Baptist Association. In 2004, Arlo R. Reichter, executive minister of the ABC of Wisconsin, claimed that a few African-American churches, whose deacon bodies consisted of men and women, tended to ordain them.[88]

Marcia J. Patton, executive minister of the Evergreen Association of ABC in Kent, Washington, claimed in 2004 that twelve of its thirty churches were African-American. Of the twelve, ten had deaconesses, and two had women deacons on a par with men and ordained their women

---

[85]"Deaconess training guides and course inspiring deaconesses to achieve excellence." <www.kineticgroupinc.com/deaconess>, accessed 11 November 2004.

[86]Robert B. Wallace, letter to author, 5 October 2004.

[87]"By-laws, First Baptist Church of Fairmont, West Virginia." <www.labs.net/fbcfairmont>, accessed 11 November 2004.

[88]Arlo R. Reichter, e-mail to author, 7 October 2004.

deacons: Mount Zion Baptist Church in Seattle, Washington, and Martin Luther King Jr. Memorial Baptist Church in Renton, Washington.[89] The latter church had a single deacon board. Linda Smith, chairperson of that board in 2002–2004, noted that another woman had earlier served as chair and that the church's bylaws took a gender-neutral approach to the selection of deacons.[90]

Seventh Day Baptists

Seventh Day Baptists have interchangeably designated females in the diaconate as "deacons" and "deaconesses," ordained those chosen to serve for life, and assigned equal duties to men and women. However, if they elected persons to the diaconate for a definite term of years, they tended not to ordain them.

In 1972, the Seventh Day Baptist General Conference published a manual of procedures. This manual clearly affirmed deaconesses and observed that they and deacons were chosen by church election after being nominated by the existing diaconate. Seventh Day Baptists used three different methods of electing and installing deacons and deaconesses. Some churches followed the traditional pattern of ordaining them for life or as long as they remained members of the church. Other churches elected them for a specific term of service, in which case they were usually not ordained. In a third approach, some churches elected and ordained deaconesses for life but rotated their periods of service on a cyclical basis of five years active, then five years inactive, followed by five years active, and so on.[91]

A 1999 update of the Seventh Day Baptist manual asserted more directly that

> Seventh Day Baptists believe women are called to the diaconate, as well as men. The possibility that the term "servant" in Romans 16:1 can be understood in a technical sense as "deaconess" (and the less likely possibility that "their wives" in 1 Tim. 3:11 can be so understood) gives some direct Scriptural evidence for this practice. In addition, there seems to be no expressed reason in Scripture why women should not, today, serve as

---

[89]Marcia J. Patton, e-mail to author, 29 September 2004.

[90]Linda Smith, e-mail to author, 24 October 2004.

[91]Wayne R. Rood, ed., *A Manual of Procedures for Seventh Day Baptist Churches* (Plainfield NJ: Seventh Day Baptist General Conference, 1972) 48.

deaconesses. The fact the first deacons were men is more a reflection of the Jewish culture of Jesus' day, than it is of any Scriptural principle.[92]

The 1999 manual followed the same three methods in the 1972 manual of electing and installing deacons and "deaconesses," except that it applied the third method to deacons and deaconesses, rather than just to deaconesses. Further, it noted that Seventh Day Baptist churches followed various patterns of nominating individuals to the diaconate. Deacons, male and female, had the same duties: advising the pastor, visiting members, leading in worship (including sometimes preaching), and assisting the pastor in administering baptism and the Lord's Supper.[93] The manual presented sample constitutions and bylaws of Seventh Day churches in Nebraska, Wisconsin, and California; all provided for women in the diaconate.[94]

Conclusion

By early 2005, Baptist women deacons had made enormous strides. Increasing numbers of churches elected them. Deacon bodies in more and more churches chose women to serve as chairs and as other deacon officers. Ironically, these patterns of advancement took place in the face of intensified opposition to ordained women deacons, particularly among Southern Baptists. As women progressed toward equality in church leadership as deacons, American Baptists, CBF Baptists, and selected other Baptists affirmed the process; Southern Baptists resisted the process; black Baptists chose deaconesses; and other Baptists worldwide took various positions. In spite of opposition, the period from 1990 to 2005 created a strong foundation for the future of Baptist women deacons.

---

[92]Rodney L. Henry and the Committee on Faith and Order, *A Manual of Procedures for Seventh Day Baptist Churches* (Janesville WI: Seventh Day Baptist General Conference of USA and Canada, 1999) H-2.

[93]Ibid., H-2, H-3.

[94]Ibid., appendix J-5, examples 1-6, 2-3, 3-10.

Chapter 7

Women Deacons/Deaconesses in Other Countries

The purpose of this short chapter is to show that Baptists in many countries worldwide use women deacons and deaconesses. This explodes the all-too-frequent notion that Baptist women in the diaconate are both rare and tied into a few liberal churches. On an international basis, churches of many theological persuasions include women in the deaconship. For them, balanced interpretations of the Bible lead inevitably to the incorporation of women into church leadership positions. Naturally, Baptists being Baptists, the dominant pattern in some countries is to deny women the right to participate in diaconal functions.

Although Baptists outside the United States vary in their attitudes toward and approaches to women deacons/deaconesses, women definitely exist in the diaconate in some countries. Baptists in certain countries use the term women *deacons*; others prefer *deaconesses*; still others use both. Similarly, some Baptists ordain women to the diaconate; others do not. The following consists of brief snapshots of the status of women deacons and deaconesses in selected areas of the world. The chapter concludes with a statement of support for women in all phases of ministry by a Canadian Baptist theological educator.

General International Presence. In the late 1980s, Beth MacClaren, executive director of the Women's Department of the Baptist World Alliance (BWA), presented to the BWA's Study and Research Division the results of a study of women's roles among Baptists in other countries. She pointed out that women "are struggling on every continent. The struggle is everywhere and takes many forms. . . . There is a lot of pain expressed. The pain comes from those who are marginalized in society and in the Church. Yet, there is power in the struggles. There is courage, determination and purpose."[1] As positive examples, she identified deaconesses in such diverse countries as Nigeria, Ghana, Korea, Denmark, and Canada.[2]

Australia. Several Baptist churches in Australia have women deacons. In the late 1990s, the Canberra Baptist Church in Kingston had twelve deacons, half of whom were women. Senior Minister Thorwald Lorenzen, also chair of the BWA Human Rights Commission, wrote: "I think for the future of this church it is imperative that all functions within the church are equally accessible to men and women. I would hate to go back to the old days of total male diaconates."[3]

Richard K. Moore, honorary archivist for the Baptist Churches of Western Australia, reported in 2004 that some Baptist churches in Western Australia affirmed and used women deacons, while others opposed them. Ordination of women deacons was nonexistent. In an earlier era, all deacons would have been men, although in some churches a separate board of deaconesses would have existed. Moore claimed that the Dalkeith Baptist Church had women deacons by 1978, assisting in distributing the Lord's Supper, and that the Como Baptist Church had them by the end of the 1980s. Other churches paralleled the Dalkeith and Como churches in adopting women deacons. However, churches like the Riverton Baptist Church and the Melville Baptist Church, even in 2004, took strong stances "against women in any roles of leadership (over men) or in what are perceived as unsubmissive roles."[4]

Canada. The 1955 *Canadian Baptist Ministers' Handbook* included one sentence regarding deaconesses: "Deaconesses are given special responsibility for work among women and girls in the congregations and often are assigned special duties such as calling [i.e., visiting]."[5] Baptists in Canada, as in the United Kingdom, typically do not formally ordain deacons, male or female. Samuel J. Mikolaski, noted Canadian Baptist scholar, remembered in 1998 that

---

[1]Beth H. MacClaren, "Women's Issues," *Faith, Life, and Witness: The Papers of the Study and Research Division of the Baptist World Alliance, 1986–1990*, ed. William H. Brackney (Birmingham AL: Samford University Press, 1990) 216-17.

[2]Ibid., 216-18, 222, 224.

[3]Thorwald Lorenzen, letter to author, 23 March 1998.

[4]Richard K. Moore, e-mail to author, 17 May 2004.

[5]*Canadian Baptist Ministers' Handbook* (N.p.: Literature Committee, Baptist Federation of Canada, 1955) 18.

in my teens in Toronto 60 years ago a separate body of deaconesses were appointed in some older traditional churches which were, as well, strongly evangelical. These women fulfilled counseling and visitation roles, not unlike the class of deaconesses in Germany, or the women who were deacons on the regular Board in my pastorate in Oxford. In some cases a single woman deacon was called as a paid staff member, chiefly for pastoral visitation and ministry to women. The formal office of deaconess has largely been given up. In many instances today women are elected to the diaconate so that men and women deacons are on the same Board, as in the UK.[6]

John E. Boyd, pastor of the First Baptist Church of Halifax, Nova Scotia, provided a list of twelve churches in Nova Scotia with women deacons, nine of which, he knew for certain, either had or had had women deacon chairs. (See the appendix for a list of the churches with female deacon chairs.) Boyd added that "I am sure there are many more churches, especially in Nova Scotia, with women deacons" and that during his sixteen years as pastor of First Halifax, "there have been five women as Chair of the Diaconate." Having served as pastor of several Nova Scotia Baptist churches, all of which had women deacons in 2004, Boyd concluded: "It is so long since I didn't work with women deacons that it always hits me when I hear that churches are still struggling over this issue! I have worked with outstanding women as deacons (as well as pastors!) and I cannot imagine going back to the old ways."[7]

Denmark. A 1990 publication claimed that "about 50 percent of the deacons are women."[8]

European Countries. In 1987, Baptist historian Leon McBeth claimed that "almost all European Baptist churches have had women deacons or deaconesses since the nineteenth century."[9]

France. An 1879 confession, revised in 1895, of French Baptists became the standard confession of the Federation of French Baptist Churches and was still used in the early 1980s. It stated that "Apart from elders or pastors, the only other officers of the local churches are the deacons and deaconesses. They must be elected by the congregation and

---

[6]Samuel J. Mikolaski, letter to author, 17 February 1998.

[7]John E. Boyd, e-mail to author, 7 May 2004.

[8]MacClaren, "Women's Issues," 224.

[9]H. Leon McBeth, *The Baptist Heritage: Four Centuries of Baptist Witness* (Nashville: Broadman Press, 1987) 821.

invested in their position by the laying on of hands. They should possess the qualities stated in the Scriptures: their job is to aid the pastors in their ministry, to serve the church by using the talents they have been given by God and they should particularly be responsible for all the material needs of the congregation."[10]

Michael Thobis, president of the federation's Commission on Historical Research, reported in 1998 on his research into the records of an early French Baptist church, the Church of Rivecourt (Oise), formed in 1840. In 1847, that church named two deacons, a man and a woman. Then in 1875, with a new name, the Church of Saint-Saveru, that church elected four deacons, one of whom was a woman. She was in charge of visiting sick female church members.[11]

The 1979 confession of faith and statement of ecclesiastical principles of the Evangelical Association of French-Speaking Baptist Churches, in common use in the 1980s, asserted that

> In addition to pastors and elders, the local church may have other responsible servants, for example deacons and deaconesses whose role it is to assist the pastors or elders in their ministry, by assuming special responsibility for everything that relates to the material interests of the congregation.[12]

Ghana. In the late 1980s, Beth MacClaren stated that "Ghana has ordained deaconesses."[13]

Hong Kong. In 1998, Chu Wood-ping, executive director of the Baptist Convention of Hong Kong, claimed that in Hong Kong "women deacons are very common, both ordained and nonordained."[14]

Korea. Fred Rolater, professor emeritus of history at Middle Tennessee State University and in 2004 professor of church history at the Korea Baptist Theological University/Seminary in Daejeon, consulted with leaders in several Korean Baptist churches in Daejeon and provided the following information. Korean Baptist churches had two types of deacons: *Chipsonim*, translated "deacon," and *Ansu Chipsonim*, translated "ordained deacon."

---

[10]G. Keith Parker, *Baptists in Europe: History and Confessions of Faith* (Nashville: Broadman Press, 1982) 131.

[11]Michael Thobois, letter to author, 28 March 1998.

[12]Parker, *Baptists in Europe,* 143.

[13]MacClaren, "Women's Issues," 217.

[14]Chu Wood-ping, letter to author, 28 March 1998.

The ordained deacons tended to be male; further, they operated somewhat like elders in Presbyterian churches, the dominant Protestant group in Korea. The nonordained *Chipsonim* included men and women. Probably about fifty percent of the *Chipsonim* in most Korean Baptist churches were women. The Dae Heung Baptist Church in Daejeon, probably the fourth largest Baptist church in Korea, had about sixty-seven percent women on the *Chipsonim* level. The *Chipsonim* deacon functioned as a church servant teaching Sunday school, doing evangelistic or hospital visitation, ministering to the handicapped, and working with children and in women's ministries. According to Rolater, "The voting members at the annual Korea Baptist Convention meetings are either ordained pastors (*moskas*) or ordained deacons who are chosen as delegates by their churches. Thus, very few women have any voting power in the convention. No woman may be ordained to the *moksanim* or pastoral level."[15]

New Zealand. In 1998, Angus MacLeod, secretary of the Aukland Baptist Association in New Zealand and past president of the Baptist Union of New Zealand, stated that "Nearly all Baptist churches in New Zealand now have women as well as men deacons. There is no difference in their roles and, in some instances, women deacons outnumber the men."[16]

Nigeria. Describing women's status in Baptist life in Nigeria, Beth MacClaren claimed in the late 1980s that "Women are filling traditional roles in the churches: Teaching, children's and women's work, tending to orphans and the poor, and, generally, working in a caring capacity. A few are deaconesses, especially in Nigeria."[17]

Scotland. David Bebbington, history professor at the University of Stirling, Scotland, referred to a 1984 "survey of 72 Baptist churches in Scotland [which] found that in 37, women held office as deacons."[18]

South Africa. In 1998, Sydney Hudson-Reed, retired area Baptist coordinator for the Western Province of South Africa, noted that "More and more of our churches have women deacons."[19]

---

[15]Fred Rolater, e-mail to author, 7 September 2004.
[16]Angus MacLeod, letter to author, 2 April 1998.
[17]MacClaren, "Women's Issues," 216.
[18]David Bebbington, letter to author, 20 March 1998.
[19]Sydney Hudson-Reed, letter to author, 5 May 1998.

USSR. As early as 1884, a Russian Baptist confession stated that "there may be deaconesses in the church."[20] In the late 1980s, deaconesses, typically older women, enjoyed considerable respect and authority in USSR Baptist churches. They assisted in church charitable activities, baptisms, weddings, funerals, and Communion preparation.[21]

West Germany. In 1983, *The Commission*, a periodical publication of the Southern Baptist Foreign Mission Board, published an article on "Baptists in West Germany: Tradition Thrust into Today." In addition to describing home missions and education, the article discussed deaconesses. Reflecting "the West German Baptist concern for Christian social responsibility," West German Baptists had three deaconess orders that supported "hospitals, nurses, homes for the elderly, [and] local church youth and education workers." The orders included the Bethel order in East Berlin, the Albertinen order in Hamburg, and the Tabea (Tabitha) order in Hamburg. These orders featured living in motherhouses and wearing uniforms. The article noted that "Changes are coming to deaconess work. More opportunities for Christian service are opening for young women that do not require the separated lifestyle of the deaconess groups. New deaconesses are fewer in number."[22]

Zimbabwe. In 1998, of the 283 churches in the Baptist Convention of Zimbabwe, less than five had women deacons, but they were all ordained, claimed J. N. Mazvigadza, secretary of that convention.[23]

A key reason why Baptists in selected countries have women deacons and deaconesses and women pastors relates to the fact that administrators and professors in theological education have trained leaders for churches by instilling in them the New Testament principles of spiritual equality between men and women, the giftedness of women, and the right of God to call women. A classic example has been Harold L. Mitton, who served for many years as a Canadian Baptist pastor and later as principal of Acadia Divinity College in Wolfville, Nova Scotia, a divinity college committed

---

[20]William L. Lumpkin, *Baptist Confessions of Faith*, rev. ed. (Valley Forge PA: Judson Press, 1969) 428.

[21]Heather Vose, "The Ministry of Women in the Baptist Churches of the USSR," *Faith, Life, and Witness: The Papers of the Study and Research Division of the Baptist World Alliance, 1986–1990*, ed. William H. Brackney (Birmingham AL: Samford University Press, 1990) 134.

[22]"Baptists in West Germany: Tradition Thrust into Today," *The Commission* 46/1 (January 1983): 43.

[23]J. N. Mazvigadza, letter to author, 22 May 1998.

to training ministers for Baptist churches in the Atlantic provinces of Canada.

In 1987, the *Atlantic Baptist* published Mitton's article, "The Place of Women in Ministry." At that time, he was principal emeritus of Acadia Divinity College. Mitton initially summarized his position by acknowledging that debates about women's place in ministry continue throughout the Christian church today, with plenty of arguments for and against, and by issuing a direct challenge to opponents of women in ministry:

> Apparently, it never occurs to many people to regard a woman as a Christian person uniquely gifted by the Spirit of God for the good of the whole body of Christ. Consequently, all manner of obstacles are placed in the way of women exercising leadership in the church. This, it seems to me, is regrettable. Is it not conceivable that God in His sovereign freedom calls whom He will to serve Him? There are women of proven gifts who humbly believe that He has laid His hand upon them. It is primarily on this high ground, and not simply on that of the equality of the sexes, that the matter should be settled. Naturally, as in the case of men, the church has a duty to scrutinize the claim, since entrance into the ministry is too vital a matter to be decided by the individual alone, whether man or woman.[24]

After claiming that "The prohibition of women in ministry, so strongly advocated by some, does not find consistent support in Holy Scripture," Mitton reviewed the three passages that he believed to be most often used to challenge the viability of women ministers, 1 Corinthians 11:4-15, 1 Corinthians 14:34-35, and 1 Timothy 2:11-15. One by one, he disputed interpretations of these passages that placed women in subjugation to men and kept women out of ministry. He concluded that "women have whole title to the order of Christian Ministry as God shall call them. Let those who scruple consider only what it has cost the church, and will cost the church, not to use the talent of women. Sexism must be seen for what it is, namely, discrimination, and discrimination in any form is a monstrous evil, robbing persons of dignity and worth."[25]

With unrelenting passion, Mitton asserted that "The issue is an important one. At the very time when women have been forging ahead in secular society as teachers, doctors, lawyers, technicians, professors, and so on, the church appears to cling to a patriarchal system or structure which places the

---

[24]Harold L. Mitton, "The Place of Women in Ministry," *Atlantic Baptist* 23/4 (April 1987): 16.

[25]Ibid., 17-18.

church's leadership firmly in masculine hands."[26] In fact, because of "the pivotal issue: the universal priesthood of all believers in Christ, female as well as male," the Bible makes plain that "There can be no true partnership and equality of the sexes in the life of the church so long as those vested with the authority to speak for God are men and men only."[27] Baptist women deacons have profited from this kind of defense on an international level.

---

[26]Ibid., 16.
[27]Ibid., 18.

Chapter 8
Women Deacons Tell Their Stories

This chapter shows what life has really been like for women deacons and their churches by letting the women and the churches do the talking. Three kinds of information are included: primarily the personal stories of selected women deacons, especially current and former deacon chairs; pastoral affirmations of women deacons and assessments of their significance and contributions; and church documents that relate to women deacons, such as a deacon covenant, a resolution relating to women in positions of service, extracts from sermons, and an ordination service.

These stories, affirmations, and documents describe vital issues and share honest views. They also reveal condescension and freedom, sadness and humor, dreams and fulfillment, pain and joy. The stories and other accounts relate to twenty-five churches in the District of Columbia and in twelve states: Alabama, Georgia, Kentucky, Maryland, Massachusetts, Mississippi, Missouri, North Carolina, Pennsylvania, South Carolina, Texas, and Virginia. North Carolina and Virginia churches have a high representation simply because they have more women deacons than other states in the South. Churches included are rural, suburban, and urban; small, medium, and large. Comprising part of the stuff of modern Baptist women's history, these stories can translate into live source material for churches considering the possibility of adding women to the diaconate.

Berea Baptist Church, Rockville, Virginia

Berea Baptist Church ordained its first female deacons in 1983. Since then, it has had several female deacon chairs. Mark E. Hughes, pastor in 2004, shared his views about women in the diaconate, assessed the values of female deacons, and described factors that led the church to adopt them.

> In my five years here at Berea Church, I have noted a very open identification with women as co-ministers in the congregation, rather than as "sub-ministers." Hearing that Berea had already moved into an open diaconate was one of the things that drew me to say yes to the call to this church.
>
> Having grown up in Orange Baptist Church, Orange, VA, with females on the deacon body as long as I could remember, it was never a thought in my mind that women could not serve in this God-called role.

My personal philosophy of deacon ministry stresses that they are staff with me in the pastoral care of this church. As such, they are my extra "eyes and ears" in the congregation, but more than that, they are ministers in their own right with their own gifts they bring to the ministry of this church. Having both male and female perspectives on church issues, theological discussions and interpersonal relationships have [has] expanded the depth of our ministry, leaving us with fewer blind spots. Men and women approach problems and solutions from different directions, and having a broad perspective has been a blessing.

Seeing women serving in this role is also important, I think, for the young women and children of our church, showing them that God may use them in many roles, be they clergy, deacons, Sunday school teachers, moderators, or other lay leaders. It creates a climate of seeking God's approval first, human approval second—always.

Berea has a history of such openness deep in its DNA. When congregations around Richmond began putting out its black members at the end of the Civil War, Berea opened its doors to those who had nowhere else to worship. Abner Church just down the road from us was born out of Berea years later from some of the descendents of those African-American members. It was a natural outgrowth of this openness that led a nominating committee to ask in the early 1980s "Can we nominate a woman as a deacon?" At that time the constitution forbade it, so the pastor invited the congregation into a process of studying for themselves the idea. After a period of education in which all were allowed to voice their opinions and interpretations, the church voted to accept the constitutional change allowing women as deacons. (On a side note, the church also hired a female interim minister in the mid-1990s.)

A few left the church for a while; most returned. And even those who never accepted the idea themselves remained in fellowship here at the church. Berea, while not perfect, seemed like a good community to remain a part of even when its members didn't always agree.

I am proud to serve alongside some of the most caring ministers, male and female, who feel called of God to serve their God and their church family.[1]

Boulevard Baptist Church, Anderson, South Carolina

Johnny F. McKinney, pastor of Boulevard Baptist Church, said in 2004 that his church had had women deacons since 1975 and that women had served

---

[1]Mark E. Hughes, e-mails to author, 8 September 2004; 14 September 2004.

as deacon chairs. Then he assessed the significance of women deacons to the church.

> Women are vital components of our church's deacon ministry. Our constitution calls for forty-two deacons, serving for a two-year term. Our deacons are not an administrative body, but rather, a ministering body. Each deacon is responsible for pastoral care for between eight and twelve family units. In addition, our deacons help lead in worship, in outreach and in various mission endeavors of our congregation.
>
> Our church affirms the gifts that are present in our all members—men and women. This inclusiveness is modeled to the community and to the church. Boulevard believes that this model is only fair and just. We are also healthier by having male and female perspectives represented in our conversations. It has been my experience that our women are often superior to our men in offering pastoral care and support for members of their family groups.[2]

Central Baptist Church, Lexington, Kentucky

Rachel Smith Childress, registrar and director of student services at Lexington Theological Seminary in 2004, was ordained a deacon at Central Baptist Church in 1984 and was named the church's first female deacon chair in 1986. She later served a second term as chair in 1995–1997. She gave some personal reactions to her two terms as chair and described some developments that occurred during those terms.

> It meant a lot to me, each time [to be elected deacon chair]. The first time, I was 29 years old—it was a sincere affirmation of my gifts and the trust these people had in me—especially since it was during a time we were without a pastor. I also felt called to the role and affirmed in it the other times I served in the leadership role. It was a wonderful opportunity for me to discover and develop gifts of leadership in the church—and to see how a church operates from a much more internal vantage point.
>
> There is occasional surprise when folks find out I am baptist (intentionally small b) and have been ordained as a deacon and chaired the group—that comes from ignorance about what it means to be baptist and is from folks who would consider themselves enlightened and "liberal." That still happens and always amazes me.
>
> We went through some difficult times during my tenures. The By-Laws Committee (which I also chaired) recommended changing our policy

---

[2]Johnny F. McKinney, letter to author, 28 September 2004.

on baptism for folks moving membership. It created such a controversy that the deacons were called to step in and research and propose a strategy. It was wonderful how the group of deacons, in spite of very different views, shared their experiences and feelings openly in the group. AND, as a group came up with a plan of church-wide education on Baptist heritage which covered a two-year period.

Childress also provided a deacon covenant, still in use in 2004, which was prepared while she served as deacon chair.

Deacon Covenant
Deacons are called of God and the local church, in keeping with the scriptures, to be servants. As a Deacon of Central Baptist Church, I covenant to:
Have an active prayer life, praying for the community of this world, my local community, my church, my family, my friends, and my own needs;
Serve this church faithfully and cheerfully, offering not only my abilities but my presence when we gather together;
Be sensitive to the needs of others and strive to meet those needs using the gifts God has given me;
Fully participate in the service of communion, remembering the name of Jesus and how his service inspired the disciples;
Read, study, and emotionally experience the scriptures;
Love and minister to our church family;
Sacrificially share my financial assets;
Be open to the desire of God, to discover and grow the gifts which God has bestowed on me to use those gifts to take my place in the body of Christ;
Find spiritual nourishment and respite in ways which will invigorate me to service;
Be an Easter person, experiencing daily the ever-presence of the resurrected Christ;
Share my intimate knowledge of the Almighty God as Creator, Redeemer, and Sustainer with those I encounter each day;
I covenant to do all I do, to the best of my abilities, to the glory of God.[3]

---

[3]Rachel Smith Childress, e-mail to author, 2 September 2004.

First Baptist Church, Auburn, Alabama

Sylvia Gossett, who in 2004 lived in Lindale, Texas, had served several years earlier as deacon chair at First Baptist Church, Auburn. She remembered a lighthearted moment:

> One funny thing I remember was that one month I was running really late and arriving in the church office just in time for the deacons' meeting. The pastor, at that time Glen Turner, was standing there getting ready to go into the meeting room and I said, "Oh, please give me just a minute to put some lipstick on." Glen laughed and said, "That's the first time a deacon chair has ever said that to me."[4]

First Baptist Church, Clemson, South Carolina

Winnie V. Williams served as deacon chair at First Baptist Church in 1986–1988. In 1993, she described some events relating to her years as chair and offered some reflections on women's roles in church life.

> Much of my life has been a "train ride," waiting to get to the station, waiting for the painful stereotypical attitudes toward women that have dominated societal thinking to diminish, waiting for churches to deal with passive indifference toward women, and waiting for a change in the male-dominated theological climate. . . .
>
> Several years ago my husband and I spent a weekend with a wonderful Christian couple that had previously been a member [members] of our church. In the matter of conversation the male friend stated that he was the Chairman of the Deacons at his Church (SBC) in the town in which they now reside. My husband then responded, "Winnie is the Chairman of Deacons of the First Baptist Church of Clemson." Our friend was appalled and quickly replied, "Not you, Winnie, that is not Biblical, that is not acceptable." "Why," he commented, "our church does not allow women to serve on any committee." His wife sarcastically responded, "Oh, yes it does—women serve on the flower committee and on the refreshment committee. . . . "
>
> On my "train ride" I no longer just wait to get to the station for I now perceive the view from my window with a different perspective. Churches are beginning to validate that through the utilization of the gifts of women, and opportunities for being the church are twofold. Churches are reshaping

---

[4]Sylvia Gossett, e-mail to author, 22 April 2004.

programs to accommodate all of God's people and women are discovering a place for themselves in the history of the church. The process is slow but women desire to fulfill God's call to be of service whatever the responsibility, whatever the sacrifice, and wherever He leads.[5]

First Baptist Church, Gaithersburg, Maryland

In July 1989, Brian Conner, pastor of Redland Baptist Church in Derwood, Maryland, wrote several Maryland Baptist pastors whose churches he knew had women deacons. He was seeking guidance for dealing with the issue in his own church. One response he received came from Charles L. Updike, pastor of the First Baptist Church of Gaithersville. Updike wrote:

> Our church ordained a woman deacon in 1979 for the first time. The wisdom of that decision has been evident many times. Although some felt we were being dishonest with the Bible, no one doubted the spiritual qualities of any of our women in the nomination process. Indeed, I believe our women nominated are under far greater scrutiny than most of the men nominated. Churches are more prone to set aside men more quickly than women. I believe this reflects a cultural rather than spiritual bias. The true quality that leads one to be called is not physical gender. God has called all his people to be servants and spiritual leaders on the basis of commitment, willingness to serve, and the desire to do what God wants. . . . Much the way some have used the Bible to justify slavery at one point in our history, we have used the Biblical text to prop up a longstanding status quo in this regard. I believe it is a misunderstanding of the true Biblical position and encourage you and your congregation to weigh heavily the actions and teachings of Jesus when it came to women and service.
>
> On a very practical basis, I want to share a beautiful witness for women's ordination. One night I received a phone call at about 3:00 AM. It was a woman who was very distressed and wanted me to come and see her. She was very frightened and anxious about her husband being out of town and felt like she was going to die. In the midst of her anxiety attack, she wasn't aware that it would be totally inappropriate for me to journey to her home in the middle of the night with her husband out of town. Instead, we talked a few minutes and then I was able to tell her that I would call one of our deacons to see if she could come and spend the rest of the night with her. She immediately took me up on the suggestion and after a phone call to one of our women deacons, the problem was solved.

---

[5]Winnie V. Williams, "Women in Ministry," *South Carolina Fellowship News* 2/2 (April 1993): 1.

The next day, she called and shared her gratitude for someone being there. I hung up and called my deacon and thanked her for being Christ to her in the midst of this lady's fears. . . .

Our world is too dark a place to squabble over anatomy. God is looking for persons who will faithfully serve.[6]

First Baptist Church, Philadelphia, Pennsylvania

Helen Hannon served on the Board of Deacons of First Baptist Church for twenty-nine years, 1975–2004. She was elected the first female "president" of the deacons in 1986 and served in that role for seven years; further, she served as vice president for fourteen years. She described a variety of experiences. She remembered the first Sunday that she served Holy Communion in 1975:

> A dear female friend rose and left the sanctuary before I reached the pew. Another dear female friend said as I approached and extended the tray of bread, "Helen, I don't like this. . . . " Her husband said, "Be quiet, Julia." (She accepted the bread.)

Hannon also remembered several occasions in which "a single, female member consistently disrupted meetings. I was a frequent target during my terms as president/vice president on the Board of Deacons."

During her presidency of the deacon body, Hannon had to deal with two delicate issues, one relating to personnel and the second concerning gays and lesbians. First, in 1986, "a complaint was made to the Board of Deacons of First Baptist Church by a young, married female member. She alleged inappropriate behavior by our co-pastor." After "a very painful, long period requiring meetings with both parties" and meetings "with experts in the field of psychology and church government," this matter was eventually resolved peacefully. Second, in 1990, Peter C. Wool, the church's pastor, and Hannon, the deacon president, received regular requests from a gay psychiatrist,

> to discuss with the Board of Deacons the feasibility of allowing a group of people to meet in the church and engage in an outreach program encouraging members of the gay and lesbian community to develop a program which would meet their spiritual needs and foster Christian fellowship. After many hours of discussion, worry, anxiety, and prayer, the

---

[6]Charles L. Updike, letter to Brian Conner, 5 September 1989.

pastor and myself realized the Board of Deacons, as leaders committed to God's ministry, needed to respond in Christian love and understanding. The Board responsively adopted a resolution establishing the "Lambda Gathering." This resolution became the foundation out of which the Lambda Gathering was founded. The first meeting was held March 17, 1991. . . . The group expanded and became active in church activities: Bible Studies, Fellowship Hour, Outreach. Once again, in its long history the First Baptist Church opened its doors and heart to those seeking a home in which to freely worship.[7]

Beryl J. Russell served as deacon at First Baptist Church in Philadelphia in 1990-96 and in 1997–2003. She also remembered the 1990 developments relating to gays and lesbians.

Within a few months of my appointment [to the deacons in 1990], the Board was asked to consider the formation of a Fellowship for Gay and Lesbian Christians to become an integral part of the church's program. It was the first time I was giving serious consideration to my position on Homosexuality and was asked to prepare a policy statement on behalf of the deacons. I welcomed the opportunity to clarify my own thinking on the subject and tried to determine from a study of the life and ministry of Jesus what He would probably do. I felt He would be sympathetic to any group of people who were being ostracized and discriminated against and so recommended strongly that as a church we should make such fellowship possible. While some members of the Board of Deacons resigned and left the church, the majority remained and for a number of years the Lambda Gathering, as it came to be known, strengthened the spiritual life of the church and many members held responsible positions.[8]

First Baptist Church, Sanford, North Carolina

Ann Noe Womble joined First Baptist Church in 1960. The church ordained its first woman deacon in 1973. Ordained in 1985, Womble served a four-year term on the deacon body, during which she served as secretary and vice-chair, and then rotated off. The following presents her reaction to being invited to serve a second term in 1992–1996, resulting in her service as deacon chair in 1992–1994. (In August 2003, her church licensed her to preach.)

---

[7]Helen Gannon, letter to author, 5 October 2004.
[8]Beryl J. Russell, letter to author, 5 October 2004.

After being off the board . . . I was asked again to serve. It was even more an honor to answer such a high calling, and I prayed for a long time as I considered the matter. I knew it required a lot of dedication and commitment, and I was not sure if I was ready for that again so soon.

After much prayer and expressing my hesitation to God several times, I responded by saying that I would come back on the board if they would allow me to be chaplain so that I could have a devotion at the beginning of each meeting. It had been and continued to be a real concern for me that so many of our meetings had been business only or talk about the Saturday ballgame or just a quick meeting to discuss certain matters. I thought that to be effective as servants in the church, we needed to be inspired and encouraged more than I felt I had been when I had previously served. The nominating committee said they would consider it and get back to me. When they responded by saying there was not a position for a chaplain but they would like for me to be chair and then I could conduct the meeting as I so desired, I was shocked and more than humbled to think they would invite me to chair this group of mostly men. I then did have a lot of praying to do. I prayed and talked to my minister and associate minister and my husband and children before I ever made a decision. But I believed that God was calling me to that position at that time for a specific purpose and that He would give me the strength, energy, and ability to do what He was calling me to do.

After the shock of me being nominated to that position, the men settled down and were very gracious to me for the two years I served as chair. Dr. Del Parkerson, senior minister, enjoyed introducing me to visitors and friends as his deacon chair and then he would say: "Ann is the only deacon chair I have ever had who came to the meetings with a plan in mind." I did enjoy working with him so much. He constantly encouraged and supported me.

The only negative thing that was ever said to me in a meeting was said one night when I mentioned that I was so pleased something that we had discussed had passed the vote in church conference. One of the men said in a rather negative way: "Well they didn't have any choice after you railroaded it through." Several deacons later apologized for his statement, but I just laughed when he said it. Later I wished I had said "thank you" for believing that I had the leadership ability to railroad the Board of Deacons and the entire church into making such an important decision. I believe that decision was to have two morning services year-round. For several years we had early service only during the summer.

During my terms of chair I presented many items of business that had been overlooked for years for different reasons. I think I was just so naïve that I didn't realize I shouldn't bring them up.

I was so pleased with the response of the deacons when I served as a deacon and as chair but especially in the position of chair, and I will cherish my time in that position for as long as I live. It was one of the most rewarding experiences of my life.[9]

First Baptist Church, Winchester, Virginia

First Baptist Church elected its first women deacons in the 1970s, and five have served as deacon chair since the early 1990s. Michele Heath, one of those chairs, described some difficult issues that she had to deal with while serving as chair.

Just as I was to begin my term as deacon chair, I realized my term would not be a normal one. A month or two before my term was to begin my church's Pastor and Associate Pastor resigned; each of them answering God's call to a different area of service. Early on as the term began I soon realized that it would be marked as a year of turmoil. A power struggle was beginning to surface and it continued even as the Interim Pastor was called. Therefore, I began my term as chair about ten days before the interim began his time of service at our church.

So many issues within the church began to surface. As each event began to unfold I tried to minister and work for the best that would honor Christ and His church. We did lose some members through each of these situations, but were able to keep some from leaving. The most damaging situation for the church was when the Interim and a church member who felt he was a self-appointed leader (he was not serving on any committees or holding any leadership positions) went to the home of a church employee who was also a member of the church and fired the member and then accused her husband of not taking his responsibility because his primary job was a seasonal one. He had another job during the winter months, but didn't earn as much during this time. This situation threatened to divide the church, but I was able to intercede in ministry to this family and through the grace of God the divide in the church did not lead to a split. Some members left but without rancor. Later, before his interim time was up, the Interim Pastor admitted to me that due to the situation and what happened, he couldn't minister to the family, but that I was able to minister effectively to this family.

During my time as chairman, the Interim Pastor and other church leaders showed little inclination to consult with me or to seek my thoughts about the spiritual health of the church or about the issues that confronted

---

[9]Ann Noe Womble, e-mail to author, 31 August 2004.

us as a church. The previously mentioned situation was one where I would have counseled caution in both action and method to prevent the hard feelings that resulted. During this time I saw the church act as an ugly bride and not as Christ would have intended. Through this experience I learned a lot and grew as a person. My prayer throughout this experience was that I be able to demonstrate God's grace and love.[10]

First Baptist Church of Christ at Macon, Georgia

The First Baptist Church of Christ ordained its first women deacons in January 1986. Connie Jones joined this church in 1989, was elected a deacon, and then served as the church's first female deacon chair in 2003 and 2004. She offered some perspectives on serving as deacon chair.

> I joined FBC Macon in 1989, after the congregation had resolved the issue of ordaining women deacons. Even so, I was surprised when asked if I would consider serving as deacon. Looking back, I would affirm the importance of faith community for discerning one's calling, because it was a significant and affirming experience for me that members of the congregation saw me as being "deacon material."
>
> There have been several layers to my experience of being Chair of Deacons and Church Council: I am very honored to be the first woman in my church to serve in that role, and at the same time, have needed to "get past" being the first.
>
> There have been moments when I struggled to balance personal convictions about a given issue, including women's issues, with being leader of the whole congregation.
>
> The respect and affirmation of my leadership by our senior pastor through the navigation of church business and politics have been vital.
>
> Hard worker that I am, I've had to balance the effort and responsibility of being chair with taking time away, having fun, and cultivating a support network both in and out of the church. Alongside that, recognizing that spiritual leadership is ultimately more about loving people and listening well than it is about "getting stuff done" has been a helpful perspective.
>
> Discovering that early Baptists were accepting of women deacons and preachers was astounding to me. Realizing that my church has reclaimed an early Baptist tradition of ordaining women has renewed my pride in

---

[10]Michele Heath, e-mail to author, 22 September 2004.

being a Baptist, being a member of First Baptist Church, Macon, Georgia, and being a woman called by God.[11]

First Baptist Church of Clarendon, Arlington, Virginia

First Baptist Church elected its first women deacons in 1980. Ellen Bartlett joined the church in 1982, was ordained as a deacon in 1995, and served as deacon chair in 1998–2000. She described events surrounding the election of the first four women deacons in 1980.

> Nineteen-eighty was the date that women began to serve. There was pretty vehement discussion about it, I've learned, but no open opposition once it happened. Only one family left the church because of that, it was reported, but some people called the new deacons "deaconesses" and had to be "educated"!
>
> One current female deacon who was asked to serve that first year wouldn't let herself be nominated because her own sister was so opposed to women deacons and she didn't want to cause a rift, but the best friend of that opposing sister was elected, and when Bernice saw that her sister didn't let it hurt her friendship with that lady, Bernice herself accepted nomination the next year and was elected, for the first of many times.
>
> Currently, we have serving as our Senior Adult minister a man who was on the FBCC staff at that time (1980), though he left to take a position at another church from about 1988 till last year. Mark could thus give me a perspective on how things changed when women became deacons, and to quote him, "Women moved the role of the deacon from a business model to a ministry model, from ruling the church to serving the people."[12]

The First Baptist Church of the City of Washington, D.C.

In September 1984, First Baptist Church approved "A Resolution on the Ordination of Women" in response to the June 1984 "Resolution on Ordination and the Role of Women in Ministry" adopted by the Southern Baptist Convention. Everett C. Goodwin, the church's pastor, had delivered a sermon titled "Does Gender Matter to God" on June 24. The resolution read:

> WHEREAS, since its founding in 1802 The First Baptist Church of the City of Washington, D.C., has sought to bear witness to the gospel of

---

[11]Connie Jones, e-mail to author, 31 August 2004.
[12]Ellen Bartlett, e-mail to author, 8 September 2004.

Jesus Christ throughout the world, to promote the fellowship of those who were united in that mission, and has, through prayer, encouragement, and training, sent forth many men and women to serve in the manner of Christ, and

WHEREAS, in the last several years this Church has been led to ordain many women to the service of the Diaconate, and several women to the calling of the Christian Ministry, and now plans to so ordain another woman in October, 1984, and

WHEREAS, this church believes that the teachings of our Lord and Savior Jesus Christ, as taught in the scriptures, show that women have equal responsibility and opportunity in servanthood and ministry in Christ's Church, and

WHEREAS, the 1984 Southern Baptist Convention at Kansas City, Missouri, adopted a resolution by a vote of 4,793 to 3,466 which opposed the service of women in pastoral functions and leadership roles entailing ordination, and

WHEREAS, this Church recognizes and reaffirms that ordination is a matter within the purview of local churches,

NOW, THEREFORE, The First Baptist Church of the City of Washington, D.C., hereby repudiates the resolution of the Southern Baptist Convention opposing the ordination of women and affirms the belief that we are one in Christ, and that this belief dictates that women should have equal access to pastoral functions and leadership roles entailing ordination.

AND, FINALLY, The First Baptist Church of the City of Washington, D.C., reaffirms its commitment to the historic Baptist heritage and witness, especially the autonomy of the local church, the presence and power of the Holy Spirit to deal individually with persons of all races, circumstances, and sex, including a call to ordained ministry in the church, and the great principles of fellowship in mission established at so great a sacrifice by the ancestors and pioneers of our faith and fellowship: By these means The First Baptist Church of the City of Washington, D.C., reaffirms its dedication to carry the Gospel of Jesus Christ to all the ends of the earth, and to all peoples, and by the ministry of all who will answer his call, and to pray and work together for the coming of the Kingdom of God.[13]

---

[13]"A Resolution on the Ordination of Women," First Baptist Church of the City of Washington DC, 19 September 1984. (Copy provided by Rev. Deborah Cochran, The First Baptist Church of the City of Washington.)

Greenlawn Baptist Church, Columbia, South Carolina

"Wrestling with Words" was the sermon title on 2 January 1993, when Pastor Marion D. Aldridge preached to the Greenlawn Baptist Church. He claimed that

> A new issue is before us today. Women—not all of them, but some of them—are saying it is time they are called by their right names. Tired of being called babes, chicks, honeys, skirts, dames, and broads, these women are asking simply that they be called what they are—women. They are also asking that they not be called "girls" or "men" or referred to as "he" or "him."

Aldridge then related the women's issue to deacons and other aspects of church life.

> This church has a history of inclusion. . . . In our deacon selection process, women and divorced persons, who are excluded from the diaconate in many other churches, are eligible to serve here. We are racially inclusive, having white, black, Hispanic, oriental, Native American and Jewish members. To say we are inclusive is not to say we condone Satan worship, idolatry, adultery, or theft.
>
> Being inclusive does mean that, in matters of justice, we would rather suffer discomfort ourselves than to cause another person, unjustly, to suffer pain. Singing new words to a familiar carol is a little uncomfortable to me. But thoughtlessly and intentionally excluding half of the congregation, when we know better, seems callous and unchristian. . . . The church staff shall make every effort to be gender-neutral. . . . This process of making our language gender-sensitive . . . is not always easy.[14]

Hominy Baptist Church, Candler, North Carolina

In 1981, Hominy Baptist Church ordained Polly M. Bryson as the church's first woman deacon. She served as deacon vice chair in 1986–1987 and as chair in 1987–1989, 1990–1992, and 1995–1996. She commented on the church's support for women deacons and on her personal involvements, and she noted how her deacon ministry led her into other ministries.

---

[14]Marion D. Aldridge, "Wrestling with Words," *Greenlawn Pulpit* (2 January 1993): 2, 4-5.

God calls us all to be ministers and I feel both women and men can be great servants for God's kingdom. The church has been very supportive of women deacons.

Serving as deacon chairperson helped me to grow spiritually. I was the deacon to the deacons. I assisted the pastor in his ministry by filling in when he was away. I helped administer the Lord's Supper. I feel that being a servant in such a way opened doors for me as later I became a volunteer associate chaplain at Mission Hospital for four years and later was hired as the ministerial secretary to the chaplains and worked for 13 years. I feel God was leading me in this direction and the experience as a leader in the church prepared me for other ministry.[15]

Knightdale Baptist Church, Knightdale, North Carolina

Knightdale Baptist Church first ordained women deacons in 1931. Rita Blackmon has served three terms as deacon chair since 1999. She described some of her feelings about her service.

It has been an honor and has meant a great deal to me to serve our church family as deacon chair. I appreciate the confidence and trust that they have placed in me by allowing me to serve in this capacity. Serving as chair has allowed me the opportunity to work much more closely with the pastor and other church staff and I have certainly learned to appreciate their work and ministry more. I pray I have been instrumental in helping our church family to more fully appreciate the efforts of the church staff. I feel one of my greatest contributions has been in supporting/encouraging the pastor/church staff. During each of my three terms as chair I have been blessed with a great group of very supportive deacons. Being chair requires a lot of a person, it is hard work, and can be stressful at times. I pray a lot! I am most willing to be part of the leadership and count it an honor to have served, not only as deacon, but as chair.

My church family has been extremely supportive of me in this ministry and has been a great source of encouragement. Even though our church has had women deacons since 1931 we have only had one, other than myself, to serve as chair. Many members of our congregation have commented to me that they appreciate the spirit and sensitive nature which the women bring to the deacon board.

Strangely enough, my first time as deacon chair was at the retirement of our long-term (31 years) pastor. Even though he had given our church

---

[15]Polly M. Bryson, e-mail to author, 1 October 2004.

a one year notice of his retirement there were many things that I had to get involved with that were unique to being without a pastor in 31 years. Our church called a new pastor in early 2000, therefore, the first part of my first term as chair I was dealing with the former pastor retiring and trying to bring on a new pastor. During my third term as chair our pastor resigned, with little notice, and in an unusual manner. The last half of this term was very stressful and demanding.

The biggest challenge for me as chair has been getting involved in the small, petty conflicts that can take away from my personal worship experience.

To be an effective leader as a woman chair requires a delicate balance of ministry and support. I could not have been an effective leader without the support/encouragement of my deacons and church family.

I am most willing to be part of the leadership within my church and I love the challenge of "getting things done." One thing is certain, as chair you learn a lot, you study, worship and pray very hard![16]

Masonboro Baptist Church, Wilmington, North Carolina

Gordon Wright, pastor of Masonboro Baptist Church, went to Masonboro in 1984 immediately upon graduation from Southeastern Baptist Theological Seminary. He then became the church's pastor in 1988. He shared some developments that took place soon after becoming pastor.

During the nominating process of '89, one of our deacons asked if we should consider the whole congregation including women when asking for deacon nominations. I said that we absolutely should. Doris McQuery was called to serve. She shook our organization from being a body that gathered to eat breakfast and confess our guilt over all that we were not doing to a body that started to do ministry. The second year of her three-year service (1990) the eleven men elected her chair. We have had numerous women serving with distinction ever since.[17]

Northside Baptist Church, Jackson, Mississippi

Northside Baptist Church first elected women deacons in 1982. It chose twenty-nine women deacons in 1982–2002. Six women served as deacon chair in 1989–2003.[18] The church ordained Lida Stark as a deacon on

[16]Rita Blackmon, e-mail to author, 25 September 2004.
[17]Gordon Wright, e-mail to author, 2 September 2004.
[18]Lucy Rushing, e-mail to author, 5 May 2004.

January 20, 2002. Following a sermon by Linda McComb, Stark's ordination service proceeded as follows:

> Leader: What we are called to see in each other is how God's grace is made manifest: "God has given some to be apostles, some prophets, some evangelists, some pastors and teachers, to equip God's people for the work of service, for the building up of the body of Christ, until we ALL attain to the unity of our faith and in our knowledge of the Son of God."
>
> *People: We see these gifts in Lida. We have chosen her to serve among us, with us, and through us, that we all might serve God together.*
>
> Leader: Is it your will then, with God's blessing, to ordain her into the deacon ministry of Northside Baptist Church?
>
> *People: It is.*
>
> Leader: Lida, you have heard the will of the church, but you, too, must see the grace of God in your own life. Is it your will then, with God's blessing and help, to undertake the ministry of deacon here at Northside Baptist Church?
>
> *Lida: It is.*
>
> Leader: Will all of you together do the work of the kingdom, healing and helping the sick and sinful, serving and strengthening the weak and wearing, learning and loving, and living in faith until God ends this age?
>
> *ALL: With God's help, we will.*
>
> Leader: Then as a sign of your union together with her, I invite as many as wish to come forward, to lay your hands on her head or shoulder, and to speak your words to her.[19]

Peakland Baptist Church, Lynchburg, Virginia

Steve McNeely, pastor of Peakland Baptist Church, which had had deaconesses and later women deacons since its constitution in 1955, strongly affirmed the values of women deacons.

> Grounded in hints within the New Testament and the clear witness of early church history, one of the advances of our contemporary context is that we have restored, in more enlightened circumstances, the vital service of women as deacons. I regret that a literal reading of selected portions of Scripture and a false view of true submission in Christ leads so many fellow Baptists to practice a nonenlightened view of women's roles of service. I regret that women are thus deprived of their calling and that the

---

[19]"A Service of Ordination," *Bulletin*, Northside Baptist Church, Jackson MS, 20 January 2002.

Body of Christ is impaired by the denial of gifts for ministry. I could not serve with a church that would so limit the gifts and call of God.[20]

Royal Lane Baptist Church, Dallas, Texas

Cookie Stokes was ordained a deacon at Royal Lane Baptist Church in 1979. She served as the church's first female deacon chair in 1986–1987 and then served again in 1994–1995. She provided two stories, the first relating to the year she was ordained as a deacon, the second to her second term as deacon chair.

In the year 1979, when I was ordained as a deacon, I was on top of the world. I was 34 years old, had been married for 16 years, had a masters degree in math, and had been vice-president of a small, but respected, computer company for 10 years. Corresponding to these 10 years was our membership and place of service at Royal Lane Baptist Church. After 10 years of marriage, we had our first child, a son, and then 4 years later, a daughter. My world was complete. Both my husband and I were active at Royal Lane. I'll never know why I was asked to serve as a deacon before he was, but I felt awkward about the situation. A year later, to my shock and to the surprise of our friends, family, and church members, my husband asked for a divorce. Although I tried to reconcile, when he became self-destructive, I saw no other choice. For a while we both attended Royal Lane and that also made it difficult for people to know about our divorce. (Royal Lane is not a gossiping church.)

Eventually the pastor and deacon chair came to me to talk about my role as a deacon. When they asked if I thought I needed to resign from the board, I answered, "No." There were never any other questions and I was not asked to resign. Though it was a dark hour in my life, I appreciated the support of my church family and tried to be Christ-like at a time when it would have been easy not to be. . . .

In February 1987 I attended the annual Dallas Baptist Association dinner and program for deacon chairs and their spouses. My friend and Royal Lane deacon, Nancy Ferrell, accompanied me. We were welcomed and had dinner in the Fellowship Hall of Wilshire Baptist Church in my East Dallas neighborhood. Following the meal we were invited into the sanctuary for a meeting. One of the first things that happened was that a man began passing out printed material to all of the men deacon chairs. I raised my hand, but was ignored. Nancy, being bolder and quicker on the uptake than me, pursued the person passing out the materials and obtained

---

[20]Steve McNeely, letter to author, 22 October 2004.

my copy. One of the other deacon chairs present was Ellis Watkins of North Dallas Baptist Church, someone I knew well professionally. . . . He lent credence to my presence. If anyone noticed or objected to my participation, it was not known to me.[21]

Second Baptist Church, Lubbock, Texas

Second Baptist Church ordained its first five women deacons in 1976. Since then, eight women have served as deacon chair or cochair.[22] In 2000, a husband-wife team, Doug and Sammie Corley (she had been ordained in 1996), served as deacon cochairs. The following presents two accounts from Second Baptist. In the first, Sammie Corley describes two events that took place while she served as cochair: the church ordained forty-three deacons on one Sunday, and she served as deacon cochair with her son-in-law as pastor. In the second, Stephanie Nash, pastor for Christian education and outreach at Second Lubbock, describes the role of women in the diaconate and general leadership of this church.

Comments of Sammie Corley:

> I was honored to be asked to serve as cochair of the deacons with my husband, Doug. Our year as chairs of the deacons in 2000 was a rather special year in that we ordained 43 new deacons at one time—and believe me, that was God's idea, not mine. Charles Johnson, my son-in-law, was our pastor at that time. To accomplish this task we used both the early and late worship services with one-half in each service. As Charlie tells it, he is the only Baptist preacher to ever have his mother-in-law as chair of the deacons, telling him what to do. Since he left our church soon after the ordination of all the deacons to become pastor of Trinity Baptist Church in San Antonio, we began to see why God wanted so many deacons. We all filled up the slack for the almost two years until we called a senior pastor.[23]

Comments of Stephanie Nash:

> Second Baptist Church has played a unique role in supporting women of faith in both professional and lay ministry. In a society fraught with denominational battles over race, gender, and lifestyle disputes, Second

---

[21]Cookie Stokes, e-mail to author, 25 August 2004.

[22]Stephanie Nash, e-mail to Philip Wise, 7 September 2004 (forwarded to author via e-mail 8 September 2004).

[23]Sammie Corley, letter to author, 7 September 2004.

Baptist Church has assumed a strong stance in support of women in a denomination traditionally reluctant to provide women with visible leadership roles. The church ordained its first five women deacons, Anita Bass, Ina May Stewart, Jane Bundock, Elsie Roberts, and Edna Weber, in 1976. Second Baptist went on to ordain its first woman minister, Dot Thompson, in October 1982, an action still rarely duplicated in any other Baptist church in West Texas. Since then several more women have been ordained as career pastoral ministers by the church, including Michelle McLendon, Elizabeth Valentine Abraham, Carmen Wong, Dawn Darwin Weaks, Stephanie Nash, and Judith Fullingim. Secondly, the church has employed ordained women to serve as members of its own pastoral team, including Nancy Campbell and Mary Anne Forehand in addition to Michelle, Elizabeth, Dawn, and Stephanie, already mentioned. This role in supporting women in professional ministry has not only encouraged these women in their lifelong call to ministry, but has also undoubtedly encouraged sister churches in other parts of the state and nation to provide a similar opportunity for women to minister professionally.

Within its own organizational structure, Second Baptist encourages the leadership development of women in the congregation by routinely offering women visible roles of leadership in worship, within its committee structure, and as principal leaders of the church's lay and business operations. Several ordained women have served as Chair or Cochair of the Diaconate including Anita Bass, Madeline Douglass, Jo Ann Wyett, Jonanna George, Pam Blassingame, Sammie Corley, Dellinda Ebeling, and Michelle Doss; and as Chair or Cochair of the Leadership Team (or Executive Board) including Stephanie Nash, Nancy Sharp, Emily Sharp, Sandy Ogletree, and Marleta Springer. Beth Pennington served as a deacon and Staff Coordinator for the church at a crucial time of transition in the staff. Currently, 50 of the church's 89 ordained deacons are women. Women serve the church in many traditional ways as well, as teachers, committee chairs, musicians, scripture readers, prayers, worship leaders, and ushers. At Second Baptist, every member is a minister, regardless of gender.

The women of Second Baptist Church have inherited the legacy of leadership bequeathed them by the many women mentioned above as well as the church at large. Although the church cannot possibly take credit for the all the accomplishments earned by these women in their individual attempts to improve the lives of their fellow women and their community, Second Baptist Church is credited with having served as a haven of encouragement, inspiration, and spiritual empowerment for them, a place where women continue to be embraced for their God-given gifts, valued for their service to others, and inspired to fulfill their true calling; in short, to make their unique contributions to Christ's Kingdom.[24]

St. John's Baptist Church, Charlotte, North Carolina

Margaret Almond concluded her service as deacon chair at St. John's Baptist Church in May 2004. A retired banker, she shared information in three e-mails about her service as deacon chair and about the church's attitudes toward women. She even offered a suggestion about how I should write this book.

> My year as chair of the Diaconate has been no different than the previous year when the chair was a male. I have presided at all church conferences, at deacon meetings monthly, prepared an agenda of actions items, etc. . . .[25]

> Women are not singled out as "women" deacons. We are all ordained deacons, have the same responsibilities, serve in all manners of church service, and answer the call of God to visit the sick, support our church mission, and pray for our neighbors around the world. I really wish you could write your book without referring to women deacons.
> I'm reminded of my days in banking. I retired after 40 years with a local Charlotte bank. At the time I was promoted to Vice President, for many years I was always introduced as the "a WOMAN Vice President" of the Charlotte Office. Finally, I began responding by saying, "I am a Vice President who happens to be a woman!! No big deal!![26]

> Please keep in mind that at St. John's, deacons are deacons . . . men, women, possibly gay males or lesbian females (we do not do a litmus test). Deacons are to be leaders of the church, care for their flocks, and support the outreach of our ministry.[27]

University Heights Baptist Church, Springfield, Missouri

University Heights Baptist Church ordained its first woman deacon in 1995; it had a woman deacon chair in 1998 and a female vice-chair in 2004.

---

[24]Stephanie Nash, e-mail to Philip Wise, 7 September 2004 (forwarded to author, 8 September 2004).

[25]Margaret Almond, e-mail to author, 28 April 2004.

[26]Margaret Almond, e-mail to author, 24 August 2004.

[27]Margaret Almond, e-mail to author, 25 August 2004.

Senior Pastor Michael K. Olmsted described the process of nominating and electing deacons, noted the steps taken to provide for women deacons, and assessed the value of women deacons to the church.

> Nominees, regardless of gender, are treated the same. Our deacon selection process begins with the election of a nominating committee, composed of two deacons from the executive board of the diaconate, two deacons from the entire body of deacons, and three representatives of the congregation. The congregation is invited to nominate candidates through a printed form. The nominating committee, operating confidentially, reviews the forms, conducts "friendly" interviews, gives a general description of responsibilities, and asks each candidate to think and pray before deciding to have their name placed on the ballot. Voting takes place on a Sunday morning.
>
> U.H.B.C. had discussed the possibility of women as deacons for several years. Because that discussion had become more intense, I did an eight-week Bible study series on what the Bible says about women as servants of God and leaders in the early church. We also had a guest scholar preach on the subject on a Sunday morning. Although there was some objection, the congregation strongly supported women as deacons. This church has always treated women as capable and valued leaders, so the step to women deacons was a logical decision.
>
> Our women deacons have continued to lead us into ever stronger servant ministries and prayer efforts. It is a delight to see our men and women struggle with issues, pray and act out their faith in positive ways. As I look back at this significant transition, I count it one of the highlights of my forty years of ministry.[28]

Walnut Grove Baptist Church, Mechanicsville, Virginia

Walnut Grove Baptist Church elected its first three women deacons in the early 1990s, one of whom was Jan Campbell. Having served two terms as deacon chair, including service in 2004, she described serving with interim pastors and shared her attitude about women in church leadership.

> Our church was formed in 1831, was used as hospital for soldiers on both sides of the Civil War during battles of Cold Harbor, and is transitioning from a small rural church to a medium-sized suburban church with two Sunday morning worship services/styles. I am serving my second term as chair; in both terms I have served during an interim without a perma-

---

[28]Michael K. Olmsted, letter to author, 27 September 2004.

nent pastor: in the first, we chose an intentional interim pastor and underwent an intense self-study as our previous pastor had served with us for 25 years before retiring; in this one, our pastor is answering a call to missions in Indonesia and I will be a member of the pastor search committee when we begin our process.

Currently we participate in both SBC and CBF ministries, with a strong devotion to Virginia Baptist missions and work. I feel fortunate and blessed that my church recognizes the value of both men and women in leadership. It is a privilege to serve my congregation, and I am confident that the basic tenets of true Baptist belief and soul competency require that each of us pick up our ministries as God has called us to do, including the spiritual leadership of our congregation. When the subject of women in ministry comes up, I refer to Galatians 3:28 which shows that all souls are equal at the foot of the cross.[29]

Warrenton Baptist Church, Warrenton, North Carolina

Barbara Overby described the Warrenton Baptist Church as a small and old church with an average Sunday attendance of about seventy-five. The church had its first women deacons between 1945 and 1955. Overby shared a story revealing a highly practical, rather than a biblical or theological reason, both for electing women deacons and later for giving them a role in distributing the elements of the Lord's Supper.

> The story goes that [at first] there were only men as deacons. Our church used a cloth over the communion set, as well as the one under the set. The men had extreme difficulty in removing and properly folding that cloth, so they decided to elect women as deacons, solely for the purpose of folding the cloths. It is believed that the women were allowed to attend the meetings, could vote and sit on the front pew for first Sunday communion; however, they did not serve communion.
>
> According to Margie Watson, one of the two who were the first to actually serve communion, this is how that event came into being: "On a Sunday morning when not enough deacons were available to serve communion, the chairman anxiously started figuring out what he could to. He sent one of the deacons to see how many 'rotated off' deacons were in the congregation. Two additional deacons were needed.
>
> "Two lady deacons were present whose responsibility had been to fold the table cloth. (Never had the ladies actually served. They sat on the bench until time to replace the cloth.) During the anxiety, one of the ladies

---

[29]Jan Campbell, e-mail to author, 10 September 2004.

said to the other, 'Don't you think we could do this?' hoping to relieve the chairman of his predicament. The other lady deacon replied, 'I do think we can.' They questioned whether the congregation would take the sacraments from women.

"When the other deacons recovered from their shock, it was decided to do it. The choices were to let the ladies serve or be number deficient. The ladies successfully served and have done so since that time."

Until 2001, our Constitution stated there would be 12 deacons, 10 men and 2 women. At that time, the Constitution was changed to read 12 deacons (no gender specified). Ever since that time, we have had as many as 6 women serving at one time.

The first and only woman chairman was Mildred Johnson, elected on January 9, 2000. She served for 2 years before rotating off the board.[30]

West Acton Baptist Church, Acton, Massachusetts

Jeff Long-Middleton, pastor of the West Acton Baptist Church, described and affirmed women deacons in his church, which is related to the American Baptist Churches, USA. He discussed the absence of ordination, the prevalence of female chairpersons, and his personal views of the value of women in the diaconate.

We have never "ordained" either women or men deacons. They are nominated through the nominating committee and voted on by the church. They do not serve "life" terms but can serve two three-year terms consecutively and then take one year off.

Our church has had several female chairpersons of the Board of Deacons. Indeed, over the past 14 years, I think they have all been female.

The meaning, significance, and contributions of women in the diaconate of our church have been profound in terms of the spiritual insight and commitment. One of the questions which underlies this issue is that of biblical interpretation. Our church sees those passages that refer to limiting the role of women within the church as largely culturally or contextually driven—much as one might argue the issue of slavery.[31]

---

[30]Barbara Overby, e-mail to author, August 31, 2004.
[31]Jeff Long-Middleton, e-mail to author, 1 November 2004.

Woodhaven Baptist Church, Apex, North Carolina

Claudia J. Dickens recently completed a term as deacon chair at Wood-haven Baptist Church. She told about a difficult situation and about her overall service as deacon chair.

> While serving as deacon chair, we had to deal with some conflict in the church that was incited by a deacon. It was a very difficult year, but with the help of the Center for Congregational Health, our church has survived and is doing well. I had to take a firm stand while moderating our deacons in concert with the personnel committee during this time. Our church is young, and this was our first issue with church discipline, so we decided that the deacons would draw up some guidelines for church conflict which were brought before the church and made a part of our church constitution. . . .
>
> One of the positive highlights of my tenure as deacon chair was the involvement of our congregation in expanding our Deacon Ministry Teams beyond just the Deacon Teams to include church members. This allowed our church to do more ministry. The deacons were leaders in ministry and not doing it by themselves.
>
> I felt very inadequate going in to serve as chair, not because I am a woman, but because I knew there were several other deacons who could do the job quite well. Our vice chairman was a retired missionary, who stood by me and encouraged me. I learned much from him and trusted his wisdom.
>
> My tenure as deacon saw me before the Lord much more than before and I feel I'm a stronger Christian and individual for that experience. I never felt being a woman was an issue with anyone I worked with or from the church as a whole.[32]

---

[32]Claudia J. Dickens, e-mail to author, 24 August 2004.

Conclusion

The Lessons of History

Ten lessons emerge from this study. The purpose for sharing them is three-fold: to affirm churches with women deacons; to urge churches without women deacons to consider electing them; and to encourage churches with deaconesses, unequal in status to deacons, to assign them a status fully equal to deacons.

1. *The Incarnation of Christ injected liberty into human history*. Early in his career, Jesus visited Nazareth, his hometown, entered the synagogue on the sabbath, took a scroll, and read from Isaiah:

> "The Spirit of the Lord is upon me,
>   because he has anointed me
>   to bring good news to the poor.
> He has sent me to proclaim release to the captives
>   and recovery of sight to the blind,
>   to let the oppressed go free,
> to proclaim the acceptable year of the Lord's favor."
>
> (Luke 4:18-19 NRSV)

Then Jesus spent the remainder of his earthly ministry liberating people from the shackles of ecclesiastical bondage, spiritual slavery, ethical failure, cultural imprisonment, and even the subjugation of sickness and death.

Jesus' life, teachings, ministry, death, resurrection, ascension, plus his call for all believers to become disciples and his announcement that he would come again, constituted the most powerful message in women's (and everyone else's) behalf the world has ever experienced. Jesus effectively mandated that the church utilize to the fullest all the gifts of all the people to help release people from shackles so that they could invest their lives by denying themselves, taking up their crosses, and following him.

2. *The New Testament concept of diakonia (service) mandates the urgency of electing women to the diaconate. Diakonia* is a critical requirement of the Christian community. Because the New Testament and church and Baptist history express *diakonia* in one of its purest forms in the diaconate, that function of the church on earth needs all the help it can get. Adding women to the cause enhances a church's ability to serve more

people. To argue that women can serve just as effectively without being deacons begs the question: Why would the same logic not apply to men? Baptist churches today need to break down all barriers (social, gender, theological) that prohibit women's participation in the diaconate. The necessity of *diakonia* at the heart of church life provides sufficient reason to make women a part of the diaconate.

The implication of biblical history is that placing women in the diaconate represents a natural expression of Christ's intention for the complete fulfillment of the service motif in the church. It also overrides the unnatural tendency (sin, if you will) to subject half the Baptist population to a male-dominated, woman-suppressing pattern of doing church. Further, it overcomes twenty centuries of misreading the intentions of the apostle Paul for women in roles of service and ministry. In Galatians 3:27-28, Paul, too, called for affirming Jesus' gifts to and expectations of men and women.

3. *The issue of women deacons has global implications.* Global Women was organized in December 2001 in Birmingham, Alabama. This impressive Baptist organization adopted as its mission statement: "Motivated by the love and mercy of Jesus Christ, Global Women exists to create worldwide friendships among women for shared learning and service."[1] The first issue of the organization's newsletter in 2002 shared some key reasons why women (and all Baptists) need to be concerned about women:

> Did you know that 33% of the world's population are non-Christian women? This means that women comprise the largest unreached people group in the world. Did you know that women are 66% of illiterates, 80% of refugees, 70% of poor, 75% of sick persons? This means that millions of women are homeless, hungry, and dying. Did you know that this year alone, 4,000,000 women will be sold as slaves?[2]

The implications of Global Women's findings are extraordinary. Women's needs worldwide are unbelievably large and widespread. It would require the ministry of every Christian in the world to begin to meet such phenomenal needs. Therefore, the refusal of many Baptists to elect women as deacons is tantamount to rejecting the giftedness God provides them to help meet human needs. Placing women in diaconal roles in church life

---

[1]Mission Statement, *Voices: A Newsletter of Global Women* 1/1 (Spring 2002): 1.

[2]"Who Are Those Global Women," *Voices: A Newsletter of Global Women* 1/1 (Spring 2002): 1.

enhances their influence and ability to exact change. As Donald F. Thomas aptly put it in *The Deacon in a Changing Church*, "It may be that the most important question is not whether women should hold positions in the church but whether the modern church can fulfill its ministry without them."[3]

4. *The right of women to serve as deacons in Baptist churches is a human rights issue and therefore a moral issue.* On 1 January 1863, President Abraham Lincoln issued the Emancipation Proclamation, a historic document that resulted in the end of slavery in the United States. Twenty-eight years later, in 1891, the Home Mission Board of the Southern Baptist Convention (SBC) presented its forty-sixth annual report. Reflecting the prejudicial and discriminatory attitudes of Southern Baptist home missions leadership, this condescending report stated in the section on "our work among the colored people":

> Nothing is plainer to any one who knows this race than its perfect willingness to accept a subordinate place, provided there be confidence that in that position of subordination it will receive justice and kindness. That is the condition it prefers above all others, and this is the condition in which it attains the highest development of every attribute of manhood. Whenever it shall understandingly and cheerfully accept this condition, the race problem is settled forever.[4]

Similarly, on 10 December 1948, the United Nations General Assembly adopted the Universal Declaration of Human Rights, a crucial document that declared that all people are born with equal dignity and rights. Thirty-six years later, in 1984, the SBC adopted a resolution denying ordination to women, including deacons. That same convention, in 1998 and 2000, adopted revised editions of the Baptist Faith and Message that denigrated women into a position of submission to men in the church and excluded them from the pastoral ministry. Then, in 2004, the SBC North American Mission Board (formerly Home Mission Board) adopted a document (described in chapter 6) to be used as a tool for defining a church and withholding funds from any church desiring to start a new congregation, if that church has women deacons.

---

[3]Donald F. Thomas, *The Deacon in a Changing Church* (Valley Forge PA: Judson Press, 1969) 114.

[4]*Proceedings*, Southern Baptist Convention, 1891, appendix B, xxxvii.

The point is this: At times, documents of American and international politics and culture have more effectively recognized the values of human rights for all than have Baptist churches and other organizations that have systematically excluded women from key roles of leadership in congregational life. Outsiders (and many insiders, for that matter) have every right to ask: Why do certain segments of the Baptist community treat women with the same indignity and inequality that Jesus Christ came to destroy? SBC leaders need to do some serious soul-searching regarding their antagonistic attitudes toward women in leadership capacities, particularly those who are ordained.

5. *Baptist origins provide solid support for women deacons as a basic Baptist ideal.* The earliest Baptists placed women deacons on a par with male deacons in nomination, election, ordination, and duties. Therefore, Baptist origins deliver a provocative question to Baptists in the twenty-first century: What are the implications of Baptist beginnings for Baptist churches today when those beginnings plainly supported women deacons? History suggests that churches need to move past all distinctions and differentiations between men and women in diaconal functions, just like the first Baptists in 1609.

6. *Futility characterizes every objection to electing women deacons.* This study has uncovered many reasons why most Baptists have opposed women deacons. Twenty-eight representative "reasons" follow.

(1) Woman's sinning first in the book of Genesis.

(2) No explicit approval of women deacons in the New Testament.

(3) Misreadings of the intentions of Jesus for women.

(4) Literal, restrictive, and noncontextual interpretations of verses in the writings of the apostle Paul (1 Corinthians 11:3-16; 14:34-35; 1 Timothy 2:11-14) and of Peter (1 Peter 3:1-3).

(5) The selection of seven men in Acts 6:3.

(6) The idea that a woman cannot be the husband of one wife (1 Timothy 3:12).

(7) Misunderstandings of the social status of women in the New Testament and transferal of that status onto women today.

(8) Influence of John Calvin.

(9) Baptist use of translations of the Bible and commentaries on the Bible that prohibit women deacons.

(10) Inadequate awareness of the presence of women deacons at certain places and times in general church history.

(11) Lack of historical knowledge about the presence and value of women deacons in various periods of the Baptist past.

(12) Insufficient awareness of the presence and contributions of women deacons in certain other Christian denominations.

(13) Misunderstanding of the priesthood of all believers.

(14) Masculinized views of church leadership.

(15) Excessive pastoral authority by male ministers.

(16) Growing presence of elders in Baptist life.

(17) Surging influence of right-wing religion in American culture.

(18) Role of fundamentalist Baptist leaders, publications, meetings, and actions.

(19) Erroneous views of ordination as conveying special authority.

(20) The act of women's ordination among Southern Baptists (typically not an issue with American Baptists).

(21) Negative resolutions and statements of faith adopted by the SBC regarding women's submission and ordination.

(22) The view that women's ordination represents a march toward apostasy, liberalism, and modernism.

(23) Actions of SBC theological seminaries and mission boards that have depreciated women by making their ordination a test of their faith, acceptability, and effectiveness.

(24) The refusal of LifeWay Christian Resources curriculum, books, and other materials to advocate women deacons.

(25) The efforts of some Baptist state convention executive directors, directors of missions, and Baptist state newspaper editors to downplay the leadership capacity of ordained women.

(26) The power of local-church tradition not to want to change.

(27) The notion that the presence of women deacons will somehow cause men to be less involved in deacon ministries and other church ministries.

(28) The refusal to deal with potential conflict in church life required to change church policies to provide for women deacons.

Here is the kicker: Not one of these twenty-eight reasons overrides the compelling presence of Christ who devoted his life and teachings to the liberation of *all* humans—including women. No man has the inalienable right to assume that only he is gifted enough to serve as deacon and that no woman possesses such qualifications. Unfortunately, most Baptist churches have made opposition to ordained women a doctrine equal to believer's baptism and the Lord's Supper. It is time for Baptist churches to abolish such discriminatory practices. No biblical, historical, or theological factor can sufficiently undercut this need; to the contrary, the Bible, Baptist history, and the doctrinal ideals of the Christian faith place high priority on the giftedness of women and their right and responsibility to exercise it in every capacity of church life.

7. *Questions continue to exist.* What are the implications for the future
of women deacons in Southern Baptist churches when all six Southern Baptist seminaries teach students that they should object to the ordination of
women in their churches and then graduate those students into those
churches to implement their objections?

What are the implications for the future of Baptist women in missions
and for churches supporting missions when the SBC North American and
International Mission Boards oppose the selection of ordained women for
service in mission roles and of nonordained women whose churches
approve the ordination of women?

What stance should Baptist churches take today toward women deacons? And how should Baptists deal with the following realities: the Old
Testament emphasis on women being created in God's image; the emancipation-based life and teachings of Christ; New Testament emphases on
women and freedom; the possibilities and practices of women deacons in
pre-Baptist church history; the presence of women in the diaconate
throughout Baptist history; and the growing patterns of adding women to
the diaconate and naming them deacon chairs?

8. *Every Baptist church that does not have women deacons has a
responsibility to consider changing church policies to provide for them.*
With decisive policy making, bylaw changes, and other actions, churches
will do well to move quickly to upgrade the whole quality of congregational life by giving women their due. Every church without women
deacons must move past the weak argument that "Our church has always
done it this way." Tradition is not sacred, even in church life, when it vio-
lates the intentions of Christ. Such churches must also cast out internal and
external prohibitions against women's ordination expressed by ultraconservative Baptists who hang all their hats on the tree of male dominance in
church leadership, teaching, and authority; stop using curriculum literature
that downgrades the ordination of women; and stand tall for the call of
Christ to put women in their places—the ultimate servant and leadership
positions the church has to offer. Women will benefit; the diaconate will
gain respect; service will be rendered; the church will prosper; Christ will
be honored.

9. *Baptists being Baptists, with local-church autonomy providing a
form of independence, churches are free to choose women deacons or
deaconesses or neither.* However, such decisions will have consequences.
Women will be treated equally with men in the diaconate and all church
leadership opportunities, or they will not. Gender equality will reflect the
purpose of God in creation, or gender inequality will reflect a modern-day

version of discrimination and prejudicial treatment within the church; and the latter will perpetuate a form of theological corruption—essentially telling God that the church disagrees with his decision to create women in his image, fully gifted to undertake any and every spiritual opportunity the church can offer. Local-church autonomy must not be used as a polity-oriented justification to overrule God's intention for half the people in Baptist life.

10. *Churches with deaconesses would do well to transition them into women deacons.* Some churches with deaconesses treat them equally with deacons. Other churches, however, and there are thousands of them, treat deaconesses separately from male deacons, view them as assistants to deacons, deprive them of ordination (when it applies to deacons), prevent them from serving as deacon officers, and do not allow them to distribute the Lord's Supper. While churches with deaconesses merit commendation for incorporating women into the diaconate, they would do well to take three additional steps: terminate the subsidiary status applied to deaconesses; start calling deaconesses deacons; and revise church policies to provide for complete equality in nomination, selection, ordination (or nonordination), duties, and election to deacon offices.

Appendix

Selected Baptist Churches with Women Deacon Chairs and/or Cochairs in the Present and/or Past

Most Baptist deacon bodies with female chairpersons have elected them since 1960, and the number of women chairs has risen dramatically since 1990. This list of selected churches focuses primarily on Baptists in the South and West related primarily to the Cooperative Baptist Fellowship and the Southern Baptist Convention, although it does contain some American Baptist churches, including African-American churches, and a few Nova Scotian churches. Intended only to be representative and illustrative, this appendix would be significantly longer if a scientific technique existed for securing comprehensive information from all Baptist churches in the United States and other countries.

This representative list includes 292 churches in twenty-five states, the District of Columbia, and Nova Scotia. The leading states are North Carolina (seventy-eight chairs or cochairs), Virginia (sixty-six), and Georgia (thirty-one). The total number of such churches is unknown because of the difficulty involved in securing this information. Hundreds of additional churches, especially those related to the American Baptist Churches, USA, have or have had women deacon chairs. Since the number of churches with women deacons that have not yet had a female chair is much larger than the number that have, it is extremely likely that thousands of Baptist churches, nationwide and worldwide, have women deacons. The number of churches with women deacons is probably much higher than most Baptists realize.

Because many churches with female deacon chairs are not included in the list, I invite churches with female chairs in the past or present that are not included to alert me to them. Should this book ever be revised, I will be glad to incorporate the additions.

Alabama
Baptist Church of the Covenant, Birmingham
Crosscreek Baptist Church, Pelham

First Baptist Church, Auburn
Hillcrest Baptist Church, Mobile
Mountain Brook Baptist Church, Birmingham
Southside Baptist Church, Birmingham
University Baptist Church, Montevallo
Vestavia Hills Baptist Church, Birmingham
Weatherly Heights Baptist Church, Huntsville
District of Columbia
First Baptist Church of Washington
California
Nineteenth Avenue Baptist Church, San Francisco
Tiburon Baptist Church, Tiburon
Florida
First Baptist Church, Cocoa
First Baptist Church, DeLand
First Baptist Church, South Miami
Georgia
Briarcliff Baptist Church, Atlanta
Carlton Baptist Church, Carlton
Cave Springs Baptist Church, Cave Springs
Dogwood Hills Baptist Church, East Point (dissolved)
Druid Hills Baptist Church, Atlanta
Emory Baptist Church, Atlanta
Fellowship Baptist Church, Americus
First Baptist Church, Athens
First Baptist Church, Carrollton
First Baptist Church, Decatur
First Baptist Church, Forsyth
First Baptist Church, Fort Oglethorpe
First Baptist Church, Gainesville
First Baptist Church of Christ at Macon
First Baptist Church, Marietta
First Baptist Church, Morrow
First Baptist Church, Roswell
First Baptist Church, Savannah
Heritage Baptist Church, Cartersville
Highland Hills Baptist Church, Macon
Memorial Baptist Church, Savannah
Milledge Avenue Baptist Church, Athens
National Heights Baptist Church, Fayetteville
North River Baptist Church, Alpharetta
Northside Drive Baptist Church, Atlanta
Oakhurst Baptist Church, Decatur

Parkway Baptist Church, Duluth
Peachtree Baptist Church, Atlanta
Smoke Rise Baptist Church, Stone Mountain
Tabernacle Baptist Church, Carrollton
Wieuca Road Baptist Church, Atlanta

Kansas
College Heights Baptist Church, Manhattan
Leawood Baptist Church, Leawood

Kentucky
Broadway Baptist Church, Louisville
Calvary Baptist Church, Lexington
Central Baptist Church, Lexington
Crescent Hill Baptist Church, Louisville
Deer Park Baptist Church, Louisville
Faith Baptist Church, Georgetown
First Baptist Church, Corbin
Highland Baptist Church, Louisville
Ridgewood Baptist Church, Louisville
St. Matthews Baptist Church, Louisville
Twenty-third and Broadway Baptist Church, Louisville

Louisiana
Broadmoor Baptist Church, Baton Rouge
Emmanuel Baptist Church, Alexandria
St. Charles Avenue Baptist Church, New Orleans
University Baptist Church, Baton Rouge

Maryland
First Baptist Church, Wheaton
Kensington Baptist Church, Kensington
Paramount Baptist Church, Hagerstown

Massachusetts
First Baptist Church, Bedford
First Baptist Church, Beverly
First Baptist Church, Greenfield
First Baptist Church, Haverhill
First Baptist Church, Jamaica Plain
Mashpee Baptist Church, Mashpee
The Baptist Church in Grafton, Grafton
The Gay Head Community Baptist Church, Vineyard Haven
West Acton Baptist Church, Acton

Mississippi
First Baptist Church, Starkville
Northminster Baptist Church, Jackson
Northside Baptist Church, Jackson

Missouri
    First Baptist Church, Jefferson City
    Kirkwood Baptist Church, Kirkwood
    Memorial Baptist Church, Columbia
    Second Baptist Church, Liberty
    University Heights Baptist Church, Springfield
    Webster Groves Baptist Church, Webster Groves
New York
    Baptist Temple, Rochester
    First Baptist Church, Rochester
    Lake Avenue Baptist Church, Rochester
    Scarsdale Community Baptist Church, Scarsdale
    York Baptist Church, York
North Carolina
    Ardmore Baptist Church, Winston-Salem
    Arlington Boulevard Baptist Church, Greenville
    Boiling Springs Baptist Church, Boiling Springs
    College Park Baptist Church, Greensboro
    College Park Baptist Church, Winston-Salem
    Cullowhee Baptist Church, Cullowhee
    First Baptist Church, Asheville
    First Baptist Church, Cary
    First Baptist Church, Elkin
    First Baptist Church, Forest City
    First Baptist Church, Gastonia
    First Baptist Church, Greensboro
    First Baptist Church, Henderson
    First Baptist Church, Hickory
    First Baptist Church, Hillsborough
    First Baptist Church, Jamestown
    First Baptist Church, Kannapolis
    First Baptist Church, Lenoir
    First Baptist Church, Lumberton
    First Baptist Church, Marion
    First Baptist Church, Monroe
    First Baptist Church, Morganton
    First Baptist Church, Mt. Gilead
    First Baptist Church, Raleigh
    First Baptist Church, Rockingham
    First Baptist Church, Sanford
    First Baptist Church, Shelby
    First Baptist Church, Spring Hope
    First Baptist Church, Sylva

First Baptist Church, Wadesboro
First Baptist Church, Wilson
First Baptist Church, Winston-Salem
First Baptist Church, Yadkinville
Forest Hills Baptist Church, Raleigh
Franklinton Baptist Church, Franklinton
Goshen Baptist Church, Leland
Grace Baptist Church, Statesville
Greystone Baptist Church, Raleigh
Hominy Baptist Church, Candler
Immanuel Baptist Church, Greenville
Knightdale Baptist Church, Knightdale
Knollwood Baptist Church, Winston-Salem
Louisburg Baptist Church, Louisburg
Lowes Grove Baptist Church, Durham
Mars Hill Baptist Church, Mars Hill
Masonboro Baptist Church, Wilmington
Memorial Baptist Church, Greenville
Memorial Baptist Church, Williamston
Mt. Carmel Baptist Church, Chapel Hill
Myers Park Baptist Church, Charlotte
North Chapel Hill Baptist Church, Chapel Hill
Oak City Baptist Church, Oak City
Park Road Baptist Church, Charlotte
Park View Baptist Church, Durham
Piney Grove Baptist Church, Williamston
Providence Baptist Church, Charlotte
Pullen Memorial Baptist Church, Raleigh
Ridge Road Baptist Church, Raleigh
Rowland Baptist Church, Rowland
Roxboro Baptist Church, Roxboro
Salem Baptist Church, Apex
Shiloh Baptist Church, Shiloh
Spilman Memorial Baptist Church, Kinston
St. John's Baptist Church, Charlotte
Viewmont Baptist Church, Hickory
Wake Forest Baptist Church, Wake Forest
Wake Forest Baptist Church, Winston-Salem
Warrenton Baptist Church, Warrenton
Warsaw Baptist Church, Warsaw
Watts Street Baptist Church, Durham
Weldon Baptist Church, Weldon
Wendell Baptist Church, Wendell

Westfield Baptist Church, Dunn
Wingate Baptist Church, Wingate
Woodhaven Baptist Church, Apex
Woodlawn Baptist Church, Apex
Yates Baptist Church, Durham
Zebulon Baptist Church, Zebulon
North Dakota
Bethel Baptist Church, Powers Lake
First Baptist Church, Bismarck
First Baptist Church, Fargo
Immanuel Baptist Church, Minot
Nova Scotia, Canada
Bayside United Baptist Church, Bayside
First Baptist Church, Amherst
First Baptist Church, Halifax
Mahone Bay United Baptist Church, Mahone Bay
New Cornwall United Baptist Church, New Cornwall
Northwest United Baptist Church, Northwest
Port Williams United Baptist Church, Port Williams
Sydney United Baptist Church, Sydney
Wolfville United Baptist Church, Wolfville
Oklahoma
First Baptist Church, Oklahoma City
First Baptist Church, Shawnee
Spring Creek Baptist Church, Oklahoma City
University Heights Baptist Church, Stillwater
Pennsylvania
First Baptist Church, Philadelphia
South Carolina
Augusta Heights Baptist Church, Greenville
Boulevard Baptist Church, Anderson
First Baptist Church, Clemson
First Baptist Church, Greenville
First Baptist Church, Pendleton
Shaws Fork Baptist Church, Aiken
Trinity Baptist Church, Seneca
South Dakota
First Baptist Church, Pierre
First Baptist Church, Sioux Falls
First Baptist Church, Vermillion
Tennessee
First Baptist Church, Chattanooga
First Baptist Church, Jefferson City

First Baptist Church, Knoxville
First Baptist Church, Oak Ridge
Immanuel Baptist Church, Knoxville
Immanuel Baptist Church, Nashville
Prescott Memorial Baptist Church, Memphis
South Gate Baptist Church, Antioch

Texas
Austin Heights Baptist Church, Nacogdoches
Broadway Baptist Church, Fort Worth
Calder Baptist Church, Beaumont
Calvary Baptist Church, Waco
DaySpring Baptist Church, Waco
First Baptist Church, Arlington
First Baptist Church, Austin
Highland Park Baptist Church, Austin
Lake Shore Baptist Church, Waco
Royal Lane Baptist Church, Dallas
Second Baptist Church, Lubbock
Seventh and James Baptist Church, Waco
South Main Baptist Church, Houston
University Baptist Church, Austin
University Baptist Church, Fort Worth
Wilshire Baptist Church, Dallas
Woodland Baptist Church, San Antonio

Vermont
Restoration Baptist Church, Burlington

Virginia
Abingdon Baptist Church, Abingdon
Alum Spring Baptist Church, Culpeper
Angel's Rest Baptist Fellowship, Pearisburg
Arlington Heights Baptist Church, Arlington
Bedford Baptist Church, Bedford
Berea Baptist Church, Rockville
Berryville Baptist Church, Berryville
Blacksburg Baptist Church, Blacksburg
Bon Air Baptist Church, Richmond
Brewington Baptist Church, Brewington
Browntown Baptist Church, Bentonville
Burkeville Baptist Church, Burkeville
Calvary Baptist Church, Fairfax
Cedar Run Baptist Church, Culpeper
Chatham Baptist Church, Chatham
Churchland Baptist Church, Chesapeake

Effort Baptist Church, Palmyra
First Baptist Church, Bristol
First Baptist Church, Newport News
First Baptist Church, Norton
First Baptist Church, Richmond
First Baptist Church, South Boston
First Baptist Church, Staunton
First Baptist Church, Waynesboro
First Baptist Church, Winchester
First Baptist Church of Clarendon, Arlington
Franklin Baptist Church, Franklin
Freemason Street Baptist Church, Norfolk
Ginter Park Baptist Church, Richmond
Glade Baptist Church, Blacksburg
Grace Baptist Church, Richmond
Grandin Court Baptist Church, Roanoke
Hampton Baptist Church, Hampton
Hatcher Memorial Baptist Church, Richmond
Heritage Baptist Church, Farmville
Hilton Baptist Church, Newport News
Ivor Baptist Church, Ivor
Larchmont Baptist Church, Norfolk
Main Street Baptist Church, Emporia
Marlow Heights Baptist Church, Front Royal
Messick Baptist Church, Poquoson
Monument Heights Baptist Church, Richmond
Mountain Baptist Church, Bluemont
North Riverside Baptist Church, Newport News
Northminster Baptist Church, Richmond
Parkwood Baptist Church, Annandale
Peakland Baptist Church, Lynchburg
Richland Baptist Church, Hartwood
River Road Baptist Church, Richmond
Rivermont Baptist Church, Danville
Saluda Baptist Church, Saluda
Second Baptist Church, Petersburg
Sycamore Baptist Church, Franklin
Taylorsville Baptist Church, Doswell
Thalia Lynn Baptist Church, Virginia Beach
Trinity Baptist Church, Norfolk
University Baptist Church, Charlottesville
Vienna Baptist Church, Vienna
Walnut Grove Baptist Church, Mechanicsville

West End Baptist Church, Suffolk
West Main Baptist Church, Danville
Westhunt Baptist Church, Richmond
White Stone Baptist Church, White Stone
Winfree Memorial Baptist Church, Midlothian
Wytheville Baptist Church, Wytheville
Zoar Baptist Church, Deltaville
Washington
Good Shepherd Baptist Church, Lynnwood
Japanese Baptist Church, Seattle
Martin Luther King Jr. Memorial Baptist Church, Renton
West Virginia
College Avenue Baptist Church, Bluefield
Summit Point Baptist Church, Summit Point
Wisconsin
First Baptist Church, Waukesha

A Selected Bibliography

Books

Adams, Sheri. *What the Bible Really Says about Women.* Macon GA: Smyth and Helwys, 1994.

Agar, Frederick A. *Church Women at Work.* Philadelphia: Judson Press, 1937.

_____. *The Deacon at Work.* Philadelphia: Judson Press, 1923.

Blevins, Carolyn D. *Women's Place in Baptist Life.* Brentwood TN: Baptist History and Heritage Society, 2003.

Brackney, William H., editor. *Baptist Life and Thought: 1600–1980—A Sourcebook.* Valley Forge PA: Judson Press, 1983.

_____, editor. *Faith, Life, and Witness: The Papers of the Study and Research Division of the Baptist World Alliance, 1986–1990.* Birmingham: Samford University Press, 1990.

Briggs, J. H. Y. *The English Baptists of the Nineteenth Century.* Volume 3 of A History of the English Baptists, edited by Roger Hayden. Didcot UK: The Baptist Historical Society, 1994.

Calvin, John. *Calvin: Theological Treatises.* Translated by J. K. S. Reid. The Library of Christian Classics 22. Philadelphia: Westminster Press, 1954.

Carlson, Leland H., editor. *The Writings of Henry Barrow, 1590–1591.* London: George Allen & Unwin, 1966.

Deweese, Charles W. *The Emerging Role of Deacons.* Nashville: Broadman Press, 1979.

Edwards, Morgan. *The Customs of Primitive Churches; or A Set of Propositions: Relative to the Name, Materials [sic], Constitution, Power, Officers, Ordinances, Rites, Business, Worship, Discipline, Government, &c of a Church, to Which Are Added Their Proofs from Scripture, and Historical Narratives of the Manner in Which Most of Them Have Been Reduced to Practice.* Philadelphia: printed by Andrew Steuart, 1768. Microfilm: (from a copy dated 1774) Nashville: Historical Commission, SBC, 1958.

Encyclopedia of Southern Baptists. 4 vols. Nashville: Broadman Press, 1958, 1971, 1982.

Flynt, Wayne. *Alabama Baptists: Southern Baptists in the Heart of Dixie.* Tuscaloosa: University of Alabama Press, 1998.

Howell, R. B. C. *The Deaconship: Its Nature, Qualifications, Relations, and Duties.* Philadelphia: American Baptist Publication Society, 1846.

Humphreys, Fisher, and Philip Wise. *Fundamentalism.* Macon GA: Smyth and Helwys, 2004.

Johnson, William Bullein. *The Gospel Developed through the Government and Order of the Churches of Jesus Christ.* Richmond: H. K. Ellyson, 1846.

Lumpkin, William L. *Baptist Confessions of Faith*. Revised edition. Valley Forge PA: Judson Press, 1969.

Maring, Norman H., and Winthrop S. Hudson. *A Baptist Manual of Polity and Practice*. Valley Forge PA: Judson Press, 1963.

Martimort, Aimé Georges. *Deaconesses: An Historical Study*. Translated by K. D. Whitehead. San Francisco: Ignatius Press, 1986.

McBeth, H. Leon. *The Baptist Heritage: Four Centuries of Baptist Witness*. Nashville: Broadman Press, 1987.

_____. *A Sourcebook for Baptist Heritage*. Nashville: Broadman Press, 1990.

_____. *Women in Baptist Life*. Nashville: Broadman Press, 1979.

Moody, J. B. *Women in the Churches: Their Rights and Restrictions*. Second edition. Martin TN: privately published, 1910.

Morgan, David T. *Southern Baptist Sisters: In Search of Status, 1845–2000*. Macon GA: Mercer University Press, 2003.

Morris, Nicola. *Sisters of the People: The Order of Baptist Deaconesses, 1890–1975*. Centre for Comparative Studies in Religion and Gender Research paper #2. Bristol, England: University of Bristol, 2002.

Nichols, Harold. *The Work of the Deacon and Deaconess*. Valley Forge PA: Judson Press, 1964; revised edition, 1984.

Niebuhr, H. Richard, and Daniel D. Williams. *The Ministry in Historical Perspectives*. New York: Harper & Row, 1956.

Olson, Jeannine E. *One Ministry, Many Roles: Deacons and Deaconesses through the Centuries*. St. Louis: Concordia Publishing House, 1992.

Parker, G. Keith. *Baptists in Europe: History and Confessions of Faith*. Nashville: Broadman Press, 1982.

Pettis, Robert L. *"Servants of Christ": A Training Guide for the Ministry of the Deacon and Deaconess*. Richmond VA: R. L. Pettis, 1995.

Riley, Maurice. *The Deaconess: Walking in Newness of Light*. Newark NJ: Christian Associates Publications, 1993.

Rose, Doris M. *Baptist Deaconesses*. London: Carey Kingsgate Press, 1954.

Sheffield, Robert. *The Ministry of Baptist Deacons*. Edited by Gary Hardin. Nashville: Convention Press, 1990; reprint, 1993.

Shurden, Walter B., editor. *The Struggle for the Soul of the SBC: Moderate Responses to the Fundamentalist Controversy*. Macon GA: Mercer University Press, 1993.

_____, and Randy Shepley, compilers and editors. *Going for the Jugular: A Documentary History of the SBC Holy War*. Macon GA: Mercer University Press, 1996.

Smyth, John. *The Works of John Smyth, Fellow of Christ's College, 1594–[159]8*. Two volumes. 1915 Tercentenary edition for the Baptist Historical Society, with notes and biography by William Thomas Whitley. Cambridge UK: University Press, 1915.

Stagg, Evelyn, and Frank Stagg. *Woman in the World of Jesus*. Philadelphia: Westminster Press, 1978.

Thomas, Donald F. *The Deacon in a Changing Church*. Valley Forge PA: Judson Press, 1969.

Trull, Audra, and Joe Trull, editors. *Putting Women in Their Place: Moving Beyond Gender Stereotypes in Church and Home*. Macon GA: Smyth and Helwys, 2003.

Articles and Essays in Books and Encyclopedias

Beasley-Murray, George R. "The Diaconate in Baptist Churches." Background paper in *The Ministry of Deacons*. World Council of Churches studies no. 2. Geneva: World Council of Churches, 1965.

Cox, Mrs. W. J. "The Woman's Part." *Official Report, Sixth Baptist World Congress*. Edited by J. H. Rushbrooke. Atlanta: Baptist World Alliance, 1939.

"Deaconess." *The Mennonite Encyclopedia*. Volume 2. Scottdale PA: Mennonite Publishing House, 1956.

"Deaconess." *The New Schaff-Herzog Encyclopedia of Religious Knowledge*. Volume 3. New York: Funk & Wagnalls, 1909.

MacClaren, Beth H. "Women's Issues." *Faith, Life, and Witness: The Papers of the Study and Research Division of the Baptist World Alliance, 1986–1990*. Edited by William H. Brackney. Birmingham AL: Samford University Press, 1990.

Marshall, Molly T. "Women's Status in Ministry Equals That of Men." *Defining Baptist Convictions: Guidelines for the Twenty-first Century*. Edited by Charles W. Deweese. Franklin TN: Providence House Publishers, 1996.

Montgomery, Helen Barrett. "The New Opportunity for Baptist Women." *Record of Proceedings, Third Baptist World Congress*. Edited by W. T. Whitley. London: Kingsgate Press, 1923.

Articles in Journals, Newspapers, Newsletters, and on Websites

"American Baptist Policy Statement on Ordained Ministry." 1989 (revised 1992, 1997). <www.abc-usa.org/resources/resol/ordain.htm>.

"American Baptist Policy Statement on Women and Men as Partners in Church and Society." 1985 (revised 1990, 1996). <www.abc-usa.org/resources/resol/women1.htm>.

"American Baptist Resolution on the Empowerment of Women in the American Baptist Churches." 1977 (revised 1981, 1990, 1995). <www.abc-usa.org/resources/resol/empwomen.htm>.

Blevins, Carolyn D. "Reflections: Baptists and Women's Issues in the Twentieth Century." *Baptist History and Heritage* 35/3 (Summer/Fall 2000): 53-66.

Briggs, John. "She-Preachers, Widows, and Other Women: The Feminine Dimension in Baptist Life since 1600." *The Baptist Quarterly* 31/7 (July 1986): 337-52.

Callahan, Yvonne H. "Mrs. Betty Galloway: Portrait of a Woman in the Deaconship." *The Deacon* 3/3 (April-June 1973): 16-18.

Carter, James E. "Dealing with Doctrinal Conflict in Associational History." *Baptist History and Heritage* 17/2 (April 1982): 33-43.

Cartledge, Tony. "Defining a Baptist (?) Church." *Biblical Recorder*, 23 October 2004, 2.

Cate, Robert. "Shall We Have Women Deacons?" *Baptist Standard*, 17 April 1974, 4.

Chandler, Charles H. "What about Women Deacons?" *The Deacon* 14/3 (April-June 1984): 45-50.

_____. "What about Women Deacons?" *Search* 8/3 (Spring 1979): 24-41.

Clanton, Jann Aldredge. "Why I Believe Southern Baptist Churches Should Ordain Women." *Baptist History and Heritage* 23/3 (July 1988): 50-55.

Clingenpeel, Mike. "The Changing Face of Leadership." *Religious Herald*, 23 March 2000, 8.

Davies, J. G. "Deacons, Deaconesses, and the Minor Orders in the Patristic Period." *The Journal of Ecclesiastical History* 14 (April 1963): 1-15.

"Deaconesses." *The Baptist Magazine* (London) 6 (1814): 401-403.

"Deaconesses." *The Baptist Magazine* (London) 33 (1841): 113.

"Deaconesses." *Western Baptist Review* (Kentucky) 1 (February 1846): 232-36.

Deweese, Charles W. "Deaconesses in Baptist History: A Preliminary Study." *Baptist History and Heritage* 12/1 (January 1977): 52-57.

_____. "Ministries of Baptist Deacons in Early America." *Baptist History and Heritage* 25/2 (April 1990): 3-14.

Dorsett, Elizabeth. "The Baptist Deaconess Society of New York City: The Deaconess on the Field." *The Baptist Commonwealth* (Pennsylvania), 12 October 1916, 19-20.

"First Baptist Church of Oklahoma City, Okla., Ordained Three Women Deacons." *The Southern Baptist Journal* 12/1 (January-February 1984): 25-26.

Garrison, Gene. "Why the First Baptist Church of Oklahoma City Ordained Women as Deacons." *Echoes from the Pulpit* (1 July 1984).

Grant, Marian. "A Number of Women Chairing Boards of Deacons." *Biblical Recorder*, 19 November 1977, 7.

Gray, James R. "Ordination: Male or Female." *The Southern Baptist Journal* 5/2 (March 1977): 9.

Griffin, Dan L. "For Women's Ordination." *Baptist Standard*, 24 April 1985, 8, 10.

Hawthorne, Melvin. "Deaconesses Ordained in Manhattan Baptist Church." *Church Administration* 13/11 (August 1971): 39.

Henderson, Charles R. "The Work of Deaconesses." *The Standard* (Chicago), 11 April 1896, 5.

Hewett, John H. "Women's Ordination: Biblical Perspectives—PRO." *Word and Way*, 17 May 1984, 6, 11.

Hinson, E. Glenn. "The Church: Liberator or Oppressor of Women?" *Review and Expositor* 72/1 (Winter 1975): 19-29.

_____. "Early Christian Practices Give Support to Ordination of Baptist Deaconesses." *Baptist Standard*, 29 March 1972, 8-9.

_____. "On the Election of Women as Deacons." *The Deacon* 3/3 (April-June 1973): 5-7.

_____. "On the Ordination of Women As Deacons." *Capital Baptist*, 8 February 1973, 3, 6.

_____. "On the Ordination of Women As Deacons." *Western Recorder*, April 1972, 3, 15.

Holcomb, Carol Crawford. " 'Coming into a New Awareness': Women Deacons at Seventh and James Baptist Church [Waco, Texas]." *The Journal of Texas Baptist History* 18 (1998): 1-25.

Hubble, Gwenyth. "Women in the Ministry." *The Fraternal: Journal of the Baptist Ministers' Fellowship* 119 (January 1961): 11-15.

Hull, William E. "Woman and the Southern Baptist Convention." *Christian Ethics Today* 6/4, issue no. 029 (August 2000). Online edition at <http://www.christianethicstoday.com/Issue/029/Issue%20029_August_2000.htm> (accessed 16 February 2005).

_____. "Woman in Her Place: Biblical Perspectives." *Review and Expositor* 72/1 (Winter 1975): 5-17.

"Illinois Church Ordains Two Women Deacons." Baptist Press, 23 January 1976.

"The Issue of 'Women Deacons.' " *The Deacon* 3/3 (April-June 1973): 4.

Jones, Peter Rhea. "The Liberating and Liberated Lord: A Biblical Essay on Freedom." *Review and Expositor* 73/3 (Summer 1976): 283-92.

King, Martin. "NAMB Trustees Meet, Approve Guidelines for Church Starts." Baptist Press, 7 October 2004.

Knight, Walker L. "Equality and Stained Glass: A Look at Woman's Changing Role in the Church." *Home Missions* 43/5 (May 1972): 2-6.

Langley, Ralph H. "The Role of Women in the Church." *Southwestern Journal of Theology* 19/2 (Spring 1977): 60-72.

Letsinger, Norman H. "The Status of Women in the Southern Baptist Convention in Historical Perspective." *Baptist History and Heritage* 12/1 (January 1977): 37-44, 51.

Loftis, John F. "The Emerging Identity of Deacons, 1800–1950." *Baptist History and Heritage* 25/2 (April 1990): 15-21.

Lumpkin, William L. "The Role of Women in 18th-Century Virginia Baptist Life." *Baptist History and Heritage* 8/3 (July 1973): 158-67.

Magee, Nell. "One Woman Speaks." *The Baptist Program* (August 1974): 8, 22.

Mann, Gerald E. "How We Got Women Deacons." *The Deacon* 5/3 (April-June 1975): 46-47.

"Many Southern Baptists Opposed to 'Women Deacons.'" *The Deacon* 3/3 (April-June 1973): 8-9.

"Mars Hill Baptist Church Elects Woman Deacon Chairman." Baptist Press, 2 February 1976.

Maston, T. B. "The Bible and Women." *The Student* 64/8 (February 1985): 4-6, 47-48.

McBeth, H. Leon. "The Ordination of Women." *Review and Expositor* 78/4 (Fall 1981): 515-30.

_____. "Perspectives on Women in Baptist Life." *Baptist History and Heritage* 22/3 (July 1987): 4-11.

_____. "The Role of Women in Southern Baptist History." *Baptist History and Heritage* 12/1 (January 1977): 3-25.

McClain, Thomas M. "Women's Ordination: Biblical Perspectives—CON." *Word and Way*, 17 May 1984, 7, 11.

McKean, May Field. "The Baptist Deaconess Home." *The Standard* (Chicago), 31 August 1907, 10-11.

_____. "Deaconesses, Ancient and Modern." *The Standard* (Chicago), 20 April 1901, 6-7.

Mitton, Harold L. "The Place of Women in Ministry." *Atlantic Baptist* 23/4 (April 1987): 16-18.

Moon, Lottie. "Ministering Women." *Religious Herald*, 23 March 1871, 1; and 13 April 1871, 1.

Morgan, S. L. "Dr. Paschal and Deaconesses." *Biblical Recorder*, 13 February 1929, 4.

Myers, Carlton L. "Deaconesses, Women Deacons, or Deacons' Wives?" *The Deacon* 3/3 (April-June 1973): 10-12.

"On Deaconesses." *The Baptist Magazine* (London) 34 (1842): 68.

"Ordaining Women." *The Southern Baptist Journal* 12/1 (January-February 1984): 3.

"Ordination of Women, A Survey." *Called and Committed* 2/2 (May 1979): 2.

Paschal, G. W. "Deaconesses." *Biblical Recorder*, 23 January 1929, 4-5.

_____. "Morgan Edwards' Materials toward a History of the Baptists in the Province of North Carolina." *The North Carolina Historical Review* 7/1 (July 1930): 365-91.

Patterson, Dorothy Kelley. "Why I Believe Southern Baptist Churches Should Not Ordain Women." *Baptist History and Heritage* 23/3 (July 1988): 56-62.

Pinckney, T. C. "BGAV Direction." *The Baptist Banner* 13/5 (May 2000)—online edition.

Powell, Paul W. "Against Women's Ordination." *Baptist Standard*, 24 April 1985, 9, 10.

Rogers, Joyce. "God's Chief Assignment to Women." *The Southern Baptist Journal* 2/1 (January 1974): 3, 9.

Ryals, DeLane M. "Southern Baptist Women Ministering in Metro New York, 1970–1995." *Baptist History and Heritage* 39/2 (Spring 2004): 90-99.

Sisk, Ron. "Women in the SBC: A Status Report." *The Student* 64/8 (February 1985): 45.

Stancil, Bill. "Recent Patterns and Contemporary Trends in Deacon Life." *Baptist History and Heritage* 25/2 (April 1990): 22-30.

Summers, Ray. "Deacons-Deacon-Deaconesses." *Baptist Standard*, 3 July 1974, 9.

Tenery, Robert M. "The Ordination of Women." *Baptists United News*, 29 December 1975, 4.

Terry, Bob. "Two Women Ordained by Faith Baptist, Georgetown [KY]." *Western Recorder*, 6 February 1969, 9.

Webb, Henry. "What about Women Deacons?" *The Deacon* 9/3 (April-June 1979): 3.

Wilson, Johanna L. "The Ministry of Women." *Southern Baptist Advocate* 1/1 (August 1980): 8-9.

Woman's Missionary Union of Virginia. "Declaration of the Dignity of Woman." *Religious Herald*, 23 September 2004, 8.

"Women in the Deaconship: A Survey of Selected Southern Baptist Churches." *The Deacon* 3/3 (April-June 1973): 13-15.

Young, J. Terry. "Baptists and the Ordination of Women." *The Theological Educator* 7/2 (Spring 1977): 7-9.

Pamphlets

Ashworth, John W. *Deacons and Deaconesses*. London: Yates and Alexander, 1881.

Baptist Deaconess Home: 312 West 54th Street, New York City. No date but probably in 1890s or early 1900s.

Deaconess Guide, A: Designed for the Organizing of the Consecrated Women of the Church. Nashville: National Baptist Publishing Board, 1960s; reprinted 1997. (Sixteen pages.)

McKinney, Mike L. *Why Women Deacons? A Biblical and Historical Rationale for Women Serving as Deacons in Baptist Churches*. 1998.

Rauschenbusch, Walter. *To the Deacons of Our Churches*. Brotherhood leaflets no. 6. No date but probably 1890s or early 1900s.

Southern Baptist Women in Ministry. *Opening Doors: A Brief History of Women in Ministry in Southern Baptist Life, 1868–1993*. 1993.

Annuals, Minutes, and a Yearbook

Annual. Arkansas Baptist State Convention. 1984.
Annual. Baptist General Association of Virginia. 1976.
Annual. Illinois Baptist State Association. 1976.
Annual. Kentucky Baptist Convention. 1984.

Annuals. Baptist State Convention of North Carolina. 1975, 1984.

Annuals. Calhoun Baptist Association (Alabama). 1988–1999.

Annuals. Capital Baptist Association (Oklahoma). 1983–1984.

Annuals. Redwood Empire Baptist Association (California). 1981–1987.

Annuals. Southern Baptist Convention. 1891, 1963, 1984, 1998, 2000.

Minutes. District of Columbia Baptist Convention. 1984.

Yearbook. American Baptist Convention. 1965–1966.

Manuscript Collections and Unpublished Materials

Brown, Caralie, and Jane Purser. "Deaconesses: A Long History of Service." Baptist history file folder, "Deacons." Southern Baptist Historical Library and Archives, Nashville.

Brown, Joseph Allen. "Ordination of Women to the Diaconate at the First Baptist Church of Shawnee, Oklahoma." D.Min. thesis, Southern Baptist Theological Seminary, 1984.

Burrows, Lansing. Lansing Burrows papers. AR 25, file folder 55, lecture 148 titled "Woman's Position in the Church, June 4, 1872." Southern Baptist Historical Library and Archives, Nashville.

Burton, Dale D., Jr. "The Northeast Baptist Church Considering the Ordination of Women as Deacons." D.Min. thesis, New Orleans Baptist Theological Seminary, 1980.

Charles Stanley papers. AR 666, box 1, file folder titled "Correspondence— Women's Ordination—1984–[19]85." Southern Baptist Historical Library and Archives, Nashville.

Cook, Ivey Clinton. "The Deacon's Role in Baptist History, 1607–1845." Th.M. thesis, Southeastern Baptist Theological Seminary, 1970.

Edwards, Morgan. "Materials towards a History of the Baptists in the Provinces of Maryland, Virginia, North Carolina, South Carolina, Georgia." 1772. Microfilm version of handwritten copy located in the Southern Baptist Historical Library and Archives, Nashville.

Norman, Stan. "Ecclesiological Guidelines to Inform Southern Baptist Church Planters." Position paper presented to North American Mission Board, 28 September 2004. <www.namb.net/news/guidelines.pdf>, accessed 20 October 2004.

Patterson, Floyd Elias. "An Issues Approach to the Closure of Conflict over the Ordination of Women as Deacons." D.Min. thesis, Southern Baptist Theological Seminary, 1985.

Pitts, William. " 'We Need You to Serve": Establishing Women Deacons at First Baptist Church, Waco, 1996." Unpublished manuscript scheduled for publication by Paternoster in 2005.

Schmucker, Glen. "A Survey of the Central Issues in the Current Debate over the Ordination of Women among Southern Baptists." D.Min. research paper, Southwestern Baptist Theological Seminary, 1984.

Scrapbook. Amity Baptist Church, New York. In the American Baptist Historical Collection, Rochester NY.

Thomas, Donald F. "The Deacons and the Deaconesses: A Case Study in Backgrounds and Present Practice among American Baptist Churches." Prepared for the Division of Evangelism, American Baptist Home Mission Society, September 1969.

Watson, George. "A Case Study of the Decision by First Baptist Church, Arlington, Texas, to Elect Women Deacons." D.Min. thesis, Bethel Theological Seminary, 2000.

Women in Baptist Life Collection. AR 160, box 1, folder 1-10 titled "Consultation on Women in Church-Related Vocations, 1978"; also box 2, folder 2-6 titled "Ordination of Women—Clippings." Southern Baptist Historical Library and Archives, Nashville.

Ziegler, Melissa A. "Women in British Baptist Life." 23 June 2003. Written in England while serving as an Oxford Scholar from Carson-Newman College.

Letters, E-mails, Faxes, Telephone Messages

Hundreds of letters, originals, copies, and/or transcripts of e-mails, faxes, and telephone calls from Baptists in the United States and other countries—women deacons, pastors, local-church historians, directors of missions, American Baptist executive ministers of ABC regions, Southern Baptist state convention executive directors, and others—are in the writer's personal files.

Indexes

Names and Topics

Scripture References